MY LIFE IN HORROR

Volume II

by

Kit Power

Cover design and interior layout © WHITEspace, 2022
www.white-space.uk

Copyright © Kit Power 2022. All rights reserved. The right of Kit Power to be identified as the Author of this work has been asserted by him in accordance with the Copyright, Designs and Patents Act 1998.

Kit Power does not have any responsibility for, or control over, 3rd party websites referred to or in this book. All internet addresses given in this book were correct at the time of going to press. The author and publisher regret any inconvenience caused if addresses have changed or sites have ceased to exist, but can accept no responsibilities for any such changes.

All rights reserved. No part of this publication may be reproduced or transmitted in any form or by any means, electronic or mechanical, including photocopy, recording, or any information storage and retrieval system, without permission in writing from the publisher.

Dedicated with love, affection, and respect to the memory of
Carole Baume.

Your good work touched tens of thousands of lives for the better, and for the hundreds of us lucky enough to know you personally, you showed us how to live a life fully and well. May your example light the way for all of us who were blessed enough to know you.

SPECIAL THANKS

The production of this book was paid for via a crowdfunding campaign, and you would not be reading it without the extraordinary generosity of the following people:

KatieTree
Doug Campbell, youtube.com/@DrDougCampbell
david-watkins.com
James Everington
RJ Barker
Kayleigh Edwards
Gryf
Benjamin Langley benjaminlangley.co.uk
Dion Winton-Polak, thefinetoothed.com
Ross Warren
Alicia White
Gavin Schofield
Beloved citizens of Writeopolis
Dute
booktrust.org.uk/ofield

CONTENTS
PRIMARY YEARS (0-11)

Can You Show Me Where It Hurts?
The Wall *19*

I Was Born a Big Strong Woman
Greenham *27*

Where There's a Will
The Tripods *33*

You've Been on my Nerves for a Long Time
Superman III *41*

I Survived the Terror
The Black Hole *49*

I'll Spend It Alone
Young Sherlock Holmes *57*

I Had a Job, I Had a Girl
Born in the USA *63*

Rode the Five Hundred
When the Wind Blows *75*

I'm a Teacher of Little Children
Ender's Game *81*

They Just Worked on Him. The Way They're Working on You
One Flew Over the Cuckoo's Nest *89*

Do or Die
Escape from Colditz *93*

Only Time Will Heal the Pain of Loss
Stan Lee / The Death of Gwen Stacy *99*

SECONDARY YEARS (11-16)

Obnoxious, Self-Righteous Sadists
   Smoking *107*

I'm Not Scared of You Anymore. You're Scared of Me
   The Wild One *115*

There's No Real Magic, Ever
   Martin. *125*

You Can't Check Out
   The Elm Street franchise. *131*

Surrender to Me
   Candyman. *139*

Entertain Us
   Nevermind. *147*

Don't They Know the Rules?
   Bodycount. *157*

I'm the Tyranny of Evil Men
   Pulp Fiction *167*

El Eye Vee, Ee Are Pee, Double Oh El
   Cracker. *173*

I Wasn't Born with Enough Middle Fingers
   Marilyn Manson. *183*

If Only There is Something We Could Have Done
   XCOM. *185*

King Killer Big Wheeler Cat Peeler
   The Great Milenko *193*

Fairness Would Be to Rip Your Insides Out and Hang You From a Tree
   Scream *201*

ALLEGED ADULTHOOD (16+)

That's Your Shadow on the Wall
  Natural Born Killers. 209

We Will Bury You
  Confessions of a Reluctant Barman 215

"Insanity is Healthy"
  Columbine. 231

Whadaya Gonna Do?
  Casino. 239

This Planet Belongs to Me and This Hippy With Long Hair
  Devil Without a Cause 245

Am I Too Loud For You?
  The Marshall Mathers LP 253

I Never Had a Son
  Gangs of New York. 265

No Turning Back
  The Ghost 271

Still, It Would Be Such a Lovely Ride
  'That Hellbound Train'. 287

I Refuse to Shut Up and Die
  Exquisite Corpse. 293

The following essays were first published at Ginger Nuts of Horror (gingernutsofhorror.com) as follows:

January 2017
I Wasn't Born with Enough Middle Fingers
I Never Had a Son

March 2017
They Just Worked on Him. The Way They're Working on You

April 2017
I Was Born a Big Strong Woman
Obnoxious, Self-Righteous Sadists

July 2017
You've Been on my Nerves for a Long Time

September 2017
There's No Real Magic, Ever
Whadaya Gonna Do?

January 2018
Can You Show Me Where It Hurts?

March 2018
We Will Bury You

October 2018
If Only There is Something We Could Have Done

December 2018
Only Time Will Heal the Pain of Loss

April 2019
I'm a Teacher of Little Children

July 2019
Rode the Five Hundred
September 2019
I Survived the Terror

October 2019
Entertain Us

January 2020
Surrender to Me

March 2020
    Do or Die
    I Had a Job, I Had a Girl

October 2020
    El Eye Vee, Ee Are Pee, Double Oh El

March 2021
    I'll Spend It Alone

June 2021
    I'm the Tyranny of Evil Men

September 2021
    "Insanity is Healthy"

March 2022
    Don't They Know the Rules?

April 2022
    Where There's a Will

May 2022
    This Planet Belongs to Me and This Hippy with Long Hair

July 2022
    That's Your Shadow on the Wall

August 2022
    King Killer Big Wheeler Cat Peeler

September 2022
    Fairness Would Be to Rip Your Insides Out and Hang You from a Tree
    I'm Not Scared of You Anymore. You're Scared of Me

October 2022
    Am I Too Loud for You?

November 2022
    No Turning Back
    Still, It Would Be Such a Lovely Ride
    I Refuse to Shut Up and Die

Previously unpublished
    You Can't Check Out

INTRODUCTION

"True horror is seeing something approach."
William Friedkin said that, and he knows a bit about horror. Friedkin's movie adaptation of *The Exorcist* is the gold standard much of the field is still measured against, and with good reason. But it's his definition, more than his movie, that has haunted my relationship with horror the way Hamlet Senior enjoys a good battlement. I've worked in the field as my day job for fifteen years as the host of *PseudoPod*, a weekly horror fiction podcast, and recently have begun working as a voice actor for other horror podcasts such as *The Secret of St Kilda* and *The Magnus Archives*. In *Pseudopod*, the fiction is delivered to me wholesale and I get to exercise my critical faculties talking about why I like it and what I find interesting. In *St. Kilda*, I am complicit, following in the footsteps of the household gods of modern horror fiction narrators; DaSilva, Dyall, Serling, Gatiss, Peele.
But the thing is, as time goes on, I've found I disagree with Friedkin. Or, perhaps, that he doesn't go far enough. Because he's not wrong: the implication, the cut-away, the hijacking of the mind's eye horror enables in the best of ways is absolutely the genre to its core.
But to see something approach, there has to be a watcher, and there is a price for filling that role that Friedkin's definition does not acknowledge. One of my earliest memories is the video to 'Lullaby' by The Cure. Robert Smith, the lead singer, is lying in the exact bed you expect a patron saint of goth to have at home, menaced by Victorian ghosts and the Spider-Man, a nightmarish version of himself. As the video finishes the spider webs spread and he's consumed by the increasingly non-Euclidean expanses of the mattress. More Little Nemo in Hell than Little Nemo in Slumberland.
No one wins the Trauma Games and the medals we all get have ragged edges. My darkest interludes have all been defined by that

immobility. See horror approach. Survive it. The simple, brutal binary of that being the only choice you have.

False binaries are having a magnificently shitty decade and this one is no exception. There is power in observation. There is strength, and agency, in the act of witnessing. Kit's work embodies that in every syllable, seeing the horror approach and staring it down. Not in that ridiculous, chin-jutting way that action movies think is the only way guys can emote. He's terrified. Just like we all are. He knows what it is, and he knows the cost of seeing it and he Does. It. Anyway. Because Kit has worked out the truth; horror isn't a weapon. It's a tool. One you can use to build better spaces in your mind and your life. Spaces where, when the horror approaches again, you can stand in safety and weather the storm. Then, and this is the genius of Kit's work, you can dissect the horror and the responses it elicited and use that to make the next wave easier.

The essays here are difficult because they're honest. Trauma, horror, whatever you want to call it is untidy, malicious, delights in upending every single one of our defences. That process is just the beginning here. Horror, personal and cultural, becomes not something to endure but something to build with. Kit's extraordinary talent is the forge in which these things are melted down, examined, understood and lessened. You aren't what's happened to you. You are what you do.

Kit has made a shelter from the storm, not just for himself but for all of us. Here, horror is foundation and fear is armour and I don't think there's a more heavy metal concept on Earth right now than that.

This is stunning work from an extraordinary talent. One who's just getting started. True horror is seeing something approach. True courage, true skill, is making something better out of that horror. Friedkin made an excellent start. Kit's here to show you what's next.

Alasdair Stuart
December 2022

Every month, I wrote about a film, album, book or event that I considered horror, and that had a warping effect on my young mind. You will discover my definition of what constitutes horror is both eclectic and elastic. Don't write in. Also, of necessity, much of this is bullshit – as in, my best recollection of things that happened anywhere from fifteen to forty years ago. Sometimes I revisited the source material contemporaneously, further compounding the potential bullshit factor. Finally, intimate familiarity with the text is assumed – to put it bluntly, here be gigantic and comprehensive spoilers. Though in the vast majority of cases, I'd recommend doing yourself a favour and checking out the original material first anyway.

This is not history. This is not journalism. This is not a review.

This is my life in horror.

Primary Years (0-11)

CAN YOU SHOW ME WHERE IT HURTS?

THE WALL

Welcome back.
Let's start with music, what do you say? Let's spin the black circle.
It's December, 1979. I am almost 18 months old. Either my mother or father (Mum ended up with custody of the record, but any divorcees in the audience will know how little that means in terms of confirming parentage) brings home a double album that will form the background soundtrack to my childhood.
I will hear it before I have language. The contours of the sounds – especially the first disc, which will obviously get more play, just because of the time involved in listening to both back to back – creates grooves in my pliable gray matter that are there still. Top slice my brain when I'm gone, take a circular cast, play it – there's a good chance this album is what you'll hear.
It's elemental. It's ground zero.
And it starts oh... so... quiet. A lullaby you have to strain to hear – indeed, that you have to turn up substantially to really make sense of. I picture myself, an infant in a nappy, crawling or sitting, head turned towards the sound – likely hearing also the faint hiss of the record underneath, overlaying the sense of broadcast, of distance. It's haunting, delicate, beautiful, and then...
You're going to have to take my word for it, but it just made me jump again, the guitars and keys crashing in counterpoint, startling me sympatico with the child I was/am; following which the dark, falling, ponderous riff breaks into a vocal. The voice is clear, the sound cold,

like an iced over lake, like the stars in a winter sky, and the words I don't understand sing

> *If you wanna find out what's behind these cold eyes,*
> *You'll just have to claw your way through this disguise*

Then the riff is back, louder, more cacophonous, a voice yelling, drums clattering and crashing, and as it pounds to a climax, an aeroplane engine howls in pain, diving towards the earth, a sound that I'll hear again and again whenever Mr Bond in the 80s is having some aviation related hijinks, but this, this is the first time, the birth of the noise, the big bang, this is the universe either beginning or ending, but either way, it's an explosion of noise and fire, and when the drums finally roll to a close and the sound cuts to an infant crying, man, I feel it right down to my socks.

The first disc, especially, there's a lot of lullabies – the intro to 'The Thin Ice' most obviously, but also in 'Mother' and 'Goodbye Blue Sky' – and that's a good part of how it captured me, I think. It's an adult terror of mortality (amongst, sure, many other things) wrapped up in a combination of gentle melodies and riffs that are the audio equivalent of fever nightmares; beautifully played, but haunting, slightly distorted, ephemeral. The childishness extends to the lyrics, too; side one is the story of a boy losing his father in the war, brutalized by school, and injected with well-meaning fears by his mother (yeah, we'll come back to that).

Listening to it now, as '…Wall pt. 1' transitions into 'The Happiest Days Of Our Lives', I'm mesmerized all over again; by the fluidity of the playing, and the incredible dynamic range of the production. I'm sure to fresher and more mature ears, discovering this with a sense of history and, well, other music, it must seem hopelessly indulgent, if very well played. But for me… for me, it's literally magic – a spell that invokes feelings that are powerful, tidal, and unnamable. Even now, I feel them moving in my chest, rolling like boulders, giant and unstoppable and featureless – powerful and mysterious.

Can we talk about the flow, here? The sound never stops, that's the thing. It's one continuous piece of music for all twenty-odd minutes of the runtime of Side One, and the dynamics are incredible, in sync with the production; gentle, quiet, muted strings giving way to razorwire distorted chords, flowing into solos that sound like the strings are bleeding as they are plucked, weeping as they are held and bent.

By the time I'm really old enough to understand the fury of *Hey! Teacher! Leave those kids alone!* Floyd will no longer be cool... but something in my chest knows anyway, doesn't it? Sure. Something in my toddler blood hears the echo of future futility and humiliation, of promises made and broken, of something wonderful and joyful crushed and mangled to fit a mould that's not really person shaped at all.

Turns out, music can take you forward it time, too. God help you. God help me.

Oh and it's 'Mother'. Ah, 'Mother'. Here's something *Mindhunter* taught me – it's always Mother's fault, right? Too much love, not enough love, the wrong kind of love, too harsh, no discipline... It's such a defining myth, we believe it, even though the key thing we know about psychopaths is that they lie and dissemble and project.

And fuck, even I'm at it. Behold! The mother who allowed her toddler to listen to Pink Floyd's *The Wall* endlessly on vinyl as a child! Cower in awestruck disgust at the freak he has become! Who shall we burn?!?!

Yeah, put the torches down. She's the best, my mum, you can't have her. Thank you Mum. Thank you for *Tommy* (see Volume I), and *The Wall*, and more importantly, for so much love that neither of them could damage me beyond repair, even though they live in the darkness of my imagination like factory machines that make infernal noise and belch dark smoke into the sky... sure they do. But not for what they were; rather because of what they warned me about what the world really was, the world beyond the small, warm ball of love and light you built for us and called home. This was a window into that world, and as 'Goodbye, Blue Sky' plays and I try not to weep, I thank you, for finding a way to show us that also kept us safe. I love you.

See what I mean? I'd forgotten, but the song transitions into 'Empty Spaces', the soundtrack of a factory spitting fire and sparks, a foundry, industrial music a decade and more before Gary Numan. It's fucking exquisite, you know – even if you don't like it, even if it's lesser or non-Floyd in your personal canon, you cannot deny the total vision, and commitment to that vision, that's playing out here. I had no words for any of this, no language for music, let alone production, but I knew it spoke to me in a way very few other records did, knew it found a way to get through my ears right into my brain and chest and monkey around in there.

And sure, with adult ears, I can lament the lack of any spark of improvisation, any sense of anything other than total control, ruthlessly executed, but let's be real – that's a million light years from the point, isn't it? We're listening to the story of a man who discovers a loathing for himself and others so deep that he embraces the ultimate brutality of fascism – of course it's overly controlled.

The phone calls – the sound effects – again, too young for language, the voices, the tones of voice, they are splashes of paint across my imagination. The discordant keyboard that finally bleeds into a tune, aw, shit...

> *Day after day, love turns grey,*
> *Like the skin of a dying man...*

You can feel the violence lurking under the surface of the deranged organ tone – it's sick, draining, cycling – of course it's going to explode, and it does. I don't jump this time, but I do flinch.

It's so bleak, so cold, as it slips into 'Don't Leave Me Now' – bleaker and colder than it's really possible for a child to feel, I think (or at least, a well cared for, loved child, and oh, brothers and sisters, I think that's a thought that's going to fester). But of course, thanks to this, I felt it anyway, intuited it, somehow – or maybe travelled forward in time, to a point in my life where I could see the contours of something this hopeless, this empty. I never quite fell in, not really – too many good friends, to much love around me, too many good values instilled in me, thank you Mum and Dad, and thank you all who saw someone worth loving and stood by me, thank you, thank you, thank you – but still... just like Springsteen will later break my ten year old heart with 'Bobby Jean', long before I'd actually fallen in love, *The Wall* showed me The Cold, and what it was like to live there. It haunted me, and it haunts me still.

There but for the grace of... well, grace, I guess. Luck? Yeah, let's call it that. Cold comfort. Lol.

Anger was my drug, for a while there – oh, hell, sometimes still is, truth be told. And I got out far enough to hit fury once or twice, and that's a scary place to be for sure, but at the same time, it saved my life at least once, so I have to respect that fire, even as I fear its power, but hate... no, thankfully, I never got to hate. Never have, and hopefully never will.

But I've seen it from the hilltop. I've felt it's breeze on my face, beckoning, and it's not warm. It's cold.

Cold, like *The Wall*.

END OF DISC ONE. PLEASE PLAY DISC TWO.

As I mentioned up top, this one got less play. Even back then, finding a full ninety minutes to listen was not easy. So much to do. But we got there often enough. I remember a skip in 'The Trial', one time, where the prosecution's down slide note into a verse kept repeating. That won't happen tonight – I've cleaned up Mum's (or possibly Dad's) record, and the tone is clear as a bell, and warm as an oven.

The dynamics are amazing. I know for classical music fans all this shit is old hat – themes that repeat with different pace or decoration, instrumentation, but I'm a rock and roller to the guts, and this stuff is, I suspect, as near as I'll ever get to that transcendence that Ken Russell felt from his beloved composers. It sweeps me up and along, that's all. The screaming sax on 'Is There Anybody Out There?' just made me shiver, and now the acoustic guitar outro is making me feel like crying, and oh shit, here's 'Nobody Home'.

It's desolate. And sure, he's a rich, white rock star with the world at his feet, doing what he loves every night of his life, cry me a fucking river, I feel you, I do... but I feel him too. I feel the yawning, gasping emptiness that owns the edges of everything, squeezing, flexing, crushing, you are alone, now and forever, welcome to the desperate hearts club, there's only one way out and no-one ever comes back to tell you if it's better or worse or nothing at all, and nothing might be better, but it might not, but here is now and now is fucking empty, and yes, yeah, I have felt it, I feel it, sure I do, once you've tasted from that river, it never entirely leaves you, it flows under everything and through you, cold and dark and mostly silent, but you'll always feel the cold a little more than others, always want to be warm, because there's that small part of you that will always be shivering and alone.

Critics hate 'Vera'. Critics can kiss my arse. Twice. WWII was a gaping, bleeding, psychic wound on the landscape and minds of everyone who grew up in the immediate aftermath of it, and if your empathy is so malnourished that you can't get to the desperate and pathetic nature of this plea... well, that's okay, but don't make an idiot out of yourself by decrying those of us who can, okay?

At least no-one is going to try and argue about 'Comfortably Numb'. The only thing for me is the oddness of hearing it out of sequence, divorced from the whole. If there ever was an album that felt basically single proof, this one would have to be it – but, so it goes. It's beautiful, and I think it's hard to fully appreciate that beauty without (*humblebrag*) having heard it without comprehension – with no conception of the existence of words, let alone what they mean. Though, of course, then you're left with a devastating shift as the guitar turns blue in the exquisite final section, and you might find yourself crying without knowing why, or feeling that painful swelling in your chest that has no words either.

Fitting that it fades to silence. End of side three.

I kind of marvel at my kid endurance. It just didn't bother me, sitting and listening to ninety minutes of music in one sitting, outside forces permitting. I do remember being weirded out by the return of the albums opening riff on side four – loving it, but still definitely thrown. Songs don't get repeated, as a rule. And of course, the fact that the vocal doesn't come in when it's supposed to... something is wrong. Fever dream again; familiarity, but fractured, twisted into unfamiliarity. Am I supposed to sing along, fill in? Is it broken somehow?

And then the familiar lyric kicks in, but the drums tell you something's gone wrong – confirmed when they build to take us back to the riff, and instead they don't. We're back to the strained, angry vocal, and something is horribly, horribly wrong. When the riff does come back, I miss the aeroplane, the sense of explosion and chaos. This is far, far worse. The familiar rendered alien, and the crowd noise – are they cheering or screaming?

The next riff has a familiar tone and rhythm too, but it also quickly goes off program, dropping into something else. The kick of the bass drum feels like a punch, like a stomping boot. I'm somewhere between two and three years old, so obviously I have no fucking clue what's really going on. Equally obviously to nearly-40-year-old me, I knew exactly what the fuck was going on. I may not have been able to articulate it, but I know where it counts.

Fuck fascism, and fuck fascists. Always and forever.

Oh, right, yeah, we're in *that* present day, aren't we? A timeline where the story of a wealthy misanthrope and possible sociopath who embraces prejudice and builds a wall around himself to keep out the world of 'undesirables' – which basically translates to 'anyone who doesn't look and sound just like me, with a million or two in the bank' – doesn't sound so much like fictitious parable as it does presidential fucking biography.

'Waiting For The Worms', infuckingdeed.

God help us.

Listening to it now, it's skin crawling, obviously – but I think even back then, the sinister combination of the loudspeaker vocal and the nightmare riff bleeding through the lullaby will have gotten to me. This is the sound I heard in my head as I watched Trump's inauguration speech. If you ever wondered to yourself what you'd do if you were a German in 1932… take a fucking look around. Time to shine.

Ah, 'The Trial'.

I have a vivid memory – connected to the aforementioned skip, but that's dangerously convenient – of pouring over the double gatefold of the album as I listened, seeing the cavorting barrister, and then looking over the others (The Mother, The Lover, my, look, all the prosecution witnesses are women, how interesting) The Judge as a giant towering… well, arsehole. Literally. It seems likely my fascination with and repulsion from caricature art stems from this oft-repeated moment. And then there's the chorus about being crazy – the band still working through their seemingly endless guilt over Syd, obviously, but to my child self, was anything more horrifying than the concept of one's own mind becoming the enemy, not to be trusted? There was not. If I'm honest, there still is not.

And then the verdict is delivered, and to the chanted demands of the crowd, The Wall is torn down.

And the lullaby from the beginning kicks in, as the rubble slowly settles.

...*the ones who really love you walk up and down, outside The Wall.*
...*the bleeding hearts and the artists take their stand.*

> *...after all, it's not easy*
> *...banging your heart against some mad bugger's Wall.*

That the album itself loops is one final twist of the knife, of course; where the lullaby of side 4 cuts out is precisely where it comes in on side 1, the monstrous implication being that the building of the wall is not merely inevitable but cyclical, each generation rebuilding the horror of self isolation, trauma rippling down into explosions of bigotry.

And I have to believe there's a better way, a way to break that cycle for good.

And I have to hope we figure it out soon.

I WAS BORN
A BIG STRONG WOMAN

GREENHAM

We're going far enough back that virtually all of this is best guess territory. In the song I'd one day write about the experience, I said I was five. Mum says five to seven. Let's split the difference and go with six.

My memory is early spring. I say that because we were woken early – hellishly early. Dark outside early. I remember the pain in my eyes, that chronically stupid feeling, akin to a mild concussion – a confusion rooted in a basic failure to understand why the world is happening at all, at that particular ungodly hour.

It's Mum who has woken us up. Her friend, Zane, has decided, in apparently the middle of the night, that We Are Going. So go we do. My memory is Weetabix for breakfast, then into a van, and off.

It's a bloody long drive. And, I mean, logic dictates there will have been wee stops and what have you, but none of that has stuck at all. When you reach back this far, it's all impressionistic, blended, with the odd outright invention thrown in.

For instance, memory has us stopping to pick up some friends on the way, another women and her kids, which Mum assures me did not happen. So my memory of getting in a rock fight with one of those kids, to the horror of all concerned, must similarly be false – or, more likely, misplaced, because I am damn sure that happened at some point around this time. The past is a fucking maze.

Anyway.

We get there. Mud. that's the next thing I remember. Driving through it, walking through it. The noise, *squelch squelch squelch*. The colour of it – exactly the same shade as slurry, similar super runny consistency. Bad enough that my nose would create a phantom smell to go with the visual, the brown fluid coming up through the green grass blades with every step. Everywhere. Black bin liners at the entrances to the tents with inner groundsheets, to leave your wellies. If you didn't have wellies... best not to think about it.

Lots of walking. I was a country kid, used to walking, but still. I don't know if it was spread out, or we just did a lot of visiting, but I distinctly remember going to sleep with tired, aching legs. Similarly, the actual, non-phantom smells were, mainly, pleasant – wood smoke, and food being cooked on open flame. To this day, a roaring campfire evokes gut level waves of pleasure and comfort for me, as well as the faint tingle of adventure.

And then there were the toilets – just in case you were wondering where the horror angle came in. I know some Glastonbury festival veterans – especially visitors to the 80's incarnation of the event – may think they've seen and smelled the worst that humanity's bowels can possibly produce. Well, I am here to tell you, those people never had to use a Greenham Common toilet in the middle of the night. In true suppressed trauma fashion, I have only the most fleeting impressions – flashes of a mountain of shit, the occasional glimpse of white toilet paper, in a pit, a smell that could be tasted, that irritated the eyes, and flies, clouds of bluebottles crawling... the rest is a blessed blankness, locked too deep into my subconscious to ever again see the light of day. I hope.

But of course, most important, there were the women.

There was Tantrum. Tantrum was a true punk – tattoos, piercings – safety pins, of course. Many. In both ears. She looked amazing, spiky, but she smiled and laughed easily and well. I liked her a lot. Zane had brought us – an abduction, she's called it, eyes bright behind her large framed glasses and a bundle of curly hair. Then there was Tomma, Freedom Cloud... And at six years old (or five, or seven) it all made perfect sense. We gain more than we lose as our critical faculties develop, I think, but I have to confess, I miss having the kind of mind that could just simply accept names like that, without the slightest impulse to raise an eyebrow, or laugh, or frown.

It was an amazing space, and an amazing time. I remember earnest conversation, laughter, singing, ah, endless singing. 'I Was Born A Big Strong Woman', 'You Can't Kill The Spirit', 'Who Are The Witches?' I sang along with great enthusiasm. I got badges, too. Lots of them. Teddybears Against The Bomb, Ladybirds Against The Bomb, Frogs Against The Bomb... you get the idea. Each of them bearing the face of the animal protestor, the CND symbol overlaid on top. My mum's favourite was 'Aging Hippies Against The Bomb', and she kept that one for herself. There was just an energy to the whole camp, a sense of shared purpose, community, and solidarity that I am not sure I've ever experienced since. It was earnest and sincere, though a million miles from humourless – laughter was a constant note in the soundtrack of my time there. No money ever changed hands, that I saw – all was communal, shared willingly and with friendship. The women just helped each other, leaned on each other, used their skills and talents for the good of the group.

I remember having The Talk with Mum, too.

Why no men? Because it was important for women to have their own space, where they could just be, and talk. But it wasn't against men, at all – in fact, men helped out with the site.

Were there men's peace camps too? Yes, there were – it was important for men to have spaces, too.

How was I allowed there? Because I was a child, and children were welcome.

How old would I have to be before I wasn't allowed there? Probably a teenager.

Could I go to the men's camp then? If I wanted.

Why were we here?

We're here because this is where they are keeping the bombs. The bombs are very powerful, and can destroy whole cities. They are very very dangerous, and we don't want them to be used. In fact, we don't want them even to be built. We don't believe they should be here. So we've come here to let the government and everyone know that we don't agree with what's happening, that we don't want these bombs to be built or used against anyone. We're here because we believe in peace.

The bombs are a part of my childhood – a subject we'll return to later in this volume. Background noise. A constant, monolithic presence –

not unlike the way a more fundamentalist, Old Testament God might be present for the children of religious extremists, I suppose. Infinite, global destruction. Built and ready to fly. Tens of thousands of them. Nothing would survive – all would be consumed either by fire or the poison that followed. This was the reality of the world I had been born into. There was no certainty, no absolutes, save that if the bombs flew, everything – everything – would end, forever.

This was my reality – hell, this *was* reality. The women I was surrounded by knew it, as surely as I did, and with the added clarity of age and knowledge. And Greenham was their response to this gibbering insanity. They marched right up to the gates where the missiles were held, and they camped and they sang and they danced and they ate and they slept and they laughed. And later, they chained themselves to gates and fences, locked arms in the path of the army vehicles, and some of them were beaten and arrested, and they kept coming back and camping and singing and protesting and laughing.

They lived. On the very edge of insanity, right in the jaws of destruction, they danced and sang.

When you talk about Greenham, there's always sneers. There's always 'Bet the Russians were shitting themselves', there's always 'How did they have time? Didn't they have jobs to go to or kids to raise?', always 'waste of bloody time and effort'. The scorn, the mockery; it's kind of amazing how strong some of it is, even this far out – how strong the impulse is for some to spit on this moment, this movement. I think it says more about those who seek to belittle the protestors than the women themselves, to be honest. And, as is often the case, by mistaking cynicism for wisdom it completely misses the point.

Because, for me, Greenham is about a feeling, something you carry inside you. A glimpse of a possibility of a different way of doing things, an alternative way of organising the world and ourselves. A glimmer of a suspicion that much of what we consider to be cast iron rules of How The World Works are no more than underexamined customs, whose perpetuation is very much in service of people whose interests are not mine, or those of virtually anyone else I personally know. At a point in time and history where it seemed a distinct possibility that the world would end, not because of some massive natural disaster, but because of a series of decisions made by a tiny number of mainly men in conditions so rarefied and remote that most of us would never even know their names, Greenham just pitched up some tents and said, nope. Not In Our Name. We reject your paradigm, and we choose another.

So, yeah. I know why they sneer. Let 'em. If their alternative is a world where nuclear holocaust is a flock of geese or an angry exchange of words away, I'm all for pitching a fucking tent and being called a fucking loon.

PS – I remember asking my mum, some years later – I think around the time all the prosecutions for trespass were overturned, after the House of Lords ruled that Greenham Common was, as the name implies, on common ground, and that, therefore, the US base should never have been sited there in the first place, and the women were actually exercising their right to access common land – whether or not she thought Greenham had actually made a difference. Her reply?

"Well, all I know is, the bombs never ended up flying, did they?"

WHERE THERE'S A WILL

THE TRIPODS

It is Saturday 15th September, 1984. I am six years old.

And, for my sins, I am at my Nan's house, in London.

Ah, Nan. See, the thing is, as a kid, I never really saw it. As a child, she was kind to me and my sister, and for me, that was the beginning and end of it. I know Dad used to make pointed jokes about her, and Mum made no secret of finding her 'difficult', but all I knew was when we went up to see her, we got to play with the skittles in her side alley (using the door of her garage as a backstop for any stray throws) and she fed us well; home-cooked dinners *and* desserts. Admittedly, on one memorable evening, we were served a baked bean, erm, bake, I guess, followed by prunes and custard, which led to an evening in front of the TV which became legendary among my mother, sister and I, capable of evoking guffaws, if not outright hysteria, as we recalled The Night Of The Long Farts.

But she really *was* a good nan to us, at least when we were little. Sure, there was some weirdly aggressive gender essentialism around me growing up to be 'a big strong man', but I distinctly remember, even as a very young child, thinking of it, indulgently, as Old Person talk, and I paid it no mind, even as Mum angrily insisted I could grow up to be whatever I wanted. Later, I'd see it; when we visited Uncle Edward (of *The Thing* infamy – see Volume I) one Christmas as teenagers, she spent the entire evening stony-faced, before saying, just before leaving, 'Well, I don't know what happened to you both, you were such beautiful children!'. It should have been hurtful, maybe even traumatic, but honestly, my abiding memory is one of amusement. By that point, I knew she hated me and my sister, and I'd been informed several times that we'd been disinherited, and I took that undertaking as my cue to have nothing to do with her (that turned out to be a lie, as it happened, a fact which, again, I must sadly report I regard with only a wry amusement). And at some point, I got my hands on one of the carefully typed letters she'd regularly send to Mum – when they were still married, my father would refer to them as 'Letters From The Deep Freeze' – and I can still remember how that particular missive closed out:

"Edith from down the road passed away last week, and I expect I shall soon be joining her. Are your dogs still tying you down?
Love,
Mum"

So, yeah. Nan, eh? Real charmer. And that bungalow; my other abiding memory is sitting on the sofa, me and my sister, with Nan and Mum on the other couch, lights down low, gas fire chucking out a stupifying level of heat, while the huge colour TV in the corner blared out at us (yeah, Nan's hearing was definitely on the way out). That was a treat, mind; we had no TV at home at this point, and when we did finally get a small portable in time for Colin Baker's final TV season as The Doctor, it was a black and white set. So outside of the school holiday trips to Dad, this was my only chance to soak up the good old CRT rays and get down with it.

My memory is that Uncle Edward and Auntie Jill were there too, but I'm not sure if that's true. Certainly, I talked about what we'd watched with Uncle Edward; but was it that evening, or had he just seen it the next time we talked? He'd agreed with me that the theme and opening credits were brilliant and creepy.

Anyway.

The opening *was* awesome; the music otherworldly, but also menacing, and there were shades of Who in terms of atmosphere, for sure, but this was something different, and that green logo, spelling out the title in giant letters… there's a thing about when you're that age, I think, and your kid brain is wide open, and some genius at the

BBC knew how to create music and images that seemed to open up a universe of sinister possibilities.

I had no idea what Tripods were. But I was *dying* to find out.

My memory is that I only saw the first episode. It seems unlikely that we'd stay with Nan longer than a week, given how hard she was on Mum, and how any trip would have been in school holidays, and thus eaten into Dad visits. I feel like I saw that first episode there, and the final one at my father's house. Which... well, it was broadcast 8th December, so clearly that can't be right. Yet I know I *did* see that last episode, in colour, as I have a vivid memory of the final shot of the story, and when I recently rewatched the show on DVD, it was exactly as I remember it. So, maybe a friend's house? Seems unlikely, but maybe...

Anyway. That Saturday evening, all I knew was I was falling, damn hard.

Sure, some of it was that Tripods had a thrilling pedigree with me, what with them being part of probably the first horror story I ever heard (see the first essay of Volume I). And yes, absolutely, the BBC/Who pedigree was also in the mix. But, beyond that, there's... well, it's like this. I spent almost my entire childhood to the date of this broadcast living in *highly* rural settings. My earliest memory of home is a farmhouse that was a 4 mile walk from the nearest (very) small town and a brief, single term of school in a town near Middlesbrough aside, it had all been small village life. So, seeing children walking around in the English countryside hit perhaps a little different with me than for many of the kids watching it. Sure, I could tell we were meant to realise this was a low tech world, what with the way a simple pocket watch is treated with almost reverential awe; still and all, it just wasn't that different, or distant, from what I saw around me every day. And, I mean, my head says I must have been too young for concerns about puberty/coming of age to have resonated in any meaningful way, but my heart says different. It whispers about just how much anxiety my young mind was capable of; that bottomless well of sadness that opened up in my centre at the fact of my father's absence, sure, but also just fundamentally my ability to imagine terrifying situations, even get a kind of perverse enjoyment from this kind of imaginative catastrophising...

And the fucking Tripods *were* terrifying. They were impossibly huge, and the fact that they took you up inside them combined my fear of heights with a constant low-grade tension generated by the simple day-to-day fact of having to move about in a world fundamentally not friendly to a child's height. I had frequent nightmares at this age, about giant railings that would in no way prevent me from falling from dangerous heights, huge walls of corrugated metal with an awful, painful, whining, grinding sound behind them...

And then, again, a Gandalf-type figure who turns up to suggest The Way Things Have Always Been is hiding a deeper truth felt precision-engineered to appeal to my child mind, especially as I was likely partway through my first read of *Lord of the Rings* around this time, my mother and I taking turns to read pages to each other as summer turned to autumn turned to winter. It's often been observed that creativity and originality are really just finding ways to collide pre-existing ideas in new ways; in this particular case, replacing the journey to Mount Doom with a trek to join the resistance to the alien invasion, across a world that is both recognisably Europe and also changed in inexplicable ways certainly blew many doors off in this kid's noggin.

I loved it so much, I bought the paperback.

It was a reissue for the TV show, with a cover featuring a photo of the actors huddled around a rock that reminded me of the County Durham moors I'd spent so many hours of my young life walking over. And within, I got so much more than that tantalising first episode; not only did I get the trip across the channel, I got the stupefying ruin of a modern city, confirming this *was* my world (or at least, had been). I got the sequence where the author pulls the stunning trick of using the reader's real-world knowledge to create a moment of extraordinary tension while the POV, first-person narrator is entirely oblivious. In fact, let's zoom in on that moment, because it's instructive; Will and the gang find themselves in a subway that has been converted for military use. Sandbags and a machine gun are described (the latter without Will having the slightest clue what he's describing, to be clear) before he talks about finding a crate 'full of little metal eggs in straw'. Will casually pulls out the inviting ring pull, then stares at the live grenade, wondering what's going to happen.

Gotta tell you, folks, in terms of screaming tension, it doesn't get much better. Utter genius.

The whole first book is like that, in fact; providing the reader with information that makes more sense to us than it does to the characters;

painting the picture of an invasion that has become an occupation, the human population clearly strictly controlled and rendered docile by the coming-of-age ceremony that installs 'caps', metal grafts attached to the skull which seem to convince the wearers of the benevolence of the Tripods. That somewhere around one in ten of the recipients are driven insane is a nicely macabre touch, as is the fact that such 'Vagrants' are treated with pity and kindness by the rest of the population. By the time Will desperately throws his final grenade up into the opening inside a Tripod that is picking him up, at the climax of Book One, I was edge-of-the-seat invested in his ragged band hooking up with the resistance.

The trilogy also escalates brilliantly; in Book Two, we learn the Tripods have built cities; humans are taken in from all over the world (boys who win some kind of athletic challenge similar to the Olympics; girls, and I wish I was making this up, from giant beauty pageants), and none ever leave. Our gang, fitted with fake caps, undergo training to compete, and once Will and the *sigh* German kid called Fritz who's all taciturn and Will doesn't like For Some Unknown Reason make it into the city, man, the whole thing just kicks into another gear. The human slaves have to wear masks because the air is toxic, the artificial gravity produces a crushing weight (which makes sense of the use of physical competition to select the entrants), and The Masters themselves are utter grotesques, with descriptions that would be difficult to realise in a movie without looking laughable, but on the page, ah, the mind's eye is free to make it all work, and it really does.

The other big escalation in Book Two is that we learn that even the remnants of humanity don't have much time left; there's a huge ship on the way, and it's going to convert the earth's atmosphere into the same poison as in the cities. There's a brilliant moment here, where Will's master expresses this plan with clear signs of anxiety; there's a lot of political disagreement amongst The Masters, about how much of a threat humanity represents, and what the ethical thing is to do about them/us. And as shitty as the setup of the women's only selection criteria for city entrance being beauty is, the payoff is monstrous, as Will is taken into a museum inside the alien city, and is suddenly brought face to face with the girl he'd fallen in love with in the first book, and who had been taken by the Tripods after being declared the queen of the tournament, her body preserved as an example of Earth beauty. I can still remember the shock of the moment, and also the sick thrill of a setup that took a whole damn book to pay off.

What I'm trying to get to here is that this trilogy taught me a lot about storytelling; not because it necessarily did anything blindingly original, but because it was well written on a sentence level, with a ferocious readability on a par with Terrance Dicks on his best days, combined with a rollocking plot that piled on event and tension and escalation in a manner most pleasing. I read it several times, wanting to revisit these kids, and their long, strange, dangerous journey. I also appreciated another entirely-new-to-me-trick; that Will, the narrator, was not actually much of a hero, and was in point of fact, somewhat of a dick – selfish, whiny, self-absorbed, and jealous of the friendship his travelling companions developed. That dickishness runs right through Book Two, with his judgmental treatment of Fritz, and it's really not until Book Three that he starts to develop maturity enough to rise to the moment; and even then, the final moment of heroism falls to his childhood frenemy, Henry, with Will bearing witness.

And with adult eyes, there's tons going on under the hood; in addition to the above, there's classic anxiety of empire (similar to *War Of The Worlds*, actually, as discussed in Volume I – what if someone landed in England with the kind of firepower and tech advantage the English were landing with on other shores?), a hell of an excoriation of liberal apologias for slavery and colonialism, as personified by Will's tentacle-wringing Master, and a brilliantly downbeat ending where, the extraterrestrial threat removed, the resistance starts crumbling and fracturing back along nation-state lines. I love how Will's final act is to turn his back on his dream of being an explorer to leverage his status as a hero of the liberation of Earth to try and hold everything together; something about that really speaks to me.

And sure, there's flaws; in addition to the gender issues highlighted (and more fundamentally, the entire absence of female characters that aren't either Will's mum or Will's love interest, FFS) there's plenty of Eurocentric 'national character' stereotyping that, erm, hasn't aged well. But, acknowledging those real and present flaws, it's absolutely still a rip-roaring narrative that's genuinely about bravery and heroic resistance to tyranny, and, you know what, I think that's an important thing for kids fiction to do.

And that's why, a couple of years ago, I sat and read this series to my daughter, as bedtime reading. Before we started, I told her that the lead character was a boy, and so were almost all the other characters, and would she like it if we changed him to a her, and if so, what name would she like me to use?

And so it was that my daughter heard the story of Alice; an angry, selfish but brave girl, who undertook a dangerous journey, joined the resistance, became a boxing champion to infiltrate an alien city, gained crucial intelligence, and finally led the guerrilla action that destroyed the enemy base once and for all.

And it fucking rocked.

PS: a few months before Nan passed away, she was taken into care; she'd lost the ability to safely prepare food for herself and was increasingly disoriented. While in care, she was given medication, and her personality transformed; Mum reported that she'd asked after myself and my sister, sent her love, and that she'd spoken kindly with Mum, too. I'd made jokes for a while, after seeing the first season of *The Sopranos*, that Olivia was exactly like Nan, and that Nan had borderline personality disorder. The joke stopped being funny after she'd been taken in and received treatment.

Given who she was, and the generation she came from, there's really very little realistic chance that she could have been diagnosed sooner. And, on a selfish level, I'm glad my mum got the closure of those last few kind chats, after a lifetime of vitriol. Still, I can't help but reflect on the enormous harm done – to Nan, and to those about her – by a lack of understanding of mental health issues. It's a mostly hidden cost and damage, I think, but it's very, very real all the same. May we all somehow receive the care we need to be the best of ourselves.

My thanks to Daniel Harper, who recorded a podcast some years ago with me on the subject of this trilogy, which allowed me space to rehearse some of the above. He's currently doing vital work documenting the American far-right via his I Don't Speak German podcast (idontspeakgerman.libsyn.com); please check out his Patreon (patreon.com/danielharper) and consider throwing him some support.

YOU'VE BEEN ON MY NERVES FOR A LONG TIME

SUPERMAN III

As I discussed when recording a podcast on the subject, I want to say I was seven or eight when I first saw this movie.

I also want to say I saw it at the cinema, but I think not, sadly. I remember the movie poster vividly, but I'd have had to be younger than seven, and that summer was *Temple of Doom* (see Volume I), and the clincher is that I only have memories of seeing it on a TV screen. Looking back over thirty years, the bullshit factor is inescapable, and has enough gravitational pull to completely obliterate the unwary, so let's stick with what I know I can know.

And I mean, there's a surprising amount that is scary here, let's start with that. The combine harvester sequence alone is a total heart-in-the-mouth moment – the unconscious child in the cornfield; those relentless, merciless rotating blades bearing down on him, fast enough and close enough that you imagine you can feel the force of the breeze they generate, like an industrial fan turned lethal. You look at the utter devastation they are wreaking on the heads of corn, and your mind extrapolates to the unconscious child... yeah, that's nightmare fuel.

The filmmakers play it out to the last second, too, and when Superman finally lands and puts his hand out to stop the blade, I remember flinching, instinctively, worried that the blade might slice through even his super-flesh.

So there's that. And, as you may have heard, there's all the fun of the fair in the final act – a machine that can learn your weakness, no matter how strong you are, one that, incidentally, is also smart enough to gain sentience and rebel against its creator, robofying anyone it can get its circuits on. Suffice it to say there's a gross tonnage of yikes going on that'd shame many of the lesser entries in any 80s horror franchise you'd care to name, frankly. And all wrapped up in a family-friendly PG bow.

Ah, the 80s. Be still, my panicked, arrhythmic heart.

For all of that, and more – the insane power of computing to cause the walk and don't walk men to engage in mortal combat, say, causing gigantic pedestrian/car pileups in the progress, or to reprogram weather *monitoring* satellites to become weather *controlling* satellites, in the process creating storms biblical enough to ruin the harvest of an entire country; acid that can melt steel if it gets hot enough (yeah, okay smartarse, *heat* can melt steel if it gets hot enough, I was seven, shut up); creepy drunken would-be father figures threatening to totally ruin your bowling date with your friends because they're trying to screw your mom, and so on – there's one sequence that, for me, towers above all to become a seminal moment of childhood existential horror; the kind of trauma, not to put too fine a point on it, that lodges so deep in your psyche that you end up obsessively writing about it thirty years later, not long after recording over two hours worth of podcast on the subject with people much, much smarter than you, because it turns out you still have shit to say and you're going to make damn sure the world hears it, like some going-to-seed Ancient Mariner with better wifi, because it just won't leave you alone and you'd really like to sleep tonight if at all possible, thanks, what with work in the morning and deadlines looming and this stupid heat that won't let go, that wraps you up like a damn python and slowly, gently, squeezes the breath out of you.

And you know what it is, right? Sure you do, if you've come this far.

It's the title fight. The ultimate showdown.

Superman vs. Superman.

We do need to talk about the setup first, though. It's important.

And it starts with dodgy Kryptonite.

Turns out, Kryptonite has a 0.5% property that cannot be read by a mass spectrometer. Our hero/villain Gus, upon discovering this, in the throes of full-on 'eager-to-please-and-please-don't-throw-me-in-jail' mode with the straight up villain/villain, does what I suspect any of us would do when faced with an unreasonable boss who won't take no for an answer but never, ever bothers checking the working: he makes some shit up.

Specifically, he substitutes the missing element with tar, a helpful suggestion he gets from looking at his cigarette package.

Insert your own 'you know, those things'll kill you' gag here. Or turn to Chapter Thirteen for much, much more on that particular thought.

I'd misremembered this as nicotine, but I don't think it really damages the premise – the fact that the substance comes from a product that is both harmful and addictive is the point, I would suggest.

Anyhow. They give the dodgy Kryptonite to Superman (Pryor, in the process, giving one of his funniest performances in the whole movie, hamming it up as the ultimate drill sergeant without a clue). And, of course, nothing happens.

At first.

Before long, though, all hell has broken loose. Superman starts turning up late to accidents because he was too busy flirting with someone's mom. He straightens up the tower of Pisa. then he's attacking oil tankers because a girl (a *baddie* girl, no less) asks him to, and he wants to kiss her, so he does.

FUBAR or what?!?

It's played as a mix of laughs and drama, but as a kid viewer, there's increasing unease, building to dread, throughout. For reasons I couldn't fully articulate, this is *wrong*. He's not just not helping, he's being *mean*.

Superman.

Mean.

Is there anything scarier than that thought?

Well, turns out, yes, kid, there is.

Now Superman is drunk, in a bar, in the afternoon. He has stubble. His suit is dark and dirty from the oil spill. He has a bottle of whiskey on the bar, and is pouring himself drinks. There's a strong sense that he has not, in fact, even paid for the drink, and also that the other people are in the bar not because they want to be, but because he's told them not to leave.

He empties a bowl of nuts onto the bar, then starts casually flicking them into the liquor bottles on the other side. The bottles shatter. The barman tries to protest, scared. Another bottle is smashed. Superman uses his heat ray to melt the mirror behind the bar, distorting his own reflection.

It's hellish. It's intolerable. It's against all laws of God and nature. It is horrifying.

Eventually he staggers from the bar, and the little boy he saved from the combines sees him, tries to talk to him. Superman doesn't want to hear it, and flies off – but he can't fly away from his own super-hearing, or the voice of that child, calling out to him to snap out of it, to get better, to be well.

Because he is still loved. Because he is still needed.

It is that – that voice, that rebuke, that intonation of innocent love and hero worship – which finally leads him to the scrapyard.

It is in this place, this industrial hellscape of broken cars and twisted metal, infernal machines and pools of acid, that I will witness the most terrifying celluloid fight sequence of my childhood.

Superman vs. Superman.

Except that's not right. As Dark!Supes screams – in rage, in pain, in fear – and the yard clears as all the people who work there suddenly remember they forgot if they left the oven on or not, he spits not into two Supermen, but into Dark!Supes and… Clark Kent.

And my seven-year-old heart doesn't just sink, it fucking craters.

See, Clark is, well, nice and all, but, let's face facts, fans, he's a loser. He's a total klutz, a tool; a pillock, as my mum might say. I get why. My seven-year-old brain grasps that just fine. How do you get away with looking like Superman and still protect your identity? Well, you have to become the opposite of him. Bumbling. Weak. Shortsighted. It's the only way it can work – the only way people can see that frame, that face, and not go 'hey, wait a minute…!'

He has to be weak. More human than human. I get it.

But now he has to fight Superman. With his superpowers.

And he's going to die.

It's a mortal certainty. No human has a prayer against Superman. That's kinda the point of Superman – the Super bit, anyway. And Clark is so painfully human.

It's going to be a massacre.

It really is hard now to convey the sheer menace and dread this moment gave me. I've always experienced narrative in an intense and immersive way – I still do, to a large degree, which is why I so rarely see a twist coming before it lands – so to be caught in a moment where I knew, bone deep, that something horrifically transgressive was about to happen, without having the language or even intellect to really understand exactly what or why...

Yeah. This was a big moment.

I feel like the filmmakers knew that, too – understood exactly the impact they were having on young minds, those magnificent bastards. How else to explain how much of the beating lands on Clark, including not one but *two* trips to industrial car crushers, where he disappears inside clanking machinery of death? Or the moment when Dark!Supes rises from the pool of acid and spits the fluid over Clark, causing him to tear off his smouldering suit jacket? Most of all, why else have Dark!Supes snarl 'You've been on my nerves a long time, Clark!' as he batters Kent around the head with a car bumper?

Yeah, those fuckers knew what they were doing.

That last line proves it. Because *I* knew that. I *knew* part of Superman must hate and despise having to play that clown day in, day out, enduring the scorn of the woman he loves and the callous indifference of his boss and the countless daily indignities of being Clark fucking Kent, journalist voted 'Which one is he again?' every single fucking year.

Of *course* Superman hates Clark. Of *course* he does. How could he not?

And all it took was one stray element – one bad for you, addictive, harmful substance, dig it – for all these uncomfortable home truths to come flooding out. For Superman to find himself locked in mortal combat with his own humanity, desperate to destroy that part of him that has to compromise and work and bow down to the world and it's petty indignities. Yearning to be free, to just fly round the world vandalising monuments and scoring with hot chicks.

I still remember the shock when he didn't win. The awe, and, yes, the fear, when Clark broke from the final machine and finally found his rage, choking Dark!Supes until he faded entirely. The lump in my throat of too-many/too-much-at-once as Clark straightened afterwards, before opening his shirt and showing his glorious riot of full technicolour had returned.

Cry? I nearly puked – with relief and joy.

We need stories like this. I'm sorry, but we do. Teenage me is sneering at that and rereading *The Dark Knight Returns* for the eleventy billionth time, and fine, but also, fuck him. He's a smart, often funny kid, but he's nowhere near as smart as he thinks he is, and I'm at this point more than a little tired of his shit and its legacy.

He's wrong – and with the greatest possible respect, if you agree with him, you're wrong too. We need this story. We need to hear about darkness and redemption. We need to know that the greatest heroes have demons. Demons they wrestle with. Demons that, with the introduction of the wrong substance, can be unleashed and wreak havoc upon their world. We need to be confronted with the knowledge we already had – that part of Superman hates Clark – but also that, ultimately, it is Clark's humanity, not Superman's rage and power, that can offer salvation.

We need this.

I need this.

This is the first My Life In Horror I've written sober in... shit, I honestly don't know. It's not impossible it *is* the first. No, wait, *Gremlins*. I wrote that one on a lunch break at work. Hadn't taken a drink then. Okay, cool, so, two years then. Almost to the day. And even in that one, I sort-of lied and pretended I'd been drinking. Wow. That's... interesting.

It was easier, that's all. That's what I told myself. Get a little stewed, the juices flow better, quicker. Less self-censorship. More naked, unintended honesty.

And, you know, there was something to it, I think, at least to start with. Some of the most fun I've had has been writing these essays, especially in the months where the fiction work in progress was kicking my arse in some fashion. I think the Queen chapter from Volume I was especially good. I drank a bottle of Prosecco while writing that, and by the end things were blurry enough that I was struggling to focus on the screen. I remember bursting into tears when I was done.

Good times.

As of right now, I've been sober for six days.

I am not – and I cannot emphasise this enough – I am **not** giving up drinking. Really, totally and utterly fuck that. What I am doing – what I am determined to fucking do – is get it back where it belongs, where it used to be. Where it's a choice, not a habit. Something I can take or leave. Something fun but fundamentally unimportant.

Something I only do in company, and never alone.

And right now, that's fucking hard. Right now, it's the second big heat wave of the British summer of 2017, and I can think of nothing that would taste finer than the first long gulp out of that ice cold can of Punk IPA sitting in my fridge. This lemon squash doesn't seem to be making so much as a dent on my thirst, no matter that I drink it until I slosh when I walk.

My last bout of talking therapy, following the minor wobble I had following the Trump win, taught me something I've long joked about but never confronted: I'm a buzz junkie. Quite a bad one. I like the edge, I like intensity, I like at the very least the simulacrum of danger. It's behind a lot of the stuff I do well, of course; this essay was written 'live' via my patreon, the words appearing in front of anyone willing to part with $3 a month to support my work in real time, spilling out truths I can't get back, sweating bullets but stone cold sober… but it's also a part of why I like not just to drink, but to get drunk, and why I am chronically unable to get my arse to bed at anything resembling a sane time, unless I'm at a point of drop down exhaustion – which all too often, I am. As I am now, as I write this, in a slightly disconnected haze.

Not unlike being drunk.

Hmm.

Also as I write this, I don't know for sure where it'll end up being published. Jim Mcleod, proprietor of Ginger Nuts of Horror and dear, dear friend, has announced the site is closing, due to personal and health reasons. Speculation would be both pointless and, I think, actively disrespectful to a man that I care about so deeply and to whom I owe so much, so I won't. I shall, however, wish him well, whatever he's wrestling with, and hope he is blessed with Superman strength and Clark love.

Also also as I write this, I don't know what my future holds – tonight, tomorrow, this year, next year. I want to be less tired, more alert, better organised. I want to do more of the things that bring me joy, and less of the things that don't. I want to be a better husband, father, son. It often feels like all those things are pulling in different directions, but maybe I'm wrong about that. Maybe it's all the same thing.

And maybe tonight, once I'm done typing, I'll be able to shut this machine down, take a (very mild, over the counter) sleeping pill and book to bed, and get that mythical early night I keep promising myself.

In a world where Clark Kent can beat Superman in a bare-knuckle fistfight, I guess anything is possible.

Postscript: I couldn't find a way to bring this one up to date without doing so much damage to the closing section that it would lose all power. Suffice to say, Jim got better, the site is still rolling... and it turns out I've had ADHD my whole life, which goes some way to explain at least some of the behaviours I was just a little tough on myself about in the summer of 2017.

Which is not to say I couldn't do with healthier sleeping habits. But at least I know why, and that it's not merely some inherent character flaw, but rather a symptom of having a brain that works a little different to others.

And, yeah, it does help to know that. And if you found yourself nodding along to some of the above... maybe look into it, if you think knowing could help.

I SURVIVED THE TERROR

THE BLACK HOLE

I wrote this essay having recently returned from Florida, along with my father, stepmum, wife, and nine-year-old daughter; following what had become a generational pilgrimage to the Land The Mouse Built. It was my third visit to Disney World/Universal Studios, having first been taken by my dad as a ten-year-old, and then ten years ago, with my step kids (now teenagers, then nine and ten).

The holiday was, as always, a trip; and one of the big ways it's a trip is a mixture of familiarity and change. There's always something new – several somethings, in fact, most significantly to me a new King Kong ride which was a thousand kinds of awesome – and inevitably, something missing (in my case, the old Kong ride, Jaws, and no more Earthquake were the biggest pangs). So there's that. But there's also the intensely, comfortingly familiar – The Indiana Jones stunt show, for example, is still running, thirty years after my first visit, and it's basically identical, even though I doubt any of the performers I saw last month will be the same as the ones I saw on that first visit – they almost can't be, in fact.

Perhaps the best example of all is Star Tours; a sit-in simulator ride with 3D glasses that's run for thirty years. You're supposed to be on a space tour shuttle, but C-3PO ends up unexpectedly piloting (with R2-D2 up top, natch) and you don't even get out of the hanger before the empire tries to stop you, and you're off on a hyperspace tour of the Star Wars universe.

The way Star Tours has managed to last so long is the same way the franchise has; new shit, all the time.

As a kid, the three jumps we went through were all connected to the original trilogy; in 1990, that's all they had, after all. Then, with the big kids, there were prequel parts added. But I need to unpack that, because when I say added, I don't mean rotated in – I mean added into the pre-existing mix.

Star Tours is rarely the same ride twice.

This time out, the queues were very low (for reasons passing understanding) and I took the ride five or six times, and whilst some sequences were repeated (I ended up in the Gungan underwater city on three occasions, and was menaced by Darth Vader and Kylo Ren twice apiece in the opening sequence), there wasn't a single ride that didn't have at least one variant; even the moment when you're informed that there's a rebel spy on board the ship who has attracted the Empire's/ First Order's attention was delivered by both Admiral Akbar and Poe Dameron, on different occasions.

It's the kind of thing you could go through life never knowing. You do the ride once and it feels complete and full experience, and sure, if you get all the prequel sequences, you might feel a bit meh about it – but only a bit, because it's still the best action sequences from those movies, and you're still flying through them with C-3PO wittering and R2 blooping and bleeping away. Bad Star Wars is like bad pizza, in other words; it's still pizza, at least when it comes to the ride.

The biggest buzz for me, this time, was finding myself flying over the climactic battle of *The Last Jedi*, with walkers sending up clouds of red-on-white dust and almost stomping us. Glorious times. I think the only thing that would have topped that would have been being dropped into the assault on the records archive in *Rogue One*, but I suspect the implied bummer of that might have been a deal breaker. Or maybe I just missed it.

Anyhow.

So the kid – my kid – is nine, and brave for nine, but she doesn't want to go upside down, and she doesn't want to go backwards; the last we discovered unfortunately after the fact, having done the yeti ride in Animal Kingdom as her first coaster. There's only a handful of attractions these restrictions eliminated, and a phenomenal time was had by all, but it did mean that I had to sneak a morning to go to the Disney Hollywood park solo, so I could single-rider the Rock and Rollercoaster and Twilight Zone Tower Of Terror.

The Rock and Rollercoaster is as good as I remember, basically, with that breath-taking 0-60 mph launch leading into a loop, and then off to the races. It's fast as hell, but smooth. Great ride. I was disappointed not to find any Aerosmith themed tat that appealed in the shop, but it's not like I don't already have four or five shirts, so.

But something funny happens on the way to The Twilight Zone.

What happens is, I get to the Tower Of Terror, and I look up at the doors opening in the side of the tower, 5 or 6 stories up, and I hear the people in the ride screaming...

And all of a sudden, I kind of don't want to do it.

It's the weirdest fucking feeling. I love thrill rides. *Love* 'em. I love being high up, scared as I am of heights, and dropped/flung/inverted at speed. I adore it. And suddenly I'm on my own, and I'm looking up at the ride, and my belly turns over, and I'm not sure I want to do it.

I examine the feeling. I don't mean I *can't* do it, I discover; not at all. Of course, I *could.* Can. Will. Probably. But...

And it's safe, right? Sure. Safer than flying, never mind crossing the road. The laws governing my safety while I sit on that ride will be among the most strenuous in the world. For the 30-40 seconds I'm sat in the ride, I'll be pretty much as safe as I'll ever be in my entire life. Stay on the ride, live forever. Ha ha.

So it's not that it's not safe. On the other hand, I hate heights. I mean, really hate them. It's a phobia that I've had since a child, linked in my mind to being abnormally short for much of my formative years (does that even make sense?) and though it's waxed and waned a bit, it's never gone away, and right now is as bad as it's ever been. And to be really clear, it's an intense fear of falling, not the height per se. I can't look over any substantial drop, under normal conditions, without experiencing a lurching sensation, as though I am falling forwards, over and down. It's fucking horrible.

So, put like that, why in the hell *do* I want to do the ride?

It's a question I ponder as I browse the tat shop, again failing to find anything to spend money on (and seriously, Disney – up your tat game, for crying out loud. If you can't sell *me* anything in either an Aerosmith *or* Twilight Zone themed shop, you are Fail). I don't have to do it. I'm on my own. I can go anytime. I can say I didn't feel like it. I can lie and say I did it. No-one need ever know. So, why?

*

It's the summer of 1984. I am six years old.

My father takes me to, as far as I can recall, my first theme park, along with my sister and step brother. I am insanely excited. I will do All The Rides.

I remember looking up at The Corkscrew. Seeing it on the horizon, as the park opened. My first thought, as my brain tried to make sense of it, was that it was some kind of oversized monkeybar setup. With the distance, I had no sense of scale, you see. I imagined the kid brave enough to climb it, swinging over the inside of the loop-the-loop. Quite how I thought that was in any way possible or sane or within a galaxy of safe is a mystery lost to me now. I can only report the memory, and kind of dig the kid whose mind came up with it.

At some point, it became clear it was a coaster. At some point, I realised I'd get to ride it.

And then, at some point, I found out I wouldn't be able too.

I mentioned being short, as a kid. Well, it turns out, too short for The Corkscrew.

I wish this was a lie, that I had a better sense of proportion from an occurrence so far distant. But I don't, and I have to tell you, I can still taste the disappointment.

Did I cry? Oh, hell, probably. It sure as shit put a crimp on what until then had been a pretty good day. Either way, I must have communicated my disappointment well enough, because when we reached the queue for The Black Hole, my dad measured me up against the 'astronauts must be at least this tall to ride' and declared me, against the evidence of my own eyes, tall enough.

And so it was that my first coaster ride was one taken indoors, under cover of darkness, and in a state of ecstatic terror.

I'm sure it would look awful to my adult eyes, but my child memory is that even the queue was cool. I'm still a sucker for sci-fi trappings and aesthetics, and back then, I was an indiscriminate fiend, so no level of shabbiness or neglect will even have registered; it was Space Shit, and I was enraptured. And the rides themselves *were* brilliant; red metal framed shuttle shapes, single file bench seats. My memory is that I sat at the front, butterflies in my stomach as my father cheerfully insisted I was tall enough as he sat down immediately behind me.

That said, I also know I dreamt about the ride a lot, after that day, so it may be a dream memory, and the reality may have been that I sat behind him. What I am certain of is that I remember feeling the enormous comfort of his immediate physical presence, his smell the most powerful reassurance in the world.

Whatever happened, I was safe.

Or was I? As the ride began, a leisurely spiral up, around a lit model of figures in a space suit alongside some asteroids, I had all the time in the world to think about the fact that I was, in point of fact, a good centimetre short of the required ride height (in the interest of fairness, I have to point out that this, too, may be false memory, in that I may have only *believed* that, so please don't assume my dad was insane. Probably he wasn't).

And boy did that weigh on me, the higher we got, oh so slowly, lazily, the model that had been above us now below, and passing out of sight... How high were we? Genius design, this; sensory deprivation to create a feeling of infinite peril. The slow pace of the elevation adding to the sense of dislocation. And then the cheesy-unless-you're-six-years-old launch warning. My heart absolutely pounding. And then, pitch black... a split second of suspension... and then a plummet into darkness, the scream forced from my throat, my blood absolutely singing with raw adrenalin.

The rest is, appropriately enough, a blur, with sharp lefts, rights, and a sudden hill the only features I have any impression of. This'll sound odd, but I have vivid memories of the vivid memories, of replaying what I could remember over and over on the car ride home, in bed that night. I had a verbal version of the story prepared that I would tell pretty much anyone I met for months afterwards.

I didn't end up with the 'I survived the terror' T-shirt, but I did get a Black Hole eraser that I kept for years. It was in the shape of a T-shirt, with blue sleeves. Funny, the things you treasure, the things you remember, and the things you remember treasuring.

*

Back at Disney World, I end up taking the ride. I do it for two conscious reasons. The first is shame. Disney are running a new digital scheme to manage the whole get-a-slip-when-your-photo-is-taken thing that so rarely leads to your picking up said picture. Now, you pay upfront, and then anytime a person or ride snaps you, you scan your wristband. The photo is then linked to your app account, and you can download it to your phone.

Pretty nifty.

But it occurs to me that it also means I can't convincingly lie about not taking the ride. We've already seen photos show up for rides where we didn't scan the wrist band. But/and/also, it means telling two lies; one, that I took the ride, and two, I didn't scan the band. And, as most people who know me could cheerfully tell you, I'm a pretty awful liar at the best of times. I *might* sail one past the fam, but two in a row?

Not hardly.

And I don't want to admit that I'm scared to do the ride. I just... don't.

And then there's the second reason, and the second reason is love.

I'll cover later in this book how I can trace my messed up relationship with sleep in large part to staying up until 3am on a Friday night to try and watch *Raw Power* (later *Noisy Mothers*), the only terrestrial broadcast TV show that featured metal music videos and interviews (though a very recent ADHD diagnosis suggests there may have been other proximate causes – ah, life, she does keep the surprises coming). An incidental side effect of this was that I ended up watching *The Word* regularly, despite hating everything about it except the live music (which is, admittedly, a big exception, because they got some off-the-hook bands on occasion). A more pleasant side effect, however, was the midnight *Twilight Zone* reruns that were often on ITV.

In glorious, grainy black and white, Rod Serling would walk me through some weird/scary/miraculous scenario. The show had a reputation that preceded it, meaning that everything about it felt familiar, from the title credits and theme to the stories themselves, even though most of it was new to me. To this day, I find episodes of the show incredibly comforting to watch, whatever the actual content – like my other great genre love, *Doctor Who*, I've not seen anything like every episode, and have no strong urge to either. Also like that show, I find that the wildly variable quality bothers me not at all. Bad pizza is still pizza, as we've previously discussed, and *The Twilight Zone* is the TV equivalent of comfort food, for me. And, despite the relative severity of the ride itself, the way the approach is dressed and presented is absolutely exquisite, even by Disney's obscenely high standards. It's is set in an old, crumbling hotel, once an exclusive venue for the brightest Hollywood stars to cavort in comfort, now dusty, cobwebbed abandoned... and, well, haunted, probably.

So in addition to the catnip of *Twilight Zone* nostalgia, we have a perfectly dressed haunted hotel to walk through – and, before the ride proper starts, we're even put into a room where a CGI Serling talks us through the history of the hotel and hints at what is to come, in glorious black and white. I'm getting emotional just thinking about it, and how fucking cool it is. It's a form of immortality for a working storyteller that you feel is genuinely affectionate, and that the man himself might have approved of. Even the slightly macabre nature of the presentation plays into it, given how he made his coin.

It's the best bit of the ride, honestly. And if I could have done it and then skipped the drop afterwards... well, I dunno, actually. Probably not. Hopefully not. Because actually, the atmosphere continued after that room, with an impeccably put together boiler room style queueing area, and an incredibly atmospheric pre-drop sequence that used the music and iconography of the series, and it filled me with joy. And, oddly, when we got to the drop, I dug that too. It felt fun, in the spirit of the material, somehow. I felt safe, wrapped up in genre, hugged tight in the arms of the imagination thrill ride of *The Twilight Zone*.

*

On our penultimate afternoon in Florida, my seventy-five-year-old father and I scored fast passes to Space Mountain. As we sat in the single file, four-to-a-car coaster seat, and the familiar rattling, clanking of the chain dragged us up towards the top of a steep slope, red lettering around the top asking us to prepare for launch... honestly, I was too in the moment to really feel the moment. Which is probably as it should be.

And this time, after the ride, I bought the damn T shirt.

MY LIFE IN HORROR VOLUME II

I'LL SPEND IT ALONE

YOUNG SHERLOCK HOLMES

It's been a year since my first experience of a horror movie at the cinema (see Volume I). I remain scarred and hungry. And since then, there's been the recently discussed, utterly remarkable *Superman III* (most likely on TV, over one Christmas, but clearly an experience that lingered). And it's the summer of 1985, and I'm staying with my father, which means it is, once again, time to Go To The Cinema.

Now, Dad's taken a bit of stick in this series, in an affectionate sort of way, and I'm not really in a position where I could roll that back and remain remotely intellectually honest; at the same time, I feel like as we're getting into the second and final volume of this work, some kind of apologia or contextualisation is needed.

So, to be fair to the man, it's not actually his fault that it took the UK five years, following the hilarious debacle of giving *Temple of Doom* the PG certificate, to realise what the US clocked immediately; the need for something in between that says, effectively, 'this one's *really* PG, go see it first'.

In the US they invented the PG-13 certificate. Over here, we had to wait until Burton's 1989 *Batman* for the existence of the now-standard movie rating for superhero movies with any kind of bite at all, the 12 certificate. I can still remember *The Sun* headlines on that, incidentally – 'Film Censors Ban Kids From *Batman*', they cried, because moral panic only extends as far as gay teachers, and not in any way towards kids seeing potentially traumatic media, like, well, let's be honest, Jack Nicholson, full stop.

And, again, the old man was strict about this stuff; if there had been 12s back then, he'd have vetted, and likely we wouldn't have seen either *Temple* or tonight's topic. And in his further defence, alongside the 'Spielberg presents' tag, practically guaranteeing family popcorn entertainment, this was also connected to a franchise which has, rightly or wrongly, both feet planted firmly in mainstream, acceptable pop culture.

So, there's that. On the other hand, Spielberg had a pretty heavy involvement in last summer's *Temple* debacle.

So, should he have known?

Anyway. The lights go down, and we're in Victoriana. I am almost certain this predates any Granada related experiences, but I'm an English child, so the imagery and iconography is, at seven years old, already familiar almost unto contempt; I can't be sure, but I suspect part of my much-lamented antipathy towards Dickens is the degree to which it seems to me that English pop culture is so infatuated with and saturated by Victoriana it feels like you're a member of the world's biggest cult.

Still, given who the lead character is, at least I know it's not going to be boring.

Hopefully.

Be careful what you wish for, kid.

So, cobbled streets, fog, gas lamps, horse-drawn carriages, yadda yadda, oh, look, it's a gentleman with one of the tall hats, guess we're following this dude, okay, let's follow him. Truth to tell, I can't picture him, even having broken with tradition and completed a rewatch recently, but the folk memory is slightly portly, ruddy cheeks, and sideburns, so let's go with that. And before long, we note that this gentleman has a shadow.

A figure, completely shrouded in a dark brown cloak that is hooded and falls to the floor, meaning the figure appears to glide as it follows the man. Also meaning we can see only darkness where the face should be.

I'm a *Doctor Who* fan, even at this age, so you can bet my SpideySense is tingling a three-alarm warning down my spine already; a feeling that spikes deliciously as… something slides into view, out of the hood.

I mean, it's clearly a weapon of some kind, probably made of wood. At the same time, the smooth motion as it appears puts in mind a robot, to me, some piece of machinery opening to a firing position.

I'LL SPEND IT ALONE

And what the hell can you shoot from your face, anyway? I mean, it's a period piece, so it can't be a robot, but... but on the other hand, I'm too young to know what canon is, but I'm not too young to understand that this story was made *now,* even though it's based on stories from *ago,* so, maybe...?

Everything about the cloaked figure screams mystery, that's the thing, and again, Whovian, mystery = alien/robot, I guess. Anyhow. The nozzle, as I think of it, comes into view, there's a noise of some kind, and the man slaps his neck, as though bitten, and the nozzle slides back into place, in a reversal of the old movement, and the figure glides away.

We follow the man into a restaurant. There he is seated at a fine table, tucks in a cloth napkin, and is brought out a succulent roast bird (it's the Victorian era; if it's roast meat, it's succulent – I'm only seven but I'm not stupid). He's clearly wealthy, clearly happy. Even at seven, I have ambivalence about that, given what I know about Victorian poverty. It's literally as I come to write this that I wonder if that wasn't actually the point; if my teachers weren't trying to smuggle in class consciousness the only way they felt safe, via the medium of Ago, when Things Were Bad. In the week this essay was first written, the Tory government of the United Kingdom had just done the not-at-all Fashy thing of declaring we should no longer teach 'a version of history' that 'does Britain down', and it was/is hard not to look back on the admittedly traumatising and in many ways indefensibly insensitive teaching I experienced as a child (see Volume I for details) with a kind of weary acceptance that, yeah, better that than this ahistorical nightmare. A nation so strong and proud we need commissars – excuse me, *freedom of speech champions,* of course – in universities to make sure the trans haters get equal time with the actual LGBTQ+ community, with presumably the flat earthers and creationists queuing up behind.

Very Unity. Much Strength. Not at all the screaming insecurity of the ignorant bully, terrified above all of being found out.

I swear to God, this fucking country.

Anyway.

He grabs his carving, erm, fork, I guess, and stabs it into the roasted carcass, knife raised in the other hand, eager to get with the delicate rending of flesh.

And that's the moment when, accompanied by a nerve-shredding attack of violins on the soundtrack, the bird *grows a head and launches himself at the man.*

It's the mental shock of the moment I remember most clearly. I can't tell you if I dropped/launched my popcorn, flinched, what have you. But I remember that stab of cold, right in my gut, as the clearly-roasted-and-dead-and-equally-clearly-very-much-not-dead-and-profoundly-cross bird launched itself at, and I really can't emphasise this enough, the man's fucking face, there to peck and scratch and draw blood.

I mean, are you out of your fucking mind? Or am I?

As I think that, *literally* as I think it, we cut away to bemused restaurateurs, staring, the soundtrack snap-cutting from strings-in-full-fucking-Psycho mode to a Christmas carol, then back to the man waving his hands in front of his face, apparently wrestling with thin air...

Except then, no, the fucking bird is in his hands, and it is *evil*, twisting and pecking and writhing at supernatural speed, and his face is bleeding and holy shit it's going to take a fucking eye out...

Sidebar: I'm watching this with kiddo, ten, and the second the cutaway happens she says, with engaged delight "Oh! He's hallucinating! He must have been drugged!"

And I don't know how to feel. I mean, glad, I guess, even proud; sure, she's a couple of years older than I was, but still, that's film literate, right enough, and that same glee carries across the rest of the sequence; for her, it's the safest possible thrill ride, and they can chuck as much scary shit they want at the screen because fundamentally, it's Not Real.

The rest of the sequence was burned on my brain, in no small part because I would describe it later, for weeks, to anyone who showed the slightest interest, and likely many who did not, doing what I always did (hell, looking at this two-volume series, what I am apparently *still* compelled to do): trying to exercise power over that which had scared me by retelling it for others, trying to convey my terror faithfully and, in doing so, by some process not entirely clear or remotely examined, to gain mastery over that fear, even as I relieved it.

So, the snakeheads on the hatstand, coming to life and attacking, the gas lamps rippling and spitting fireballs, the man's final, frantic plunge from his apartment window – there's a good chance that some of the kids I went to school with have nightmares about what they imagined that film was like, based on my telling.

Or, I dunno, maybe not, maybe that's hubris. Probably that's hubris. Nice to imagine, though, that my world's youngest Ancient Mariner shtick had a shelf life beyond the immediate. But the truth was, and is, that it's a compulsion, nothing more. When something gets as deep under my skin and fucks me up as gloriously and completely as *Young Sherlock Holmes* did, I'm going to speak to it. Repeatedly. At length.

Welcome :)

And I think kiddo ultimately nailed it; she got it, straight away, and I... didn't. This movie may have introduced the notion of hallucinogenic substances to me; it's certainly clear that the idea was obscure enough, and the immediate impact of the moment so visceral and all-consuming that my own kid's simple, obvious observation didn't occur to me.

Which left me with... what?

Was the chicken invisible? Had the alien/robot shot the man with something that meant he'd be attacked by furious undead chickens and hatstand snakes that *only he could see?* To which the answer, from a certain point of view, was yes, but that was how my kid brain interpreted the moment when the man was flapping his arms in front of his face, clawing at the air. Not that there was nothing there, but that the others *couldn't see it.*

My memory is that I didn't finally work out what was going on until the characters did, which was some way into the narrative, and by that point, I'd half-watched several more hallucination sequences, peeking between fingers that I could snap shut over my eyes at the slightest provocation, and sure, some of that was no doubt *Temple* trauma revisited, but also, this damn film earned its keep, I think. The stained-glass window Knight was eerie as hell, of course, but oddly, it was the ostensibly more light-hearted moment of Watson being attacked by cream cakes (no, really, that happens) that drove the terror levels all the way back up, for reasons I'm not sure, even now, that I can fully articulate.

Well, okay, fair enough, I should try, shouldn't I?

So as a kid I had a somewhat uneasy relationship with food. I'm not sure why, but restaurant dining especially would, sometimes, lead to me becoming suddenly nauseous and throwing up. Sometimes, I'm sure, it was a simple case of overeating food slightly too rich for me; and I think, over time, some kind of low-level negative feedback/anxiety loop was kicking in.

Which means a kid being attacked by food is going to inherently ring a little more sinister for me than maybe the average kid. Also, though, it *is* a sinister sequence; the cream cakes have tiny, black, angry/evil eyes, and the chittering non-language is skin crawling, and they do end up using one of their own number as a cream horn battering ram, trying to literally ram it down Watson's throat and make him choke, and, oh, look, I can hear you laughing from here, ok, fine, I was a weird kid, let's just leave it there, but it freaked the fuck out of me. Again.

Despite (or let's be honest, because of) the abject fear, and many, many nightmares, *Young Sherlock Holmes* became a vital part of my childhood pantheon of cherished movie memories, and though the relationship with the source material is, oh, let's be charitable and call it tenuous, nonetheless I'm sure the film was at least part of the reason I ended up diving into the complete short stories as a young teenager. I loved them then, and love them still; enough that Patreon backers are getting to hear Jack Graham and I discuss each of the stories, in order, via a podcast series.

So, there's that.

But I think I've discovered, in the process of writing this, that it's that first moment of pure shock, the jump scare in the opening of the feast-turned-predator, that did the most damage. Both on its own terms, as a terrifying and inexplicable image, and for the deeper horror that lurked behind it; the notion that the world didn't have to make *any sense at all;* that, something incomprehensibly weird and awful could not only happen, without warning, but happen *and then immediately try and eat your face off while everyone else stared at you, bemused.*

In retrospect, a pretty good warning, for secondary school, adolescence, and the world of 'gainful employment' in general – all of which we'll get to in due course. And, perhaps, the perfect object lesson for someone who wants to write about what scares him, and you.

You just never know when your Sunday Roast is going to decide *you're* on the menu.

I HAD A JOB, I HAD A GIRL

BORN IN THE USA

The album came out in June of '84, about a week before the birthday I share with my father. I don't know when he got it, just that it appeared on cassette at some point, and made heavy rotation as part of the frequent long car journeys that seemed to take up so much of our time together.

I was five years old when my parents split up, and I have no concrete memory of them living together. What I *do* remember is the subsequent geographical distance between them, my mother living first in rural County Durham, then rural North Devon with my sister and I, Dad living in London. The immediate impact of this was that we only saw him at half term and school holidays, and one of the further consequences was that those holidays seemed to consist to a quite unreasonable degree of eleventy billion hour long car journeys, sat on the back seat across from my *highly* irritating sister, while my dad and stepmum sat up front, having conversations from which all I could make out were tones of voice.

The journeys out weren't as bad, of course – lots to look forward to: cinema trips, as we've just discussed; McDonalds; my beloved ZX Spectrum; video rentals. Good times. And we had the cassette tapes to keep us company: Bonnie Tyler's *Faster Than The Speed Of Night*, an AOR compilation called *American Heartbeat*, *Now That's What I Call Music 1*, and the BBC adaptation of *Genesis Of The Daleks*, which ended up being rationed to one listen per trip, so total was my addiction to that narrative.

Them, and one other.

The journey home, though. Man, that *sucked*. Hours of boredom and/or agitation, with the pain of parting at the end, weeks of school stretching ahead before we'd see him again. It was wretched; and worse, a lot of those same albums that'd seemed so full of sunlight and joy, promising easy good times and fun, turned suddenly, became cold and melancholic. To this day, Bonnie Tyler's 'Take Me Back' will raise a lump in my throat, as I'm suddenly a child again, seatbelt resting on my cheek, the grey motorway streaming past my window, the sentiment of the song perfectly matching the bitter tears on my cheeks.

And this album. Man, this album.

Before the big Guns N' Roses revolution of '89 tore up the rule book for me (see Volume I), I was already casting about for new music, trying to find something that spoke to me on a level more substantial than the pop songs I'd hear on the school bus radio. I'm pretty sure Dad made me a copy of the *American Heartbeat* compilation, and I know for sure he ran me off copies of what was then the entire Dire Straits back catalogue. I loved the shit out of that, too; especially the *Money For Nothing* greatest hits compilation. I was obsessed with the storytelling noir of 'Private Investigations', the sheer scope of 'Telegraph Road', and the doomed romanticism of 'Romeo and Juliet' and 'Tunnel Of Love'. I very self-consciously disowned Dire Straits when I entered my teenage metal phase, and just as self-consciously got back into them in my 30s, picking up the back catalogue on vinyl, eBay sale by eBay sale. It's too bland for the missus, which is fair; they are unapologetic dad rock, by far the least cool band I'm into. But they will still get a spin, on the rare occasions I have the house to myself.

And then, there was Bruce Springsteen's *Born in the USA*.

Dad for-sure made me a copy of this. I remember, because he also photocopied the inner sleeve of the cassette, cutting it out to fit the jewel case of the C60 he'd copied it on to. It was a staple of the long journeys, and perfectly captured that duel emotional state, dependant on the direction of travel; on the way out, the sha-na-nas of 'Darlington County' and swagger of 'Glory Days' sang in sympatico with the rhythms of my soaring heart, the almost uncontainable excitement of by-God going-to-Dad's; and, of course, when it was time for that long, crawling, miserable journey home, 'Bobby Jean' and 'Downbound Train' were right there to wrap me up in sweet misery.

I swear, this fucking album.

It became totemic, to me; a connection to a man I loved so much, missed so deeply and totally; hearing it would put me back into those car journeys, both trips: the joy and the pain, the anticipation and the loss, an inseparable mixture. I'd hear it, and imagine he was listening too, *knowing* he was, somewhere, taking the trip with me through these stories of love and loss and melancholy and depression and goofy joy. It hurt. It helped. I'd often cry, and it felt good, cleansing, and after I'd feel hollowed out, the pain purged, ready to fill up on something else, something better.

It also taught me so much; made me feel so many things that an eight-year-old kid had no business knowing and feeling. In its own way, *Born in the USA* was as explosive a work in my life as King's *IT* (see Volume I) – every bit as transgressive, as transformative – and several years before that particular gang of Losers would march into my imagination and take up residence in my heart. And because it was, ostensibly, just a slice of pop rock – just some big 80s megahit record from Bruce frikkin' Springsteen, for crying out loud – I was left alone with it, to marinade in it, playing it over and over and over. I remember having a pair of speakers that worked off a headphone jack, meaning you could turn your Walkman into a pretty crappy but functional stereo, and doing that, turning the volume up to maximum, and clamping the speakers to my ears. I wanted to feel like I was *inside* the sound, inside the album. Part of it.

For those of you not familiar, *Born in the USA* is one of the finest short story collections in American literature. It is one of the very, very few musical cultural artifacts of the 80s that manages to be both unapologetically of that era and still unambiguously brilliant; seering, insightful, heartfelt and afraid. The collection of tales are as varied as the characters that populate them: road tripping New Yorkers, depressed divorcees, lonely storytellers, young parents, broken-down war veterans – oh, yes, and at least one convicted pederast, just to make sure you're still awake at the back. Yes, you read that correctly. No, it's not a joke – though it is, implausibly, the punchline to one of the songs.

The album opens with the title track, 'Born in the USA', a song infamously adopted by Reagan on his first campaign trail, and still thought of as a chest-beating patriotic anthem by anybody who hasn't sat still for long enough to hear a single word of the song outside of the chorus. Now to be fair to those people, Springsteen sings with an unapologetic New Jersey accent and a voice not short of bark or gravel; my missus can't make out a word of it, and she's far from alone. The cassette came with a folded up lyric sheet, which I remember studying at Dad's house, and I either stole it at some point, or he made me a copy; either way, a lot of those early listens were with the sheet across my lap, absorbing the words, integrating them into my understanding of the songs.

And once you did that, everything about the song changed.

> *Born down in a dead man's town,*
> *The first kick I took was when I hit the ground,*
> *You end up like a dog that's been beat too much,*
> *Till you spend half your life just coverin' up.*

I'm eight years old.

I picture it. A dust and cinder parking lot. The impact of a fist on my face, then the jolt up my spine as I fall on my arse, kicking up a cloud of pale dust. Over and over. Till it becomes a way of life, just part of the day. You get hit. You fall. Over and over. Dead man's town – friends and neighbours, even at eight years old, I was living in a population 450 village in North Devon, and I got *that* just fine.

Dead men. Dead ends. No way out. No escape. And sure, as part of the wider Springsteen canon, you can see how some of this juxtaposes with the earlier optimism and fire of 'Born To Run', or even the more equivocal but still ultimately absolving resolution of 'Racing In The Street', but that's context that's decades in the coming; for now, there is only this album, that opens with these words, this image.

> *Got in a little hometown jam,*
> *So they put a rifle in my hand,*
> *Sent me off to a foreign land,*
> *To go and kill the yellow man.*

I HAD A JOB, I HAD A GIRL

See, here's the thing. To this point in my education, I know about, at most, three wars, full stop. The English Civil War, where the Goodies Won And We Got Democracy (and was Long Ago), World War One (which was against the Germans and Was Just Generally Bad) and World War Two (which was also against the Germans, who were definitely The Baddies this time, and which We, The Goodies, Won). War is a conflict of values, in other words. And while the silence on the relative merits of WWI might have given a more curious mind pause, my own thoughts skated clear over that with nary a skip. War was a clash of Values. War was about Goodies and Baddies. If We were in a War, We were the Goodies. Clearly. And the Goodies always won.

And then there's this verse.

Twenty-eight words, and my entire conception of armed conflict is upended forever, cast asunder, and the world that flows in to fill the space is infinitely murkier and scarier than that which it replaced. No Goodies here – even at eight, a 'hometown jam' is ominous, evocative of trouble, maybe even violence. *Put a rifle in my hand* felt dangerously perfunctory, if not outright sociopathic; and then there's the absolute gut-punch of a final line, rendering the subtext text, surfacing the ugly truth with a brutal, casual racism that rings with an awful resonance.

Yeah, Reagan really used this song on his campaign. And he really won. Twice.

Fuck the 80s.

Anyway. The song goes on, as our returning vet discovers no work, no help from the VA. The war's taken his brother – *They're still there, he's all gone.* – and that final verse, man:

Down in the shadow of the penitentiary,
Out by the gas fires of the refinery,
I'm ten years burning down the road,
Nowhere to run, ain't got nowhere to go.

I didn't know what either a penitentiary or refinery were, not for sure, but I knew about fires and shadows, and the invocation of Hell felt real enough, as did the desolation of 'nowhere to run', even without having the 'Born To Run' connection to draw on.

So, one song in, at eight years old, my dreams of the land of bubble gum and movies and dollars and apple pie have now to contend with racist wars, mistreated soldiers, devastated small town economics, and an American Dream that crushes lives rather than elevating them, leading to an ending where the anthem becomes a cacophony, a dirge, a cry of rage at stillborn hope in a land of hypocrisy and lies.

Nice one, Dad. Nice one, Bruce. What you got next?

Well, as it happens, you've got 'Cover Me', a song about the other side of that coin; a song about love as isolation, a small bubble of light in an increasingly scary world. 'Cover Me' takes the romantic notion of 'you and me against the world' and turns it into a desperate prayer – *promise me baby, you won't let them find us* – and a willful closing off from any wider sense of community – *hold me in your arms, let's let our love blind us*. It's chilling, the minor key and razor wire blues guitar lick sending goosebumps rippling down my young arms. The paranoia and inarticulate fear that would curdle throughout the Reagan era (and, arguably, reach an apotheosis in the seemingly bottomless rage of the Trump juggernaut) is given powerful voice here, and if Springsteen doesn't celebrate, nor does he judge. And here, I learn about love as an act of desperation and need, a claustrophobic and ultimately futile bulwark against the uncaring and frozen void of the outside world.

Two songs in.

Next up is 'Darlington County', ostensibly a cheerier tune about two New York boys (or New Jersey, claiming New York, more likely) taking a road trip to South Carolina in search of union work, pretty girls, and good times (*We got two hundred dollars / We wanna rock all night!*). As a young kid, my nearest local town was Darlington, so you can bet my imagination scrambled this one pretty good. For all that, though, it's still a song that captures a mood and vibe, namely the indestructibility of youth and youthful optimism, damn near flawlessly, before slipping a stiletto blade between the ribs on the final line of the song with a punchline so smooth you'd be forgiven for not even realising you've been cut.

'Working On The Highway' is a masterclass in short storytelling. The set-up is simple; men cleaning up after a week of work (on, you'll be shocked to learn, the highway), *some heading home to their families, some are looking to get hurt*. Our narrator works the red flag on the Highway 9 detail, but he assures us that *In my head I hold a picture of a pretty little miss / Someday, mister, I'm gonna lead a better life than this.*

After the chorus, we learn more about this particular 'pretty little miss' – how the narrator met her at a union hall, her brothers watching on, and how one day, he 'looked straight at her, and she looked straight back'.

The middle eight has our man putting his money away, and having an unsuccessful interview with the girl's father (*son, can't you see that she's just a little girl? She don't know nothin' 'bout this cruel, cruel world?*)

Springsteen is such a sincere, earnest narrator, we're right here with our man and his doomed romance, the dash to Florida... right up to the moment when we realise he's been prosecuted for crossing state lines for immoral purposes, and he's Workin' On The Highway as a convicted sex offender in a chain gang. The smile in Springsteen's voice as he sings the final line of the last verse (*Me and the warden go a-swingin' on the Charlotte county road gang*) has to be heard to be believed. Gotcha! It's all going on here, man: unreliable narrator, a story that plays a straight bat, but pulls you down the wrong path with a sympathetic voice and a misleading setup, and then pow! Right in the kisser with that suckerpunch last line. Mugged.

Comedy. Horror. Con artistry. It's all setup and punchline. Biff, bang, wallop.

And then, holy fuck, for our considerable sins, we have 'Downbound Train'.

This song guts me and leaves me out to dry every damn time, without fail. The desolation of a failed marriage, the cold, monotonous depression of a day to day existence with this gaping, bleeding hole in its centre. The storytelling is so simple and matter-of-fact – *She just said "Joe, I gotta go, we had it once, we ain't got it any more* – no judgement, no recrimination, but also no understanding, just a gulf opening up in the world our man thought he knew. I think – *I think* – it's just possible this one lays it on a little thick, if you weren't 8 years old the first time you heard it; certainly I've never met another Springsteen fan who considers it a top 10 like I do. *Now I work down at the carwash / Where all it ever does is rain* – is that too on the nose? Maybe, but I gotta tell you, friends, it cuts right the hell through *me*. And that's before you get to the extended middle, where the instruments drop right back and we get a long riff about a nightmare leading the narrator out on a futile nighttime run to the 'wedding house'. The passage begins *Well last night, I heard your voice / You were cryin', cryin', you were so alone*, and honestly, I know every word, but I've never gotten through singing it without cracking up. The inevitable crashing reaffirmation of loneliness is devastating. It's the hope that kills you. Every time.

Side one (!!!) closes out with 'I'm On Fire', almost certainly not a second song about a pederast, though the opening lines of the song are *Hey little girl, is your Daddy home? / Did he go and leave you all alone? / I got a bad desire / Oh, I'm on fire*, so, you know, there's that. It's slight, ethereal, but haunting, and also contains the line *sometimes it's like someone took a knife, baby, edgy and dull / and cut a six inch valley through the middle of my soul*, which is another authentic goosebump moment for me.

And yes, correct – we're only halfway through.

Side 2 opens with one of my anthems, a song on the shortlist for either the funeral or the wake. It's a song that almost guarantees I'll be putting another band together at some point, just so I can sing this on stage (The Gonzos covered 'Thunder Road' and 'Born To Run', and at my wedding we played a storming version of 'Two Hearts', but never this, and I can't die having not done it).

No, I'm not fucking kidding.

'No Surrender' is just The One. In an album full of heartache, melancholy, conflicted emotions, alienation, longing, loss, Springsteen kicks off side two with four minutes of pure, life affirming love; a statement of intent, a tempestuous raging against the dying of the light, a refutation of death, a glorious insistence in the power of passion to conquer the very process and notion of aging, to deny it, defy it; to not just be born again, but to live forever, within the bars of a song and the grooves of a record. *We learned more from a three-minute record, baby / than we ever learned in school* – brother, sister, neither and both, I am here to tell you that no truer words have been sung in the entire history of rock and roll. I was eight years old, and it'd be about four or five years before I tasted the bitter truth of this one for myself; still, Bruce had given me fair warning, and at least when the realisation bit, I had the cushion of it being a moment of realisation rather than shock: The Boss had called it, right enough. It's a trick he pulls on 'Thunder Road', and later on this record in 'Glory Days', but

I think never with more power than here: when he sings the line *Now young faces grow sad and old / And hearts of fire grow cold / We swore blood brothers against the wind / I'm ready to grow young again*, I just lose it. It's a meditation on aging that ripples and resonates down the timeline, ringing truer and rawer every year. I saw Springsteen on *The River* anniversary tour a few years back, and I was both longing and dreading hearing 'Independence Day', because I knew it'd make me sob my guts out. Well, he took pity on me and called an audible right before it. Instead, I got 'No Surrender', and I cried through that instead. He sings it like he means it, like it's the most important thing he'll ever tell you. And it just might be; it just might.

Man, I miss my band.

And then comes 'Bobby Jean', a song that broke my heart clean in two at eight years old, years before even the first stirring of pre-puberty introduced me to the crushes King captures so perfectly in Ben's love for Bev in *IT*. I'm not kidding about that, either – this song would make me cry every time I heard it (and I heard it a lot) and my heart ached for the singer, as though his pain was my own. It's all there in the opening verse, pure and clean as the pain of loss can be:

> *Well I came by your house the other day,*
> *Your mother said you went away,*
> *She said there was nothing that I could have done,*
> *There was nothin' nobody could say.*

And if that doesn't carve its own little valley in your heart, dig the plaintive acceptance of the refrain

> *I wish I would have known,*
> *I wish I could have called you,*
> *Just to say goodbye...*

Ah, fuck me, he's crying again.

On the page like that, it could read angry, or passive-aggressive, begging, 100 different flavours of the toxic male entitlement/pain thing and man, it's *none* of that, it's just raw vulnerability, acceptance, loss.

I'm just calling, just one last time,
Not to change your mind,
But just to say that I miss you baby,
Good luck,
Goodbye.

And the sax and slow fade carry me off. Seriously. It would be another eight years before I'd really fall in love, nine before my heart was broken for real, and I can't say it helped, exactly, but I can tell you it was *real,* how this song made me feel – makes me feel – and at least when that pain settled on me as a teenager, it had a familiarity. I knew what it was. I'd been there before.

'I'm Going Down' is practically light relief after that, even as it walks you through the futility of a relationship on the slide with no clear way out. *You let out one of your bored sighs / but lately when I look into your eyes / I'm going down* – and not in a good way. The lyrical rhythm here is exquisite, the words slotting into place like they always belonged there, and the sax solo before the drop out is a Big Man special – my dad always says "Clarence only really has the one trick; but it's a damn good one". Again, it'd be a number of years before I'd experience first-hand this feeling of something good turned bad, with no real idea why or how, but at least when I got there, I had this wry little number to remind me it was maybe not a totally uncommon experience.

Back in short story land, 'Glory Days' serves up two in two verses, with one of the greatest bitter-sweet choruses of all time (*Glory days / well, they'll pass you by / Glory days / in the wink of a young girl's eye / Glory days*) followed by a self-aware peroration in the third that ties the theme together with a wry smile and a sly punchline (*While the time slips away / Leavin' you with nothin' mister / but boring stories of / Glory days*). I think this is how a lot of people think of Springsteen, this kind of roadhouse good time rock and roller, but scratch the surface of this one even slightly, and mortality and the stark passage of time are right there behind the smile lines.

Talking of, 'Dancing In The Dark' is another apparently perfect pop song moment that's got an ocean of emotion bubbling just underneath. Because of a peculiarity of how the two sides of the C60 lined up, I remember discovering at some point that I could turn the tape over after

I HAD A JOB, I HAD A GIRL

this and get straight into 'Downbound Train' on the other side. I'd often do this for hours, switching between the two songs, obsessed with the longing in both – 'Downbound' for the crushing of hope, 'Dancing' for the fragility, the yearning. The beating heart of 'Dancing In The Dark' is naked vulnerability; the need for love, connection, companionship, without which even success feels empty, unsatisfying. So sure, it's a love song, and a pop song, but we're a long way out from 'Lick My Love Pump' and a lot of the macho bullshit I'd later come to adore; this is a song that's alive to the *risk* of love, the danger of love; it's a song about bravery and fear. It's beautiful. I loved it – then, and now.

'My Hometown' closes out with another story, this time of generational change, social struggle, and neighbourhood transformation. That could read like some MAGA/UKIP fever dream of awfulness, but this is Springsteen, and he knows the score; the factors that are causing the unwelcome changes are economic in nature (*Foreman says "These jobs are going, boys / and they ain't coming back"*). The neoliberalism of Reagan's America, Thatcher's Britain, the same short-sighted forces that still dominate our politics in 2020, even as the global temperatures rise and the rainforests burn, and we move to some awful endgame of capitalism's blind pursuit of profit über *alles*, and the seemingly inevitable environmental holocaust already begun, are all seen here in 1984; already giving birth to devastation, chewing up small-town economies and spitting out damaged people with uncertain futures and dwindling hopes. Again, you could read it as a paean to a lost 50s era of plenty, and if you stopped at the end of the first verse, that might even be a somewhat valid criticism, but you don't, and neither does Bruce, and by the melancholic final verse, as the father expresses by implication his fears about the world he will be leaving behind for his son... well, let's just say this one doesn't get any easier to listen to as the years go by.

So there you have it. *Born in the USA*, by Bruce Springsteen. One of the finest short story collections in the English language – and among those, some of the darkest horror I've encountered before or since. Seen through a more objective lens, in may not be Springsteen's best horror collection – that would probably go to *Devils And Dust*, *The Ghost Of Tom Joad*, or my own personal choice, *Nebraska*, that demo production howl of pain that is genuinely haunting in both form and content – but I'd discover none of those records until I was much, much older.

Born in the USA got me at eight. And it's never let me go.

RODE THE FIVE HUNDRED

WHEN THE WIND BLOWS

As we recently discussed, most of my childhood fascination and terror regarding what appeared then to be the likelihood of dying in an irradiated hellscape a couple of weeks after a nuclear war between the US and Soviet Russia came from my mother, and her peace activism. That's true, Teddy Bears Against The Bomb and all, but it's also true that at least one major piece of the puzzle came from my father.

And I was young – nine or ten. I remember discussing the book with a school friend – the same one who got hooked on *The Dark Knight Returns* and started producing drawings based on it, now I think about it (see Volume I) – and by then it was a revisit. So, yeah, childhood. A time when all art is vivid and exciting, because it's *all* new – every idea exciting, every character fresh, every joke funny. It's a pretty amazing state of being, and I think explains why children always seem at least mildly drunk or high, because in a very real sense, they are.

And in that sense, *When the Wind Blows* is a very bad trip indeed.

Part of what makes it so devastating is contextual, of course. Raymond Briggs was a writer and artist whose familiarity to the children of the 80s can hardly be overstated. The comics *Gentleman Jim* (about a janitor of a public lavatory) and *Fungus the Bogeyman* (I can't even – look it up if you don't know) were staples of pretty much every school library or book corner in the country, despite (or, perhaps, because of) the grossness and subversive nature of the latter title. Fungus looms large in my childhood, even though I have little memory of the narrative itself, mainly because of the incredible green art of the lead character; surely the inspiration for Shrek – though Fungus is, for my money, the spikier and more interesting of the two characters.

And then, of course, there was *The Snowman*.

I guess here we could take a moment to reflect on how much of the art we aim at children contains traumatic scenes of loss. *Bambi* and *Dumbo*, of course, feature scenes of parental loss that are shatteringly sad, and represent the elemental fear of all children of loving parents. UK kids in particular will also recall with a shudder the utterly nightmarish visions and prophecies of *Watership Down*, as well as some keenly felt casualties during the central quest of that narrative. And you can't swing a cat in a Roald Dahl story without hitting something frightful that the humour does little, if anything, to mitigate. Children's entertainment has transformed in any number of ways in the last thirty to forty years, and as someone with a nine-year-old who has consumed a fair amount of 'kids movies' over the last few years, this seems like one of the principle ways it's changed, because they just don't, generally, do trauma like this anymore. It's rare anybody dies, and even rarer that they stay dead, especially in the age of the superhero blockbusters, whose source materials, with the necessity for monthly story production, seem to bounce from dramatic death to rebirth every couple of years.

Is that for the best? Oh, hell if I know. I'm not a child psychologist, and despite eight years of archaeology on my own childhood traumas as they relate to art, I feel no more qualified to even begin to formulate a response to that than I did at the start.

What I do know is that when I watched *The Snowman* with my kid for the first time one Christmas, she burst into tears at the end.

And, I mean, you can't possibly need me to recap it. Suffice to say, both the film and the book were childhood staples, even beyond the other works mentioned herein, as much a part of the Christmas TV tradition as *Star Wars* was, the adults loving the hand drawn art style and music, the kids the story... right up to that final shot of a scarf sitting in a puddle, anyway.

The reason I bring all this up is it's important to understand the context of how I came, as a child, to *When the Wind Blows*. Even as a kid, I was starting to recognise the names of authors, and given how large *The Snowman* and *Fungus* loomed, both the writer and the art style were instantly recognisable to me. Known, and trusted – again, while both works had elements that in retrospect are clearly subversive and/or emotionally mature and complex, they were unambiguously labelled as children's entertainment. So when I found my father's hardback edition of *When the Wind Blows*, at whatever probably-single-digit-age I was, I knew it'd be okay for me to read.

Well, not so much.

It's tricky, too. It's a slow build, with the first third just being a painstaking, soft focus depiction of domestic rural life – cooked breakfasts, reading the paper at the local library, catching the bus, notes out for the milkman. It's maybe just a touch overplayed, but as someone who grew up in rural UK (mainly south west rather than up north, but still), maybe not. Certainly, I recognised the contours of the slightly-too-much-time-on-your-hands conversations and snail's pace of activity all too well – in fact it's giving me a mild but definite unpleasant visceral reaction right now, as I recall it.

Similarly, the speech patterns and malapropisms of our two leads are clearly both played for laughs, and/but with affection. Jim is often adrift when discussing world affairs, and Briggs conveys this in a number of ways – by inserting capital letters as Jim reels off the names of the various missile systems and defence protocols, sometimes having him hy-fer-nate the words as he sounds them out. It's also fun how his wife veers between being mildly impressed, disinterested, and baffled – and again, it's played for laughs, but it feels like only the mildest of fun is being poked at the couple; certainly they seem both harmless and sweet, the kinds of people nobody writes a story about.

As a child, I absorbed this with delight, even as I skimmed over the technical details (as, I suspect, I was supposed to), and, also as a child, I had no conception of just how beautifully crafted the whole thing was; how skillfully the couple were evoked, how pitch perfect the dialogue was, how brilliantly observed some of Jim's reaction faces were to remarks from the missus.

There's even a humour over the construction of the fallout shelter, as the absurdity of the advice collides with Jim's well-meaning nature, including an epically hilarious bit of cringe as he tries delicately to explain to his wife what, exactly, the sand bucket is for. The edge does start to creep in here, though. Jim's description of the bombs, the force of the blast, and the terms megadeath and overkill are delivered in the same, repeating-stuff-I've-read-without-really-engaging-with-the-substance way as before, and it's left to the reader to experience the chill of recognition, and the creeping fear that grows as Jim calmly places a series of doors at a 30 degree angle from the wall, and paints the windows of the house white to help deflect the blast.

In a really canny piece of writing; World War II is invoked, with both remembering fondly a war where 'you knew where you were', and it's really hard in 2022 not to read it and think of the crop of Brexiteers who blithely intoned that we'd survive Brexit 'the way we survived the Blitz', in the process neatly ignoring a) not all of us fucking survived, actually, and b) we didn't have any fucking choice about the Blitz – it wasn't self-inflicted, people didn't campaign for it. Certainly in this book, as in the current day, the comfort blanket of our national myth – courage in the face of adversity, keep calm and carry on, and all the rest of that shit – sits very uneasily with the scale of what's going on outside the cottage, and the juxtaposition of the nostalgic reminiscences with the uncomfortable reality is an object lesson in building tension for the reader, while the characters blithely bimble through their lives, carrying on as normal.

And then, the bomb goes off. Following which, over the space of a few days, we get to watch these sweet, good natured, not-too-bright but utterly harmless people die of radiation sickness, as they bear witness to the initial changes that will soon lead to most, if not all, life on earth dying off, leaving us an empty rock floating in an unimaginable void, nothing left to view the buildings and rubble and remains that will become a mute monument to what once was.

And he doesn't spare us any detail. They get sick, then better, then sick again. There are stomach upsets, and later skin conditions, bleeding gums. With the water off, dehydration becomes an issue. And sure, they make 'mistakes' – leaving the 'Inner-core-or-refuge' before the allotted two weeks, and later drinking captured rainwater – but part of what's being skewered here is the government survival guide, a real document that is laughable in its inadequacy, in terms of actual protection from even a limited exchange, and which poor old Jim is faithfully following to the letter. Throughout, it's his simple faith in The-Powers-That-Be that is the bitterest pill to swallow, in a lot of ways; he literally dies without that faith apparently diminishing, leaving us, the readers, with a sense of helpless rage and sorrow that finds no expression within the book. There is a single moment where Jim appears, momentarily, to snap, as he realises they've run out of water, but it's there and gone, his humanity and desire to comfort his wife immediately reasserting themselves.

It's wretched, and heart-breaking. Mawkish? I mean, it should be, but it doesn't feel that way to me – perhaps because of the age I was when I first read it, perhaps because it really does manage to transcend that by sheer force of talent. But the decision to leave the rage with the reader, unexpressed on the page (that I believe was entirely deliberate on the part of the writer) is what elevates the piece to the level of genius.

In an interview discussing the making of the movie of *Easy Rider*, Peter Fonda described watching the film with Bob Dylan, prior to release. After the shocking final five minutes, Fonda reports Bob was sad and angry – 'Why can't he turn the bike around and drive into the truck, take them both out, have that be the end?" Fonda grins. "Payback! You want payback! Well, the move ain't gonna give you that. You're gonna to have to go out into the world and get it."

I think – I am sure – that's what's going on here. Briggs gives us horror without resolution, shock without release, anger without catharsis, and then just sits back and says 'yup, this is how it ends'.

When the Wind Blows stands as a towering rebuke to anyone that claims art and politics can't or shouldn't co-exist. This is unapologetically political, and undeniably art. And by letting the story end as it does, as it *would*, Briggs challenges the reader to go out into the world and find a different ending; to break the prophecy.

I was – maybe – nine years old.

And sure, this particular horror is firmly in the rearview mirror, these days. It's mainly images of my daughter swimming in an endless sea, surrounded by the floating detritus of our flooded cities, that haunt my dreams, rather than the flash-bang of light and mushroom cloud on the horizon. My novella, *The Finite*, which would not exist without *When the Wind Blows*, is in many ways a callback to that old nightmare, an attempt to wrestle with the childhood trauma of this then-seemingly-inevitable apocalypse.

But the end of the world is still on the agenda, and if the science is close to right, still very much on the cards, absent an international effort the likes of which we've never seen. We may yet simply pollute ourselves out of existence.

And if that scares the living piss out of you, as it does me, I'm not going to sit here and tell you it's going to be okay.

Because it won't be. Unless you go out into the world and make a difference, this is how it will end.

I'M A TEACHER OF LITTLE CHILDREN

ENDER'S GAME

It's entirely possible I was eleven. Ten feels more likely, but not certain.

I am still at junior school, and still blissfully unaware of how the benign neglect of my regular teachers is soon to convert to an order-of-magnitude-more-damaging form of indifferent, impersonal violence, taking in both active and willful neglect, as I transition to secondary school.

I know I was that age because I can still visualise the ten-or-eleven-year-old bullies who I was at that time facing on a daily basis, as I read about the fictional six-year-old bullies in the opening scenes of this book. Which isn't a surprise. One of the brilliant qualities of Orson Scott Card's writing that is often unfairly overlooked, I think, is his deep understanding of how unimportant physical descriptions of people are, in prose; he has a perfect grasp of just how little you need to say (and what that little should be) in order to allow the reader to fill in their own life experiences. He's a master of getting out of the way of the reader's imaginations, inviting you to project and build your own version of the characters he's telling you about.

That's far from the only brilliant thing about *Ender's Game*. Indeed, with the admittedly rather large exception of the politics in general (and especially and specifically the gender and racial politics, which are so backwards that Card's writing IQ plummets at times, with a shocking suddenness, to Lovecraft-writing-German-U-Boat-Commander levels of terrible), most of this book is either quietly or loudly brilliant.

What I mean by the quiet part is that, as Card discusses in the gloriously defensive and passive aggressive intro to the revised edition of the book – I mean, seriously, dude, you won the Hugo and Nebula for this puppy and you're *still* this absurdly angry about the criticisms? – he shares Stephen King's disdain for much of the "gimmicks that make 'fine' writing so impenetrable to the general audience". And yes, that's an actual Card quote, and yes, we could indeed spend a considerable chunk of time unpacking the layers it reveals, but that's not the essay I'm writing today, so I will leave that as an exercise for the reader.

Astonishingly chippy phrasing (and questionable reverse snobbery w/r/t literary fiction) aside, the core truth behind the claim, one borne out beyond doubt by the text, is that Card writes lethally readable prose. The pages and chapters fly by, and they do so not because the story and themes are not weighty or impressive or difficult, but because on a sentence level, Card is an incredibly highly skilled craftsman who understands how to write prose that is pleasurable and easy to read. It's a talent that for my money goes massively undervalued in general criticism, and I think many critics dismiss it as something that anyone can do, despite the evidence of, like, the vast majority of books written in the entire history of, well, history.

Additionally, as Daniel Harper noted when we recorded a podcast on the subject of this novel recently, this book is, amongst other things, a stunning and pretty devastating portrait of a child suffering sustained psychological, emotional, and physical abuse. It's interesting how, as a child reading it, I mainly focussed on Ender's suffering at the hands of the other children, but missed entirely the brutalities his training is inflicting upon him. I think it's very telling (and not especially to my credit) that I took General Graff very much at face value, as a conflicted father figure morally agonising about the suffering he was causing his surrogate son, and I think I ended up concurring with his assessment that what was going on was ultimately necessary.

As I reflect upon that now, and the relationship between Graff and the ghost who haunts this book, I am struck with great force by the dangers inherent in the near-universal myth of the older, wise man and his child apprentice.

Anyway.

It's worth digging a little deeper here into why I bought into this for-your-own-good bullshit so uncritically, at ten/eleven years old – an ideology now I consider to be howlingly immoral, and actively cancerous to the human experience.

And the answer is, in part, that Card is a really fucking good writer, and also because he's especially good at writing about bullying.

The opening chapter of the book sets up the morality of the entire narrative in a perfect microcosm – because, again, for whatever the laundry list of things is that are wrong with Card, this cat can Write. Ender has been protected for three years by the 'monitor', a device the government attaches to promising children to assess their potential to join Battle School. The longer a monitor is left in place, the closer you are to being selected. The device 'sees what you see and hears what you hear', and as those outputs are being monitored by the military (who are also the government) the opportunity for bullies to make life difficult are severely limited – even though Ender's birth circumstances as a third child make him a prime target for such treatment, as overpopulation has meant there's a general prohibition on having more than two kids.

(And I know I keep going on about it, but seriously, the way all the above is crammed into 3 or 4 pages of the opening chapter, walking you through it all without ever once feeling clumsy or like an info dump, as Ender moves through the process of having the monitor removed and returning to his class, is an object lesson in How To Write Genre Fiction Amazingly Well Without Showing Off Even A Little Bit).

So, Ender no longer has Big Brother directly looking out for him, and sure enough, on his way out of class, three mean kids block his way, making it clear that there will be violence. We're inside Ender's mind for this sequence, sharing his thought processes. And, yes, for six years old, they're definitely a bit too sophisticated, but ten-or-eleven-year-old me had absolutely no trouble tracking the contours of his argument, or agreeing with the basic thrust of it.

Ender decides he has to win not just this fight, but *all* the fights. He has to not just beat the other kid, but beat him badly – so badly, so decisively, that the other kids will simply be too scared of him from then on to ever mess with him again. His assessment of the bullies is that only a display of overwhelming force will keep them away from him for good.

And as a bullied kid – hell, as a man in his 40's who is a former bullied kid – it feels like a seductive argument.

So much of it is true; that's part of it. Bullies *do* thrive on fear as much as anything else; most bullies are not interested in a fight, but exerting dominance – by which I mean, simply, bullies want to beat you, not get in a fight with you. A conflict where they could also be hurt, or even lose, doesn't generally appeal. That's not universal, of course – for a relatively small subset, sadism is the overriding motivation, and for a similarly small group, there may be an indifference to personal pain (though again that can often be performative, to a degree). Still and all, the notion that one should 'stand up to bullies' (should one be fortunate enough to have both the physical and psychological tools to do so, of course, which is far from all of us and not something to feel a second's shame about if you don't possess them for whatever reason – it is *never* your fault if you are bullied) has, at least situationally and subject to the above caveats, some merit.

There's an element of wish fulfilment too, let's just own that. As a child, especially once I started attending a secondary school where the bullying was more widespread, systemic (and to some degree even institutionally sanctioned, through a laughably ineptly implemented Prefect system), I would often indulge in savage, bloody fantasies involving my inflicting severe violence against my tormentors, in a suspiciously similar style to Ender (this is a thought that will return to me with some force in my early 20's, due to shocking real life events – see Chapter 27). I don't suppose there's anything unusual about me in that regard, psychologically speaking – apart from being prepared to admit it in writing, perhaps – and I am sure a lot of bullied kids will have had a similar reaction to the book: essentially, *give him one from us, Ender.*

And I believe absolutely in the right to self-defence, and the right to employ violence to defend your person from violent attack. Your rights end at the precise moment your fist meets my nose – or, more accurately, at the precise moment I see the fist coming and can reasonably assume it's intended destination is my nose. And this revenge power fantasy builds on that entirely reasonable notion, adds in the rocket fuel of aggrieved injustice, and then whispers in your ear *turnabout is fair play* and retires to a safe distance.

This is dark and bloody stuff, right here; the intersection of justice and violence, the notion of the righteous infliction of pain and humiliation, beating a bully to a bloody pulp to send a message. *Because he started it.* This is the fantasy we tell ourselves, over and over, especially in cinema – *Death Wish, Dirty Harry, Pale Rider, The Brave One, Taken,* on and on and on, the bullies finally messing with The Wrong Guy, and hell itself – the righteous fury of the victimised – being visited upon them.

And again, as a man who was once a bullied child, I'm basically fine with that. I think power fantasies for people who've been victimised are probably healthy forms of entertainment – a way to indulge the darker parts of our emotional imagination without actually doing something crazy and unforgivable in the real world. The problem with this scene in *Ender's Game* is not that Ender beats the kid, nor even that, as we later discover, he beat the kid to death; the problem is that the book wants us to believe that Ender was right to do it.

Well, okay – that's where the problems *begin.*

And again, I give Card credit for his psychological honesty here; Ender isn't happy about it. Throughout the book, Ender suffers many of the symptoms of PTSD as he relives the beating he gave his bully (and the others that inevitably follow, given the highly militarised environment he is thrust into and the meteoric nature of his success there). It is one of the primary sources of psychological torment that both plagues and drives Ender through the entire narrative. And on this score, Card does not censor or cheapen; as a psychological portrait of a bullied and victimised child, *Ender's Game* is unflinching and devastating. In this regard, I would even argue the portrayal is moral; far more so than the many revenge fantasy movies I talked about above. One of the biggest lies action movies tell us (sure, in the name of entertainment, and I love the genre, but still) is that violence – righteous, good guy violence, anyway – is, in psychological terms, consequence free. If such storytellers were remotely interested in a realistic portrayal of violence (and again, I know they are not, and am not suggesting they should be) the sequel business would consist almost entirely of watching the heroes of the prior film disintegrate under various PTSD symptoms, and the addictions and erratic behaviour such symptoms often cause.

And yes, this is *exactly* why *First Blood* is one of my favourite movies of all time.

So, Card does way, way better than Hollywood on this one, and way, way better than a lot of genre fiction, especially military SF, of which this book is, I would argue, both a foundational text and a pinnacle of what that genre has so far achieved. He does it by displaying incredible empathy for Ender, and also by digging deep into human psychology – asking himself *what would* really *happen?* – and then reporting back what he saw as honestly as he could.

The problem – and really, that's too weak a word for it – is that the book then extrapolates from this personal conflict to justify genocide.

No, really.

See, there's aliens (called, and I wish I was making this up, The Buggers) – insect type humanoid creatures (controlled, of course, by a queen hive mind) who attacked earth's colonies some time before our story began. They were beaten back, barely, and now there's a world government lead by a global military holding an uneasy truce based entirely on the fear that the aliens will be back – indeed, it's precisely to find the leaders of tomorrow that the monitors and the Battle School system exist in the first place.

Those of you familiar with Verhoeven's *Starship Troopers* will likely already be seeing the startling parallels, but what's scary here is that Card is clearly batting for the Federation, and he doesn't seem to realise that's the wrong side to be on.

Because what Card does, over and over, is have the adults in Ender's life put him in situations where there is no help coming, and he has to fight as hard as he can – to kill – to survive. And he does. And eventually, he uses that same training to commit xenocide, using a chain reaction weapon to destroy the alien homeworld. And yes, he's tricked into doing it, told that he's fighting a simulation program created as the ultimate training tool; but the fact remains that he's morally extrapolated from those earlier fights, and applied that same logic – I have to win not just this fight, but all future fights – to its logical conclusion.

And when you strip away the *they started it* justification – a line we're taught as children to treat with disdain, as some of our most rudimentary moral upbringing – what we're really talking about here is the raw brutality of might making right.

I'M A TEACHER OF LITTLE CHILDREN

Because it's not okay for me to murder you and your family and enslave your children just because you threw a rock at me – even if you threw it first. Lurking barely beneath the surface of this exciting tale of How A Bullied Child Became The Saviour Of Mankind is a pretty straight no-chaser moral justification for colonisation and genocide. That last is made utterly explicit, by the way, when we learn that Earth is going to send out colony ships to the fertile planets that used to home the aliens and are now conveniently mapped out and empty. It's one thing for a bullied kid to stand up for himself, use violence against the violent, even take it too far out of fear or misguided logic. It's quite another to treat an entire group of intelligent beings as existential threats just because you can't communicate with them.

That's what's so insidious, so morally troubling about the narrative of this book, above and beyond the awful gender and racial stereotyping (though it is, of course, of a piece with those instincts). It mercilessly plays on our strongest moral instincts to manipulate us into accepting acts of evil as morally justified.

I suspect the author would deny it – or at least, hedge. Sure, it's evil, but the lesser of two – kill them before they eat you. Leaving aside how in the real world, for most of the history of colonisation, the fight is between gunpowder and spears, and the ones with gunpowder were *also* the ones aggressively seeking out people to murder and enslave, even on the terms of the book's own narrative this justification fails.

Because the aliens *can* communicate. Turns out, via a computer program, they've been doing it all along, sending messages to Ender through a game he's been obsessed with in his downtime. Now, the book uses this to absolve Ender, both by letting him off the hook for the genocide by leading him to a queen egg, and also, in a passage that makes me want to vomit with rage, by having the queen, via telepathic link, forgive Ender for murdering her species on the basis that she understands that they just didn't understand and it was all a simple communication issue.

But here's the thing – the humans knew the aliens were intelligent. Indeed, we learn towards the end they'd even cracked the queen/hive mind thing, and won the first war by killing the queen. And, as the book tells us, the aliens were trying to communicate with us, and had even found a way to obliquely do so.

So what if, instead of turning the entire planet into a resource-gathering machine for a world army, they'd spent anything like the same effort just trying to figure out the coms? What if they'd taken a child as gifted and troubled as Ender and developed his empathy rather than his brutality?

When all you have is a hammer, every problem looks like a nail.

Ender's Game is a story about evil. It's a story about an evil society, driven by evil men, who do evil things to children in order to manipulate them to commit evil acts. That the evil men who do these evil deeds agonise and argue and weep over their decisions does not change the fact of their culpability, or the harm of their actions. It's a story of how the human instinct for self protection and survival is manipulated to create child soldiers who are capable of committing acts of genocide. It is also – grossly, unforgivably – a story that has the victims of colonisation and genocide forgive those who have brutalised and oppressed them – words put into the mouths of the murdered by a man who, for all of his considerable skills of empathy for those who share his gender and skin colour, is utterly incapable of seeing the other as of equal worth.

And that really is what it comes down to. The notion that *we* and our lives are worth infinitely more than *theirs*. One of the most unoriginal ideas in all of human history, and one of the most blood-soaked. *Ender's Game* is an agonising, sentimental, but ultimately powerful endorsement of and justification for that position.

As such, it's an incredibly powerful study of the anatomy of evil, and how that evil ingratiates itself into the minds of men. It's brilliant. It's superb. It's utterly, utterly vile.

And it's a story that I will always carry with me.

THEY JUST WORKED ON HIM. THE WAY THEY'RE WORKING ON YOU

ONE FLEW OVER THE CUCKOO'S NEST

Didn't revisit the source material, this time out. This is childhood trauma writ large, and while I have rewatched as an adult, it's probably been a decade. Let's see how deep we can get with the aid of memory and alcohol.

And though Dad's come in for his share of stick in this column, this month it's Mum's turn to sit on the naughty step. As previously discussed, Dad was pretty strict when it came to movies, but was quite happy for books to do some damage (he's almost certainly the person who put *Ender's Game* in my ten-year-old hands, for instance – see Chapter 9). When it came to cinematic trauma, Mum had him beat all to hell. No fan of horror, she still somehow managed a couple of really spectacular failures of judgement for which I am eternally grateful – hell, one of them I literally ended up writing a book about (*Tommy*, out now via Electric Dreamhouse Publications) – so, you know, no complaints.

Because here's the thing. Mum may have had little tolerance for straight up blood and guts horror, but she had a blind spot a mile wide when it came to movies she considered Classics. If it was Classic, it was Culture, and if it was Culture, there was no such thing as too young. That shit was made to be absorbed.

And, you know, mostly it was fine. The deal was, bedtime became optional on the rare occasions one of Mum's predefined Classics came on telly. A real treat. Stay up late, watch the Classic. Winner.

Butch and Sundance was one. *The Sting* was another. *Gone with the Wind*. Later, *Dances with Wolves* made the list, at least until we picked it up on VHS.

And then there was *One Flew Over the Cuckoo's Nest*.

And, you know, five Oscar wins, nine nominations. You can see her point. Pretty classic.

On the other hand...

I can't remember how old I was when I first saw it. I remember it in colour, so I was definitely in double digits. I suspect it was one of those films that was split by the nine or ten o'clock news broadcast, too – an odd artifact of the olden days when if a film had a more explicit second half, 'part one' could be shown pre-watershed and the rest afterwards.

But to me, this just shows the total inadequacy of these kinds of 'age restricted' ratings of movies or TV. Because sure, there's no blood, guts, swearing or nudity in the first hour of *Cuckoo's Nest*. But even in that first hour, there's a ton of disturbing-as-hell material, especially for a young mind. Leaving aside the sexual content of the conversations entirely (McMurphy is sectioned having first been jailed for sex with a minor, an act he justifies and celebrates in salacious detail in his opening scene), which may well have passed over my head on a first viewing, there is something deeply disturbing about this entire movie, and that's there, if not from the opening shot, then certainly as soon as McMurphy joins the ward proper.

And knowing what I know now about filmmaking, there's a shit-ton of work that went into creating that effect – lighting, choice of camera shot, the sounds, the costume, the location – it's just one of those movies where every single element is employed in ruthless service to the atmosphere and the story.

But back then, the main thing that fucked me up was the cast.

They're just brilliant. As a kid, I remember that terrible, indefinable sense that there was something... off about them. And that sense of offness seemed to carry with it a constant level of danger, of threat. As the group therapy sessions rolled around, and I witnessed hysteria and meltdowns, I kept expecting some explosion of violence, and spent most of the time watching in a state of flinching terror.

Because... oh shit, might as well. We're in a freefall with honesty here, so let's just go there. The sad truth is, as a kid, I was generally terrified of disabled people. Horrified, even. Watching footage of people with physical or mental disabilities would make me very uncomfortable, and in-person encounters would fill me with a combination of acute embarrassment and fear.

I think – I *think* – looking back, it was largely, surprise surprise, about ignorance. Education wasn't what it is now, and while my mum was pretty good on racial politics, and shit hot on feminism, disability just wasn't something we talked about. And the sad, pathetic, ugly truth, is this – I was terrified that disability was catching. That it could be transmitted, by physical contact. Certainly as a young child, I held this as a moral certainty.

I never voiced this fear – truth to tell, I've told no-one about it prior to writing this down. This is in the nature of a confession – this is to my deep shame. And a consequence of that silence is that nobody knew, so nobody could kindly but firmly disabuse me of this notion. I don't know how long it took me to shake this particular hang up, but it certainly lasted well into my late teens, and therefore my first few viewings of this movie.

Fun times.

Add into the mix a mortal terror of mental illness itself, brought about largely by my very young exposure to Pink Floyd (as discussed in Chapter 1), and we're already deep into nightmare territory.

Then we get to throw arbitrary authority and power into the mix.

Not being able to pinpoint my age makes this trickier, but I suspect that I was in my first year of secondary education. If so, the trap had already been sprung, and I was well on my way to obtaining the psychological scars that still inform my behaviour to a degree I find simultaneously infuriating and kind of pathetic, but it's possible I was only dimly beginning to realise it when this movie first entered my life. I was likely still at that stage where I believed this was where I would be Stretched, and Taken Seriously, where I would have my Chance To Shine, and be Challenged, and was still at least a few months away from the crashing realisation that all I really was was meat in a mincer, with the degree to which I would be considered good or useful measured purely by how smoothly I allowed the shredding process to complete.

How little I resisted.

So this movie must have had all the feeling of a dreadful premonition, or prediction.

Because, check it: Arbitrary authority. Regulated movement, eating, existence, participation. Nowhere to hide. No privacy. A cold authority figure who saw you as a square peg, and would use the hammer of her authority to make you fit in that round hole.

Imagination and creativity viewed with deep suspicion, humour with outright hostility. Punishments that were vicious, medieval – and worse, would rob you of your sense of self, take away that part of you that made you really *you*, kill the light behind your eyes, temporarily to start with, but if you kept pushing, sure, eventually, for good.

Because nothing – *nothing* – is more important than conformity. It is the most rewarded trait, and the only thing that is *really* valued by authority. With it, all perks and baubles are yours for the asking, and without it, you have no value – worse, you are a threat, a danger, an agent of disorder straying from the One True Path.

And then, even God can't help you. Then, you're absolutely at the mercy of arbitrary authority and punishment. And they will just keep pushing, and pushing, and pushing, until, one way or another, you break. And the hell of it is, they really don't care which way it goes. It's all the same, in the end, all the square pegs mashed neatly into round holes.

Except even that's not the bottom of it. That's not even the worst part. Not quite.

Because beneath even the electroshock 'therapy', the weaponisation of shame to induce suicide in a sweet kid whose only crime was wanting to get laid, and the horror of the final inevitable lobotomy, is this: they are doing it all for your own good.

Because Nurse Ratched, as evil as she is (and I realise there's books to be written about the gender politics of this movie, but it's late and I'm drunk), is utterly unaware of her own monstrosity. She is motivated by a sincere desire to help, to cure. Her driving principle is compassion. And it is that awful compassion that is her ultimate weapon, that gives her the strength, the conviction, to squeeze and crush and shatter – and, ultimately, kill.

Nothing is more dangerous than someone with authority and a moral certainty that they are Doing Good, without any recourse to such troubling notions as the desirability of difference and diversity. That, fairly precisely, is how humanity leads itself through the gates of Hell, over and over.

So, yeah, try and tell me this isn't a fucking horror movie.

DO OR DIE

ESCAPE FROM COLDITZ

It's Christmas, 2019. I'm more than old enough to know better, and yet here we are.

My board game habit has gotten moderately out of control in the last 18 months: the discovery that my daughter liked to play and was able to grasp very advanced rule sets with little difficulty led me to revisit Kickstarter like a crackhead returning to an old dealer after a long absence. Kickstarter being what it is, some of the titles I backed in that initial burst of enthusiasm have yet to arrive, but enough have that storage has become an issue, and at a fast enough rate that the bottom of my kid's enthusiasm for learning yet another new game was found substantially before the boxes stopped arriving.

It's a classic bit of parental overenthusiasm, in other words – hardly a hanging offence, but frustrating both on its own terms and as a representation of a deeper immaturity on my part; I was just *so* excited at the thought of endless blissful weekends spent bent over dice, cards and gigantic boards, not even thinking through the likelihood that a) learning new games constantly can generate fatigue after a while and b) the kid might actually want to do other things, from time to time.

Future me, here, breaking in to laugh at recently-diagnosed ADHD. Carry on.

So, no *Legendary* expansions on my Santa list this time, and my sole purchase for her was *RoboRally*, which she fell in love with last year when we played the original at a friend's house. Got *Concept* for the family, because the missus likes that one. And, yes, okay, *Atlantis Rising* for me. I'm not made of stone.

Anyhow.

A couple of years back, my missus managed to score a copy of *Lost Valley Of The Dinosaurs* for me, which was a huge treat, and it was a pleasure to discover that while it was certainly luck based to a degree you simply wouldn't allow in modern game design, it did have that wonderful quality of generating *stories* – moments or strings of coincidence that would stay with you, and invoke joy.

And, Christ, I was so tired when I made my Christmas list this year. The truth is I don't really *want* anything; except more time to write, and that's not something you can put under a tree. So I threw together half a dozen DVDs, vinyl titles, CDs, and books and called it good.

I swear, I don't remember putting the game on there, or why. I know I did, but…

And in between writing the list and the big day, I find myself in the vicinity of some second hand books, and end up picking up a King title in hardback, the re-read of which becomes my Christmas treat; total comfort food, reading with no thought of a review or essay to follow, just wrapping the story around me like a comfort blanket and snuggling in.

And then the big day comes, and in amongst the parcels for me is a suspiciously large box. I'm honestly mystified. And then, as the wrapping paper parts under my hands and I read the words *Escape From Colditz…*

It's the late 80s. I am yet to turn ten years old. And I am playing at Ben's house.

Ben is Alice's son, and she and my mother have been friends since Ben and I were both 2 years old; which means, functionally, we have been friends that long, too.

The nature of that friendship remains mysterious to me to this day. We *were* friends, of that I have no doubt. I liked him, and enjoyed his company, and he mine. We never had a huge amount in common: he was physical, practical and well built; I was small, bookish, and lived, then as now, largely in my own head. For all that, though, we rubbed along well enough together. Part of that was a sense of shared heritage. Both our mothers were very rooted in a kind of New Age Paganism that crossed over with 2nd Wave Feminism (see Chapter 2), and as a result of that, we'd both been brought up on a diet of Winnie the Pooh, Tolkien, Beatrix Potter, *Wind In The Willows*, and so on. I don't know at what age a TV was finally allowed into Ben's home, but I know it was later than mine, and he filled that entertainment gap with books and physical activities.

On the other hand, he was allowed cap guns to play with, and I never was, so, you know. Swings and roundabouts.

It was a common feature of my trips to his house (and it only occurs to me as I write that it seems like it always went that way; I can't remember Ben ever sleeping over at my house) that we'd go out to play, which in his case meant to roam far and wide across the countryside surrounding the village he lived in. And I was okay with that, but it was never something I'd have chosen to do under my own steam; as a kid, the outside was something I had to pass through to get to a friend's house, or endure as part of the slow torture of a weekend dog walk.

But Ben, man, he loved it.

Kid had a fishing rod. Like, age 10 or 11, he had a rod. His Mum didn't fish, and nor did Don, his stepdad (a wonderful man – tall, big grey beard, bushy eyebrows, wonderful rich deep voice, gentle manner – he'd often do storytelling at the local library), but Ben had a rod and taught himself. As we went down to the stream, he showed me the scar on his hand where he'd caught the hook on a prior occasion, and we took turns casting the line as he explained how the lure worked, the spinner that would catch the sunlight and look to the fish like the belly of a small fish in distress; prey, in other words.

We spent an afternoon down there, caught and released the same small salmon a couple of times, and then had to leave – almost certainly because I fucked up a casting and the line caught in a tree. I can't swear to it, but that feels right; certainly the kind of goofball shit I am still capable of on a bad day.

He had knives, too; multiple. Pen knives, hunting knives, one 'commando' knife with a black rubber coated blade to protect the metal from rust, and a hollow handle with a sewing kit/fishing line and waterproof matches. Kid was obsessed with waterproof matches, showing me how they worked by holding the head of the match in his mouth before striking it to prove it worked.

One time, he built a bomb.

He'd filled it with a combination of flammable materials he'd stolen from the garage. I genuinely can't recall everything he said was in the glass jar with the metal lid, except they were all combustible fluids. I want to say there was turps, some lighter fluid, but I'm not sure what else. Quite a cocktail, anyway. And he'd drilled a hole in the top of the jar, in order to have a fuse – some cloth he'd been soaking in, shit, I can't remember, something else flammable.

We took that one down to the field near the stream, and buried the jar up to the lid (my memory is there was a convenient rabbit hole that had done most of the work for us, but who the hell knows, this far out?). I had visions of a huge explosion, a gout of earth thrown up in the air, like out of a war movie or the A-Team. In the event, it was a huge anticlimax – the fuse burned out but the content didn't catch, though Ben reported to me, after he'd gone back to inspect the unexploded device over my strident protests, that vapour had formed inside the jar, which *should* have ignited. I was just relieved he hadn't lost an eye going back to inspect the damn thing. Thinking on it now, it's probably a lack of oxygen in the jar that prevented ignition.

Probably just as well.

When we turned, oh, I dunno, eleven or twelve, something like that, our mothers decided that we should undergo a rite of passage ritual, to mark our passage to adulthood. I clearly remember thinking that it was transparently too early; that ritual or no, I was still a good 40 or 50 years away from anything resembling adulthood (and lo, it has proven to be so), but also that it sounded like a fun adventure, so we went for it. We were to camp out overnight on Dartmoor, with Don acting as guardian, undergo a 24 hour fast (Ben wasn't wild about that, he always liked his food, but I wasn't bothered – as we discussed earlier, I had a somewhat uncomfortable relationship with eating, back then, and 24 hours without actually held a kind of appeal). Of the event itself I remember very little. It was cold, I think, and I feel like it rained overnight, but that may just be an ur-memory of the sound of rain on canvas, which in my mind *is* the sound of camping. We had some chat with Don, and went off on our own for an hour or two for some half-arsed vision quest nonsense. I spent most of it halfway up a tree I'd climbed. Which wasn't a bad way to spend time. Afterwards, there was a feast, and both Ben and I were given silver rings as signs of our transition. We'd both lost those rings within a month, in testament to the boys we still were.

The only thing I do remember clearly from that trip, I remember very clearly indeed; an image with a quality so stark it feels hyperreal, hallucinatory. While Don set up the tent, the clouds were dark and roiling in the direction I looked. Whether or not there was lightning, I don't recall, but the cold air had that prickly quality you sometimes get before a storm. And then I saw a pair of wild horses – one black, one brown – galloping across the hillside, along the ridge above the dip in which our tent sat. They were *magnificent*, huge, powerful, their muscles rippling under fur that seemed to gleam in the light, the sound of the hooves audible even over the rising wind. Their manes rippled as the wind caught them, and their heads tossed as they whinnied and ran on, wild, free, towards the storm.

It's one of the most amazing things these eyes have ever seen.

Anyway.

As you've probably guessed, Ben had a copy of *Escape From Colditz* – the original version, which featured not the German eagle but swastikas on the back of the escape and security cards, in stark red, black and white.

I was captivated by the game. The sheer scale of it, for starters – the board came on four pieces, each as big as a usual board, which fit together like a jigsaw, creating what the extensive game manual assured us was a reasonably accurate floor plan of the infamous castle. There were all the rooms the prisoners had access to, tunnels, guard houses, indicators to show which walls could be scaled, and how much rope you'd need to do so – even a staff car in the courtyard.

The game itself was sufficiently complex that it couldn't be played out of the box, as *Monopoly* or *Sorry!* might. But we didn't know that, so we just played it anyway, making up our own rules, taking it in turns to play the Germans or the escapees. Our basic disregard for the rules gave more of an edge to the prisoners than the guards, I think, but not straightforwardly so; and in any case, I can't recall that we ever actually finished a game, so it scarcely mattered. The point was, I loved it, and thought of it often when I wasn't there, and I was never allowed to borrow it.

Ben and I drifted apart once we came of age and were no longer living at home. It was that odd period when the internet and mobile phones hadn't quite fully arrived, and it was still possible to lose touch with someone via a kind of neutral drift and just not making the effort;

a skill I developed into a talent as a teenager and young adult, for a variety of utterly banal reasons relating to mental health which we'll cover more in part 3. It was mutual; he never made an effort to get in touch with me, either, and that was fine. Like I say, the friendship was odd; it was real, but it was never remotely intense, and truth to tell, when we were apart I certainly thought of *Colditz* more than Ben.

And then, a few years ago, Mum told me Ben had passed away. In his sleep, as far as anyone could tell, in his 30s. He had no wife, or girlfriend. His body wasn't found for a few days. No known history of drug use or excessive drinking, and no signs of that with the body. Just... gone.

Alice never recovered. She's now in assisted living; dementia. Don still lives in the house they'd all shared, in that same North Devon village.

And on Christmas day, in 2019, I open – at last – my very own copy of *Escape From Colditz*, along with a wave of emotion that has a surprising strength and ferocity.

Life comes at you fast, I think. And I smile.

PS: We played *Colditz* a couple of times, but it turns out, a game where one of you has the job of stopping the others from winning isn't actually a lot of fun – at least not for our family. The gameplay design *is* really good – when you're an escapee, you spend every turn trying to work out how to make the best of the roll you get, and you can spend a lot of time getting all your pieces in position to make an escape attempt. Similarly, playing the guards, you have good but not perfect knowledge, and if the players coordinate attempts, you have to be very lucky to stop them all. In short, the mechanics do a very good job of capturing the themes and subject matter – maybe a little too good. I will certainly play it again, but probably not with the kid.

Oh, and the King novel I was rereading on the day I opened my copy of *Escape From Colditz* was, of course, *Needful Things*.

Because when it's real life, the metaphors don't have to be remotely subtle.

ONLY TIME WILL HEAL THE PAIN OF LOSS

STAN LEE / THE DEATH OF GWEN STACY

So, let's say I'm eleven. Could be ten, could be twelve at the outside. We've finally moved to the small village that I'll see out my childhood in, transitioning to the teenager that I apparently still am (functionally, if not chronologically).

Small village life is one of those things. My mum loves it – to this day she lives in a rural community of a few hundred people out in the countryside. For her, there's a sense of belonging; that everyone knows everyone, neighbours look out for each other (even if they don't especially get on), day to day is for the most part very routine and predictable.

For myself, it was hellish, for exactly the same reasons – I found the 'everyone knows everyone' thing smothering and creepy, the constant feeling of being under surveillance claustrophobic (and the forced bonhomie with people I had nothing in common with or actively disliked even worse), the routine stultifying and excruciating.

It'll come as zero surprise to those of you who've come this far that I took refuge in various forms of escapism: books, movies, music, computer games… and of course comics.

Getting hold of US comics was functionally impossible for me until the age of 15 or so, when I was finally allowed to take the bus into Exeter of a weekend solo, therein to spend my pocket money on ether a new album in HMV or a book at Waterstones, where they'd carry the trade collections of my beloved Batman (see the final essay of Volume I for more). Other than that, I had a very small handful of trades my dad had picked up god-knows-where, which I would reread until they collapsed... and the annuals.

The annuals were a few-and-far-between thing also. The ones I'd be gifted each Christmas were inevitably *Beano* or *Dandy* types. I'd consume them, but they certainly didn't do a lot for me beyond providing a sense of vague amusement and time passing – which, again, given the circumstances, not nothing, but in retrospect a kind of sad memory, of accommodating blandness as an improvement on outright boredom.

But then there were the US ones.

I owned only a small handful of these – a couple of *Spider-Man*s, a *Superman* from '83 or '84, and *The Mighty World of Marvel* from 1979, starring Daredevil and also featuring Black Panther and Namor the Sub-Mariner. The Superman was okay, but even back then, I was much more of a Batman fan – possibly as much for the amazing rogues gallery as the hero himself – and so it was the Marvel books I returned to most. I picked them up exclusively at bring and buy and jumble sales, church or local school fundraisers where parents would offload unwanted toys, games and books. They'd often still have the names of their previous owners written in the front – and sometimes graffiti inside as well. I cared not a bit. All I was interested in was the stories.

The stories contained within the annuals were reprints, selecting standout stories from the previous 12 months (or often, I would later discover, significantly older). As such, they offered a tantalising window into a wider world forever out of reach, even as they were, for the most part, deeply satisfying collections on their own terms. The Daredevil collection is a good example of what I'm talking about. The A story is a two or three issue arc featuring a kidnapping story that's complicated by the fact that the father of the kidnapped kid is also trying to build a controversial new power station that Namor is worried will cause irreparable harm to ocean temperatures (and therefore marine life). Additionally, Namor (who the comic makes clear is short tempered at the best of times) is on some kind of day release from forced servitude to Dr. Doom (the reasons for which are not made clear, but do a wonderful job of creating a sense of a wider narrative universe, with stories weaving together to create a tapestry I would only ever be able to glimpse parts of). Later, in my teenage years, I'd come to sneer at this approach, both in terms of the soap opera feel of it, and in what I'd by then see as a rather cynical marketing ploy that meant you had to buy All The Damn Comics in order to know what was going on – and in fairness to teenage me, both are accurate charges. But back then as a child, and now, again, as an adult, I find myself in love with the idea, and faintly in awe of it... at least partly because I'm at peace with not having to know it all, content to enjoy the implications of the bigger story.

The story *is* a belter, though, with Black Panther eventually solving the issue by agreeing not to supply the industrialist with the vibranium the station needs to function, before crashing the kidnapper party, beating up the baddies, and creating and then defeating a new supervillain in the space of about 12 action filled pages.

The B story, *Death Times Two*, features a teamup of The Beetle and Gladiator, as they hijack a train and crash it into Grand Central station – all, apparently, just to get the attention of DD so they can beat him to a bloody smear. It should be a hollow action slugfest, but the art and writing elevate a basically-not-there plot into a thrill ride, the action of the big punch up flowing effortlessly, with the power balance between the villains and hero shifting almost on a panel by panel basis. And the ending resists triumphalism, instead having DD express a surprising sadness – a sense of futility, even. It cuts against all the cliches the genre is criticised for, and seems to be trying to honestly answer the question 'what would it really feel like?'. For a kid stuck in the real world version of Tatooine, it was a window into two worlds – the fictional world of Marvel, of course, but also the equally fictional feeling world of America – land of skyscrapers, dollars, and these amazing stories that spanned out across dozens of titles every single month. It engendered a yearning that stayed with me well into my teenage years, for a country that seemed impossibly massive, and wealthy, and exciting.

And then there was the '83 *Spider-Man* annual.

It's a reprint of a '73 story, in that classic Silver Age art style that I still think of as How Comics Look. And it has so many of those brilliant Spidey ingredients – his troubled friendship with Harry Osbourne, the awkward Sarah-Jane/Gwen Stacy triangle – hell, even JJJ makes an appearance, chewing out Peter Parker for coming to work ill, before reluctantly paying him for photos of The Hulk.

It's *archetypal*, is what I'm trying to say – none more Spidey. The virus Parker is suffering from feels crucial, somehow. Like, superheroes basically never get ill. It's I guess one of the assumed by-products of superpowers; the idea that your immune system can suddenly fight off the common cold is just one of those untested assumptions of the genre.

Well, not here. Here, Peter is definitely under the weather – bad enough that he slaps on the Spidey suit to get home quicker, even though he's struggling with his coordination. It's that famous vulnerability that Stan Lee would talk about in interviews, a canard that was repeated so routinely it's easy to forget the simple force of it in narrative terms, how much impact it can have, way beyond simple colour or added tension.

It can mean the difference between life and death.

So sure, when Gwen is kidnapped by a newly-snapped Osbourne senior, we assume that Peter's illness is there to add a bit of extra tension, as the two battle it out over the George Washington bridge, while Miss Stacy is held Fay Wray-like at the top of one of the support towers. And it certainly plays out that way to start with, as Green Goblin and Spiderman trade blows and gymnastics as they web sling and glide around the superstructure of the bridge. It's thrilling stuff, for sure, but it's the kind of safe excitement we've come to know and love from the franchise.

So when Goblin knocks Gwen's unconscious body off the top of the tower, we're worried, but we're not afraid. We – I – have been to this rodeo before. I'm all but yelling at Spidey to do the webslinger thing, and it's a punch-the-air moment as the webbing catches Gwen's ankle, with several feet to spare before she hits the water.

Hardly even close.

The final panel of the page shows Spidey pulling Gwen up, crowing about his spidey powers, and I can feel the familiar endorphin rush of the hero pulling it out in the nick of time...

And then I turn the page.

And the world ends.

It's all in the first frame. Spidey stops, mid-quip, and just says, 'Gwen?'. There's the Spidey sense lines around his head, but the danger here is not to Spidey's physical self – it's to his entire being. He's lost. He's lost *her.* The mask is the mask, iconic, impenetrable, but I see pain. So much pain.

The ground shifts underneath my feet. The impossible has happened. Spiderman has failed.

This is *The Night Gwen Stacy Died*.

Stan Lee was not an uncontroversial figure. He took too much credit (and probably more cash) than he deserved. He was a shameless self-promoter, and in some ways a bit of a pirate. But he was also a spokesman, an ambassador, and a key creative force behind one of the most impressive and pervasive storytelling universes in modern culture – a statement that was true well before the decade-plus juggernaut of the Marvel Cinematic Universe arrived to lay waste to box office receipts worldwide.

He reached all the way across the ocean from New York, into the bedroom of a Devon boy who was already feeling hemmed in and hungry for stories with a bit more bite, and the characters he'd helped create showed me that no hero is too big to fail, and fail big. That even superpowers don't make you immune to tragedy. And, in the second act of the same story, that vengeance offers no guarantee of satisfaction or closure.

I mean, what the hell are any of us in this business for, if not to try and have that kind of reach, make that kind of connection?

Rest easy, Mr. Lee. And for whatever part you played in bringing those stories into the world – thank you.

Secondary Years (12-16)

OBNOXIOUS, SELF-RIGHTEOUS SADISTS

SMOKING

Bit of a challenge, this. The ghost is right up in my face. Tell the story of how I became a teenage smoker while skipping over the guy who gave me my first cigarette, as well as intoning the sounds-superficially-good-but-is-actually-total-bullshit advice of 'if you feel like you're getting addicted, cut down, and if it starts to affect your breathing, really stop'.

Superficial challenge, though, when you think on it for a while. In fiction, we have the luxury of identifying root causes – that one powerful, transformative event or situation or choice about which our whole life pivots – but this is the really real world, and it's more like terminally matted and unkempt hair – a snarl of strands that feed in and create the unpickable mess that is our psyches.

So the guy who gave me my first smoke can go sit in the corner and rattle his chains in disgust at the bourbon I'm drinking instead of scotch as I pour this one out. Fuck him. I suspect we'll get there, before this book is out, but I'm in no hurry at all.

Especially as there was a girl.

I've spoken of her before – we'll call her Bev. King fans will grok to what that means immediately. And I guess it's worth reiterating that the context is North Devon, and a village with a population just over the 500 mark. So there's Bev, my age, and Freddie, a year younger, and that's it. The older kids hate me – hate us – the way you hate the dogshit you didn't realise you stood in. It's not personal, in other words, but it is heartfelt.

So the three of us band together. Bev is asthmatic, but that didn't stop her from starting smoking when she was eleven or so, quitting again after a while. And as for Freddie, well… You know how your parents always said 'And if your friends jumped off a cliff, would you?' Freddie would. Hell, he'd jump off first, hoping to set a trend.

So that's one strand. Closely tied in on that is, of course, Guns N' Roses.

As I've previously mentioned, it's basically impossible to understate the importance of this band to my development during those crucial years. Music is what I have instead of religion or sport – it fills the same hole, and a good live show is absolutely my church. And GnR was the first time I heard The Word. And while I may now be able to situate them, with greater perspective, in a place and time, and recognise the huge debt of influences they owed to, by any sane measure, far more talented bands, you never quite get over that first crush, do you? I mean, I can say all that about context and mean it, but I can also hear 'Sweet Child' playing on the stereo behind me as I type, and it still sounds like a work of impossible magic.

And back then, they were everything. Alpha and Omega and all points in between.

And they smoked. Marlboro reds.

Slash, of course. The human cartoon rock guitarist – black leather boots, JD bottle propped to one side, black leather trousers, black leather jacket over a bare chest, Gibson slung over the neck, mirror cop shades under outrageously curly fringe rammed into place with a top hat… and that smouldering cigarette dangling from the corner of his mouth, sending up a thin ribbon of smoke. And again, I know intellectually this kind of thing is subjective, but for my money, when you combine that look with his sheer talent as a guitar player, you're simply dealing with the coolest motherfucker on God's Green Earth, and it's lightyears to second place.

So there was that. And, of course, I was smart enough to know wanting to be Slash was sheer folly – to imitate would be to immediately bankrupt yourself, and to no purpose – the position was well and truly filled.

But I was more than stupid enough to want to be Axl.

Because as Slash was to guitar, Axl was to vocals – for me, at least. Sure, he didn't have that Mount Rushmore-of-rock look that Slash had, but holy shit, that boy could *sing*. The range, sure, but also the tone; that shredded, raw sound. I still think his voice on those first two records is a rock instrument of unsurpassed majesty, and I also think most people have no conception of just what an amazing feat they represent (especially, playing the old man card for a second, in the era before autotune) – there's maybe half a dozen other people on the planet who could sing those vocals, that way, with anything like that tone. And to be honest, none of them would sound any better than he did, back then in his prime.

And he smoked.

I mean, the rumours were, outrageously so. The story I remember hearing on the playground was that he actually smoked for money – that he'd been paid by researchers to sit in a room and smoke, so they could observe the effects.

I always wanted to be a singer in a rock band – 'always', in this case, being 'from the moment I heard Axl singing 'Reckless Life' on *Lies*', now I think about it – and the fact that my own personal Prometheus of the art smoked practically sealed the deal. After all, back then, I could sing along perfectly in key with my idol (at least up until the moment my voice broke, and I lost basically my entire accumulated knowledge of how to sing at a stroke a couple of weeks before my Music GCSE final performance exams, which, you know, fun times), but I was, as you may imagine, somewhat lacking in the tone department. I figured smoking might help with that. And hell, maybe it did – I did not, alas, retain the Axl range post-break, but my singing voice does have a pleasing gravel tone when I go for it (more Bruce than Axl, but better than Bieber, am I right?), and that's as likely to have been caused by the fact that I smoked when it was breaking as anything else.

Anyway, it's a moot point. By then, smoking was just a part of who I was.

And, I mean, I found my post-facto justifications. Fitz from *Cracker* (see Chapter 21) had a good line on it ("When you quit smoking, you don't live longer, it just... *feels* longer.") I can't deny having a bit of a yen for Denis Leary's *No Cure for Cancer* routine either – especially before I got properly familiar with the superior source material of Hicks.

Ah, Bill fucking Hicks. What a comedian. What a fucking force of nature. One of the things I love most about him now is his commitment to a given position – he had a huge love/hate relationship with smoking and not smoking, but wherever he was at a given moment in his life, he was fucking *committed* to it. So when he'd given up he was all like "People keep asking me why I quit. Isn't that a fucking odd question? 'Hey, man, why d'you take your mouth off the tailpipe? You almost had it!'" And when he was smoking, he'd be all like "you non-smokers are self-righteous, obnoxious sadists. Shit, I'd quit smoking if I wasn't scared I'd become one of you." If you're anywhere near the kind of obsessive fan I was (and it seems like most Hicks fans are dosed with at least a mild obsession, at least for a while) you know what I am talking about. If not, YouTube is your friend, and I envy you the ride.

But like I said, post-facto, all of it. I can't blame Hicks, and I can't blame Bev, and I can't even blame Slash. Fuck, even the ghost is only, at best, a proximate cause. He didn't put the smoke in my mouth, or light it. That was a conscious choice, made by a reasonably bright 14-year-old, in a full understanding of the stupidity of that choice.

And so it is, 1500 words in that we get to *really* why. And I'm afraid it's going to be as crushingly predictable as you might expect.

Because what all of the above kind of circles hopelessly, like dirty water around a plug hole, is identity.

I had my two friends. Mostly. And my rock/metal love garnered me maybe half a dozen more kids who'd give the nod of respect in the corridors. Not much, but a little. Just enough to keep your head above water, make you look slightly less weak and a mark than the poor fucker who didn't have that threadbare tribalism. And for the first couple of years it served. Not as anything so grand as protection – I still took the odd lump when the fancy took the wrong kids and I was about – but it moved me up the totem poll just a couple of precious notches. It made a difference, if for no other reason than it gave me something to talk about with a couple of the really scary/cool kids. It didn't make me 'cool' or 'in' – but it did make it just a little bit harder to use me as a convenient punchbag.

There's a reason we don't name farm animals, after all.

And that holds until fairly precisely the autumn of 1991, at which point, out of fucking nowhere, dance music and rave culture, grunge, and hip-hop all hit the school, apparently simultaneously, and I know I am a horseman short but that doesn't stop the apocalypse in the slightest. Suddenly, my acceptable edgy fringe taste has become utterly and irredeemably Uncool, now and forever. The GnR back patch is replaced with Nirvana, Damage Inc. with Public Enemy, and I am up cultural shit creek without a single paddle of cachet.

You know what's funny? It's only now, as I write at more than thirty years' distance, that I realise that I had options. I never really hated Nirvana, even back then. There was no reason on earth I couldn't have gone with the flow, cut my long hair into a Cobain bob, and kept right on trucking.

But it never even occurred to me. What I'd found was that the music I'd embraced (and to my credit, by '91 it also included Rage Against the Machine, The Black Crowes, and Queen, with The Sex Pistols coming any day) spoke directly to me on a level I'd previously not known existed. It was who I was. And I can't help but feel a little pride in that dipshit kid that he – that I – never for a second even considered faking it.

Good for you, kid.

Not so good; smoking became the cure for my social ills.

Because, check it: there's no environment on earth more tribal than a secondary school – except maybe prison, and I trust you can taste my bitterness from here. But in a school, there are tribes within tribes, and tribes *across* tribes. Music has tribes, and tribal overlaps, as well as oppositions. Sports fandom functions similarly, I'd imagine. Teams, sure, but also types. It's a complicated as fuck Venn diagram of loyalties and antagonisms, in other words, that would make George RR Martin look like a dull and facile plotter.

And it may not have been 100% conscious, but one of the tribes with the widest coverage across other groups, and with a particularly high population of misfits and troublemakers was, of course, the smokers.

And as soon as I started, it became my tribe. And pretty much overnight, the amount of static I got on a day-to-day basis dropped by 80%.

I wasn't buying favours, to be clear – I was not generous with my smokes, and I'd light yours for you, holding on to the lighter itself the whole time. I didn't become that kid. It was just that I became more acceptable. It was the mutual respect of the outlaw, I think now – which sounds pompous and ridiculous, and it is, but also, it isn't, it's real and it's what was. We – the smokers – had a shared pursuit that put us apart from the other kids. Most of us would have been in some kind of trouble if our parents knew. All of us would catch some moderately serious shit if a teacher caught us. Under those circumstances, your fellow smokers do become a gang, with a shared loyalty, albeit one born of common purpose rather than friendship – but, fuck, when you're a lonely 14-year-old kid, you'll take what you can get and be grateful for it.

And I was.

That's tough to look back on, now, but it's the truth. I voluntarily got myself addicted to inhaling poison, at substantial risk to my own long-term health and a non-trivial chance of giving myself something actually fatal, not out of pleasure principle, or bravado, or even to sing like Axl fucking Rose – not really – but simply out a desire to feel just a little less alone.

And, I mean, things are different now, in several important ways. I'm happier in my own skin. My long hair has gone through badge of honour and defiance to something even more useful – a filter. It keeps away from me people who don't like men with long hair, and that's just as fine as paint with me. In fact, between us, I don't know what the fuck I am gonna do when it finally falls out, as it will soon. Tattoos, I guess.

More fundamentally, that gnawing hunger for company, to be unalone, has been sated by the many, many wonderful friends I now have in my life – first and most important being my wife, and my kids, but I'm blessed with a wonderful chosen extended family too – and chances are, if you're reading this, you know who you are.

Thank you.

But I mean, also, if any of this reads like a shoot for sympathy, I'm Doing It Wrong. I'm well aware of the utter banality and relatively tame nature of this story (no change there then, haha). I have people closer to me who went way deeper and darker on this stuff. Some of them didn't come back (see Volume I). And again, if you're reading this, I'm sure you have too.

I do, however, think there remains some value in reflecting on the very banality of that horror – the notion that we are so collectively fucked up that we absorb the reality of stories like this without horror, without comment, barely without any notice whatsoever. It becomes background noise, static on the radio, unheard against the grander horrors we inflict, as a species, on the world stage, and on each other.

And in terms of priorities, it should. There's a shitload more wrong with the world than the self-inflicted wounds of a teenager a little too keen to fit in. And it's not like, in my case at least, anyone died.

Still, it is kind of fucked up, I think.

PS: Why did I quit? Well, that's where my 'God-is-a-shitty-novelist' theory kicks in. I finally started singing in a band, and learned I'd gain half an octave in range and about 15 seconds more note per lungful if I quit. So I did.

I know, I know. But it's true. And while I miss it, and still dream of it periodically, especially when I'm in my cups (one of the things I wanted to get into but didn't was the cigarette as a fetish object, because God fucking damn, there's something demonically perfect about just about every aspect of them apart from the, you know, killing you part) I still love singing more. And I think – I hope – I always will. So, yeah. Rock and roll saved my life. :)

I'M NOT SCARED OF YOU ANYMORE. YOU'RE SCARED OF ME

THE WILD ONE

Shit, man, I dunno. Young. Probably just teen or cusping it.

It's Devon. The village. Population 450. And my memory has it that it's a late night showing my mum's let me stay up for. Like for *The Sting* (and, for no reason I can fathom at this stage, the Eastwood flick *FireFox*). It feels like one of those, but maybe I'm cross-referencing from seeing a later TV listing for a late-night showing; shit, maybe it was a lazy Sunday afternoon.

No reason why not, after all. This may have been banned for 13 years in the UK upon release, only scoring an X certificate thereafter, but there's nothing in here you couldn't show at teatime on TV in 1990/1/2/3, in all honesty. The past isn't just another country, it's another fucking planet.

And yet.

Years later, I'll see *Rebel Without a Cause*, as part of a *Moviedrome* season. And, you know, it's fine. Good, even. James Dean is everything you've read, for sure; angst and pain and strength and vulnerability and fundamentally a lost puppy in a world that makes no sense to him. At the same time... Well, let me put it like this; I watched these movies on consecutive weekends with a friend of mine, the essay subject first and *Rebel* second, and her observation after *Rebel* was 'It's good, but you could tell it was made by normies'.

And she was – is – right. That's not to damn *Rebel,* nor to yuck anybody's yum, but *Rebel* is, at heart, 'A Very Special Episode Of...' Sure, done about as well as anyone has ever managed such a format, but that's what it is.

And then, there's... this.

We open with black and white on that most American of images: an open highway, stretching back as far as the eye can see. Some text appears on screen, strongly implying what we're about to see is both a true story and carries with it the whiff of scandal. The final line of text reads "It is a public challenge not to let this happen again". Which, you know, points for being possibly misleading and definitely ominous.

And then we get the voice-over.

"Mostly, I remember the girl."

And, I mean, come on.

By this age, I'm sure of very little. Two facts I am pretty confident about are that I am a massive Springsteen fan, and that I'm basically heterosexual; or at least, that women hold an at this stage not well-explored but absolutely soul-deep fascination to me; a fact that, in my case, I can date with some confidence to seeing Belinda Carlisle perform 'Heaven is a Place on Earth' on *Top of the Pops* in 1987. I was 9, but I'll never forget how that moment made me feel. If you know, you know.

Anyway, the point is this; we're combining two of my essential cultural obsessions in one single line/image combo here – the open road of the US fucking A, legendary backdrop to so much of Springsteen's epic triumph and heartache (often both in the same song), and 'the girl'; a Springsteen staple (Mary, Wendy, Bobby Jean et al), of course, but also a pop culture and pulp fiction staple that has captivated me since long before puberty (if, indeed, I'm meaningfully through that process by the time this movie surfaces, which I frankly doubt). This is not just totemic, in other words – it's close to elemental. And, sure, with adult eyes, there's a ton of deconstruction work I could do on literally every single element we're talking about, here; but I'm not an adult, I'm a kid, and, for whatever the word even means, these concepts are still pure; by which I may mean nothing grander than 'uncomplicated', but okay, whatever, this is feelings we're into, and I am *feeling it.*

And then there's this *voice*. It's beautiful. *He's* beautiful. I mean, in about 60 seconds or so, we're going to be hit full bore with that fact, as the muttering becomes a rumble becomes a roar and the dark cloud on the horizon line becomes a swarm of bikes that hurtle towards us before passing with seemingly inches to spare, and then a smash cut to Brando in the jacket and hat and shades and the score crashes in and the title *The Wild One* appears over that impossible figure in words that feel 100 foot tall and written in fire…

But even before then, there's this disembodied voice, talking about The Girl, wondering at her and how she affected him, before going on to muse about fate and happenstance and odds. And the tone, the delivery, they are velvet. Soft. Almost musical. It's the voice of a man so utterly secure in who he is that he doesn't have to worry about sounding high or even effeminate; the voice is confident because it's sexy and sexy because it's confident, and, among many other things, I'm suddenly even more secure in my sexuality than I was five minutes before.

Because I don't think it would be possible to have even a minimal attraction to men and not find Brando in this movie anything less than devastatingly sexy.

And I don't.

I understand, intellectually, that he is, to be clear. And I do periodically catch myself wishing I had an ounce of his swagger, his appeal, his apparently effortless cool – especially as a teenager, but, let's be real, even now, once in a while, sure. And my heart fucking soars pretty much every time he's in the frame, throughout the running time of the movie. But, without wishing to be crude, my heart is the only part that does soar. I wouldn't be ashamed if it were other. But it isn't.

(Sidebar to gay men reading this; I'm doing a bit. Of course you're still gay if you don't want to fuck Brando in *The Wild One*. Though if you also don't want to fuck Slash, I do Have Questions)

(Second sidebar: That was also a bit. Sorry. I'll shut up now)

Anyway.

Following the frankly stupendous opening, we follow Johnny and his club – B.R.M.C. on the back of the leather jackets, and not a fucking clue, but I wanted one so, so bad – to a speedway racing meet. They watch the racers, for a while, Brando theatrically blinking dust from his eyes as the racers scream past... And then, seemingly on a whim, he walks across the racetrack, hands nonchalantly in his jacket pockets, elbows sticking out. Of course, the rest of the club immediately follows him, causing at least one contestant to almost crash, disrupting his run, and causing an announcement across the tannoy: "Please, don't cross the track!"

At this point, one of the club climbs a few steps up a nearby ladder on the side of one of the PA towers and, leaning forward with a mocking voice says "Please, don't cross the track! We wouldn't want you to get hurt! Blood makes everything slippery!", which earns a round of laughter from the club. Following this moment, they have a confrontation with one of the officials, then one of the racers, then finally a cop, who moves them on.

I want to zoom in on this moment because it happens early in the film and it serves as a microcosm of so much of what is to follow.

The first is the positioning of the film's sympathies and the way that positioning is passed to the audience. So let's get into what I first heard Joe Hill talk about as 'duckling theory' – the idea that an audience will imprint, like the eponymous duckling, on whatever character they first encounter. It's not a cast iron law of storytelling or anything (pulp horror writers like James Herbert delighted in playing with it, for example; not to spoil any Herbert books for you, but I'd advise against getting emotionally attached to anyone you meet in chapter one of most of his novels, and God help anyone in a prologue); but it is a tendency, and one that I feel like even in '53, movie makers had to understand. Given this, having Brando's voiceover be the first thing we hear, and the man/icon on his bike the first we see is pretty suggestive. I don't want to keep banging on about how he looks in this movie, because we'll be here all day, but if that overused word iconic has any meaning left, it must surely apply to Brando in biking leathers astride a road hog. I mean, come *on.*

So. Of course I've imprinted on Brando at this point, especially as a budding metalhead in a tiny rural village all but surrounded by Squares who Just Don't Understand – but I'm pretty sure that not only am I meant to, but so are *you,* whoever you are. And let's just take a moment to admire the enormous balls of making a film in 1953 that invites the audience to primarily identify/sympathise (both weasel words, but still driving at something real, I think) with an antisocial biker club.

And then, look at how this scene plays out. Firstly, the official who confronts them is effectively mocked out of the conversation. Next, the racer, initially dismissive, is forced to walk away when faced with a straight-up challenge to try his skills against Johnny one on one. Finally, the cop does exert authority, moving the club on.

The cop figure echoes very neatly the movie's conclusion, of course, but it's the first two confrontations I want to focus on, because I rewatched this recently, and it was the damndest thing, in that I found myself seeing the scene via two conflicting perspectives at once, whereas as a kid, I'd only had one.

Because, dig it; as a kid, the duckling principle was in maximum effect. Hell, I *had* a leather jacket; the BMRC were my tribe, spiritually. I felt this to my core. So when they walked across the track and fucked up the race, my heart sang, and when they mocked the safety announcement and the racer, I laughed along with them. Because, yeah, man, fuck these squares and their cornball races-by-the-rules. Johnny can beat them all. He just don't wanna, because he's too damn cool. And as a kid with undiagnosed ADHD in a rural secondary school who had enough raw intelligence to be able to coast on the class and homework, and who'd just started to develop a sense that maybe all of it was bullshit hoop-jumping for hoop jumping's sake, let me count the ways I related. I loved it. I loved Johnny and the boys Sticking It To The Man, and fuck that cop moving them on, they weren't doing nothing.

And I still agree with that last part, for the record.

But.

I think that old saw about how you drift right politically as you get older is mostly bullshit. Personally speaking, I've never held more radical politics than I do in the year of our lord 2022, at age 44. But I think the kernel of truth around which that particular puffball popcorn of bullshit has grown is that as you get older, you do get more tired of *all* forms of bullshit, including cynicism, and maybe especially youthful cynicism. It's not that I can't, still, relate to the nihilistic impulse to just walk the fuck across the track because you feel like it; it's just that tempered against that is an understanding of the futility of it, the pointlessness, a feeling that there are more important, meaningful conventions to fuck with that might have more impact and power, and that, given the current state of play, this kind of adolescent nonsense feels like... well, adolescent nonsense.

And I can feel him howling in my breast as I type that; the scared kid with a stomach full of lies that he's desperate to puke up and a heart full of fuck you for everybody and everything that conforms to a system that's trying to kill him. I feel him. And his heart is absolutely in the right place.

But there is such a thing as wisdom. And that's not an old man cop-out. That's life experience, an understanding of The Finite that's almost impossible for the young, immortal mind to grasp. It's a calm, kind, rational voice, but not one devoid of the rage that fuels the entirely justified youthful piss and vinegar, and it simply says 'pick your battles'.

God, I'm so fucking tired.

Anyhow. Point is, watching it now, sure, fuck the cop moving them on. And sure, fuck the racer, too; there's a gatekeeper quality to his arrogance, and at this point in my life, I'm so very far over wankers who have expertise in one area acting like it makes them lords of all creation. He chickens out because he knows Johnny will hand his arse to him, and also because he has everything to lose and Johnny has nothing, and fuck him for that, too.

But then there's the official.

And what's changed between then and now is I've been given shit jobs to do, and I can't help but feel for the guy. Not to put too fine a point on it, I've been required as part of a paying role to tell people things they don't want to hear and even gotten a bit of verbal and physical abuse as a result; nothing serious, nothing life-changing, but enough that my instinctive sympathies rest, these days, with anyone in a customer facing role. Because I know from first-hand that a person in that spot is never responsible for the rules they're being asked to enforce. 'You can always pay one half of the poor to kill the other half', as the old saying goes, and this ain't that, of course, but it's somewhere on the spectrum that has that as the endpoint. And it fucking sucks. So, as much as my gut instinct pulls me towards the BRMC, yeah, I'm going to allow that being dicks to the official is, well, a dick move.

I'M NOT SCARED OF YOU ANYMORE...

As I think about it more, there's this riff in *Easy Rider* where Jack Nicholson's lawyer talks about how the reason people hate Fonda and Hopper's bikers is because they represent freedom, and how everyone likes to talk about it, but nobody likes to see people actually living it, *embodying it*, and here's the BRMC in '53, personifying what *Easy Rider* didn't have the confidence to keep as subtext, and that's... interesting.

The bike meet is important for two main reasons; firstly, it's the source of the stolen racing trophy that'll instigate so many of the fateful (and fatal, I guess) turning points of the narrative, right down to the final scene denouement, and the smile that broke a million hearts. The fact that it's stolen is enormously important, and delivers layers throughout; for now, let's just observe that it serves a duel symbolism from the get-go. On the one hand, it's literally Stolen Valour, that most dishonourable of deceits, giving Johnny an entirely bogus and unearned aura of achievement – sure, his crew is in on the gag, but wild horses wouldn't drag it from them to an outsider, they stole it for him, and his valour is theirs. But there's a flip side to that, right? We're back to 'fuck your rules'. Why shouldn't Johnny steal it, wear it, wield it over the squares? It's *all* meaningless, *all* stolen valour. It only means something because we say (pretend) it does. By stealing it (well, it's stolen for him, which in some ways is more poetic), Johnny underlies the trophy is what it always was: a lump of dipped-gold metal, just like a sheriff's badge is a lump of shaped tin, just like a uniform or flag is... ah, you get the idea.

And you know what I'm realising, kids? We're nearly three thousand words in and we're barely past the first scene. Meaning if I'm gonna say everything I want to about this movie, it's gonna end up as a damn book. Okay, so let's not do that (at least not here – if you're an editor and you like the idea of Kit Power on *The Wild One*, drop me a line and we'll talk).

Let's just zoom in on The Girl.

Because I think part of why this story hit me so hard was that I was on both sides of the love story. Johnny spoke to my soul; angry, lost, bright enough to see the size and depth of the hole, but not clue one how to get out, angry at the world for simply existing, configured as it was, and utterly convinced of the impossibility of anything resembling happiness, let alone contentment. A man for whom there is only the temporary relief brought when rage is allowed to drive action, burning out, temporarily, the baseline feelings of futility.

But then there's Mary Murphy's Kathie.

And I was her, too.

I didn't have the same deep roots in the village I was mostly raised in, and looking back, that was my saving grace; I knew I didn't *belong,* and it was the most basic article of my faith, so solid as to go utterly unexamined, that I would, one day, *leave.* Still, though, at age twelve or thirteen, the gap between here and now and *leaving* is essentially infinite. So, sure, it'll happen, of course… but if Now is Forever, what, exactly, is going to be left of me, by the time my life finally has a chance to begin?

So, sure, I'm Johnny. But I'm Kathie, too. And I'm sure an analyst would have a field day with that, but it is what it is. Her doe-eyed romanticism is mine, her naivety is mine, but so is the war between those desires, hopes, dreams… and the crushing mundanity of day-to-day life, closing off thought and possibility, feeding the romanticism whilst also underlining the essential fantasy nature of the dream. It's just now striking me that I can't think of any narrative convention that gender swaps this situation very often; and I can't help but wonder what a romantic female biker club leader might have done to my young heart and libido, (except exploding it beyond any possible repair, obviously). So, maybe it's just as well. Regardless, what the BRMC represent to Kathie is exactly what they represent to me; a kind of impossible freedom that is both desperately attractive and clearly utterly unachievable; they may as well have come from the moon, for all the good their visit will do me when they inevitably roll out of town.

And that's kind of my relationship with music, with movies, with art, at this age, in this time and place. I'm perpetually drawn, moth to a flame, to the art that lights up a whole different way of being, a mode of existence I can romanticise with a fiery passion and ache, because I know it's forever unattainable. There's pain there, of course, but there's a safety in that pain; it reinforces the inevitability of the status quo, which, sure, is shit, but at least, underneath that knowledge/pain, the sneaky voice that says *there's nothing you can do.*

And, of course, if you believe that, it's true.

And it's a pretty potent horror story, I think.

The Wild One is, I have discovered on a recent rewatch, about enough things that I'd need a book to do it all justice (and, seriously; commission me, my rates are very reasonable). I've only touched on how the entire piece is suffused with a sense of alienation; sure, between tribes, but also *within* them; the BRMC may have started off as Beetles, but it's clear Johnny feels almost as distant from the rest of his current crew as he does from his old club; Kathie is alienated from her father, and her town, but also Johnny, the object of her desire, the fantasy-made-flesh-rendered-nightmare-but-still-yearned-for (a journey that you can track based on her peeling back the layers of meaning in the racing trophy, as I think about it). The townsfolk and the BRMC are mutually alienated, of course; but the town is equally clearly as fractured as the bikers, if not more so, with ancient animosities and cycles of behaviour playing out against the psychodrama of The Night The BRMC Came To Town. That *Easy Rider* riff about the nature of freedom is here, as is everything *Rebel Without a Cause* didn't have the bottle to keep subtext, and there's also a nihilism that leaks out from Johnny himself, infecting everything and everyone he comes into contact with.

But for young teenage me, I think it was mainly about the impossibility of romantic love, both on its own terms, and as a stand-in for all the things I might desire for myself and could never, ever have. The freedom I knew I'd never have the courage to even try and live. The inevitability of a life of indentured servitude to the almighty Machine we pretend is called society, but whose true purpose is to grind us to dust and extract and syphon our life force as Value, to be drunk by an elite to whom we, in the words of Henry Rollins, 'look like ants, and our flesh takes just like chicken'.

And do you know, in one way, I was kinda sorta right?

But in many other far more important ways, I was as wrong as it's only possible to be when you're young, and you're burning with a fear that All That Is is not just Awful, but Inevitable.

There are things this project has reminded me about being young that I've been glad to rediscover, to savour, and to try and nurture anew in my adult life. But that particular feeling?

Sorry, kid. You can keep it.

It does get better.

THERE'S NO REAL MAGIC, EVER

MARTIN

Because here's the deal: the second your kid has a TV in their room – or, shit, a PC, iPad, any device that can connect to broadcast medium, the war is over. You waved the white flag. They can pour literally anything into their brains, now. Whatever human horror you can conceive, they can watch, in 1080 resolution. And almost certainly in porn parody form. All you can do is hope that whatever you've given them to that point, whatever you've nurtured inside them, will be enough for them to tell right from wrong, know their own limits, to survive whatever cultural assault they're about to self-inflict.

Truly, hope. That's all you've got.

Do you know it, as a parent? Sure you do. As long as you remember being a kid, how could you not?

No internet in the bedroom for *this* kid. Back when I were a boy, dinosaurs roamed the earth, and the internet only existed to tell a computer scientist in some posh university that the kettle in the other room had boiled.

All I had in my room was a black and white portable TV (with, crucially, a headphone socket) that I'd bought from a neighbour for the princely sum of £25, and the 4 terrestrial channels it could pick up.

Turns out, that was plenty.

I'm pretty sure I can trace back my lifelong issues with maintaining a sleep pattern, and in particular my seemingly chronic inability to get to sleep on a Friday night prior to 2am even now, at 44, back to that giant heavy lump of plastic, wire and glass.

Well, that and undiagnosed ADHD, not to endlessly repeat myself.

There was this program called *Raw Power*, see. On at 3am, it was the only broadcast show in the UK dedicated to rock and metal. Every week, it sat there in the listings, a mortal challenge to my tired pre-teen arse – you want the life source? Gotta stay up late.

And more often than not, I did.

But we're not here to talk about *Raw Power* (or the replacement show *Noisy Mothers*). Nope, this is about what I'd sometimes end up watching while completing my lonely vigil to the hallowed hour of 3am.

This is about Channel 4 running a series of previously banned or censored films, and the night I'd catch one that would cut me deep enough that, even on a recent rewatch, I'd still find myself stunned by its power, its darkness.

We need to talk about *Martin*.

The film opens with a woman getting on a train. She's beautiful. She's being followed by a strange-looking young man. He's... not ugly, but odd. My 11/12/13 year old mind latches onto him instinctively. I, like I suspect 95% of the rest of the population, was an awkward kid. I knew I liked girls – even at 11, I knew that. But I was, as is normal, not equipped emotionally or biologically to really know what that meant, or to do anything about it.

And yet, I yearned.

I was drawn to girls I perceived to be pretty or beautiful. I wanted to be someone's boyfriend, without knowing that meant or could mean any more than holding hands, (or maybe, in a fever dream, a kiss on the lips). I guess that innocence is something to be grateful for – I wonder how many post-internet children get to stay that innocent, that long.

Still, I felt... something. And I couldn't understand it or explain it, but thanks to pop culture, I knew what it was called: love.

So I loved. A lot. From a distance, after a couple of utterly crushing instant rejections. I loved, and I yearned to be loved, and I didn't have a fucking clue what any of it meant.

So then there's this boy. And the title card helpfully tells us he's called Martin. And he looks at the pretty girl, just like I look at pretty girls, knowing they do not, will not, look back.

He finds out where she's sleeping – it's a sleeper train, which I know all about, on account of being a male child in Britain in the 80s and this chap called James Bond.

Then he goes into a bathroom. Opens a wash kit, which contains razor blades, syringes, and drugs. He fills a syringe with fluid. And between Bond and *Casualty*, I know what's going on here – he's going to drug the girl, knock her out. It's what the baddies do in Bond films, like, a *lot*.

Only he's Martin. He's not a baddie – almost can't be, he's practically still a kid, very childlike, and there are not bad kids in movies, ever.

Until now.

Because, of course, Martin goes to her carriage, and after a brief black and white shot (which even at the time I read to be his imagining what was happening behind the door, the pretty girl in a nightgown calling his name), he breaks in and attacks her, drugs her, struggles with her until she passes out, then strips her naked, has sex with her, and for an encore takes a razor to her wrist and drinks her blood.

We've yet to pass the ten-minute mark.

The assault is horrific, by the way. It's a scene that would have to make most women's top 3 worst nightmares, I'd have thought. She physically fights him off, he wrestles her to the ground. She panics as the drug starts to take effect, pleading to be told what it is, and he gives gentle calm assurances that he's 'careful', that she'll just fall asleep and then wake up again.

And the worst part is, you believe him.

No, the worst part is; *I* believed him.

And sure, it's an amazing performance. John Amplas is all big eyes, sad vulnerability. Even when he's telling her not to scream, it comes out as pleading – as though he's more concerned about her inner panic than the chance of getting caught. That apparent empathy for his victim is so sincerely delivered that, first time around, I was half convinced he meant it, that this was all some kind of misunderstanding.

This is where we must pause, and admire the horror of the moment. Because as a young woman is drugged, raped and murdered, my 11-year-old boy brain is centered, not on her and her terror, pain, and violation, but on the apparent 'sensitivity' of her attacker.

Because fucking hell, George Romero, man.

And look, sure – this is not a movie for 11-year-olds. Emphatically not. But just take a look at some of the cultural criticism made of this movie, and you'll see variations of this theme, again and again – however much the male critics know what's going on is sick, wrong, evil... there's this massive sympathy, bordering on identification, with Martin.

Do we see more of Martin? Sure we do. A lot more. The movie is, in a sense, his life story. We get to see the different sides to him, his struggle to fit in, his possibly-crazed family situation. The performance opens up like a flower, and the rest of the cast is superb, and there's a home invasion sequence which, forgive me for the meme punchline, actually *should* be taught in film school, as an example of what you can achieve on a low budget with enough skill, vision, and editing skills.

Still, though, the film starts with a basically contextless assault, sex crime, and murder.

And it was Martin my mind went to.

I've mentioned earlier that I was raised feminist, and some of what that meant. And, like I said up top, parents do their best, then set you loose and hope. And between you and me, I think Mum did a pretty fucking good job.

But *Martin* happened. And at the time, I thought it was a brilliant movie, but also at the time I didn't have the tools necessary to realise just what a monstrous, incredible feat of filmmaking it represented.

There's this saying that I absolutely hate, that goes like this: porn tells lies about women and the truth about men. Well, fuck that gender essentialist bullshit, and fuck you if you believe it.

But. And. Also.

I think no matter how well we are raised, there's a wider culture. And while it's vibrant and messy and complex and multifaceted and self-contradictory and even often in argument with itself, there are a metric shit-ton of untested assumptions that underpin a lot of it, about gender and what being a man means and what being a woman means. And as much as I recoil in horror from the notion of objectification, the idea that we can see another human being not as a funhouse mirror of ourselves, but instead as a thing to be enjoyed or consumed...

Well, there's 11-year-old me. Watching *Martin*. Watching Martin rape and murder a girl, and thinking only about Martin.

Martin was George Romero's favourite of his own movies, according to the always-reliable Wikipedia entry on the subject. I have no idea if it's true or not, but I believe it. Certainly of all his works, it's far and away my favourite.

Not – to be crystal clear– because Romero was any kind of misogynist or rape apologist or objectifier of women. That's the very opposite of what I believe.

No, because he knew how to make a movie that would force us – us men – to examine that part of ourselves that is capable of objectification. He did it in the way that's true genius – the way that makes you slap your forehead and say 'well, of *course*!'

He makes the protagonist like you. Like virtually any male that's ever lived. A child, yearning. Reaching for something he cannot understand, but craves. Desire, without understanding. 'Love' without awareness.

Hunger with only a facsimile of compassion.

I love the Dead movies, and *The Crazies*. And I know that, with *Night*, Romero damn near invented a genre of horror fiction that is, at this point, probably a billion-dollar entertainment industry. And honestly, as much as I love good zombie fiction, for my money nobody has ever beaten the source for sheer visceral impact. He was a monumental talent, a world-class storyteller, and by all accounts, a lovely man in person, too.

But for my money, if the only movie he'd ever made was *Martin*, he'd still deserve the mantle of genius.

It's that fucking good.

And so was he.

YOU CAN'T CHECK OUT

THE ELM STREET FRANCHISE

We never really got into it about Freddie, did we?
 I don't mean Krueger – him, we'll cover right here, right now – I'm talking about the kid from the village, a year younger than Bev and I, who came up back when I was talking about my love affair with Marlboro Reds.
 Back then, as you may recall, I described him thusly: "you know how your parents always asked 'And if your friends jumped off a cliff, would you?' Freddie would. Hell, he'd jump off first, hoping to set a trend."
 He was *such* a strange kid.
 Like, okay, dig it: it's literally my first day being shown around the primary school in my new village. And on the way back from being shown the lunch hall and the toilets, my guide pauses to let me take in the game of British Bulldog happening on the playground. "See that kid?" He's pointing at a boy, blond curly locks, NHS thick-frame glasses, milky white complexion. I nod. I do, indeed, see that kid. As I watch, the crowd start their run across the playground, trying to avoid being caught by the players in the middle. The kid starts yelling and charges, arms pinwheeling about, fists clenched. The Bulldogs part to let him through.
 "That's Freddie. He's the worst kid in the school. Even the teachers say so. Stay away from him."
 Reader, you will be shocked to learn that I did not, in fact, stay away from him.
 Our friendship ran through our teenage years, but it wasn't without its ups and downs; and I do think it's telling that once I made it to

6th-form college and moved out of the village, it fell away entirely and very quickly. I suspect for both of us, we were making a virtue of necessity – which hey, what are you going to do? Beats being alone by yourself, and all that.

And we did have some common tastes; rock and metal, though his taste ran heavier than mine; *The Young Ones* (we watched the shit out of his VHS copy of the two series)... and, of course, wildly unsuitable horror and action movies.

Freddie wasn't exactly well off, but his family was clearly doing a little better than mine financially; he had a Nintendo Entertainment System, years before Bev got her SNES (I struggled on with my Amstrad CPC464 right up until college, though Dad had an Amega 500 that I loved almost beyond words) and, most importantly, a VHS player in his room... and the movies to go with it.

Specifically and most importantly, there were the *Elm Street*s.

At the time I first started hanging out with him, he had the first five movies – *Freddy's Dead* wasn't out yet. And he was a year younger than me. So, 11 at the absolute oldest. In other words, we were both far, far too young, basically.

Where were the parents? Getting stoned in the living room, I suspect. Mum was an Avon lady; Dad, I have no idea, but when I got older I discovered they were pretty serious potheads, and it's not impossible that generated another income stream. They seemed mostly kind people, with no real clue how to handle their basically ungovernable son. I spent a fair amount of time in their home (on sunny days, Freddie's mum would often sit on the stone front step of the house in a bikini, working on her tan), and I saw no evidence either of cruelty or anything resembling discipline.

Certainly, there were no objections to sleepovers, which would happen with some frequency, especially during the summer, when we'd pull all-nighters in well-planned campaigns to beat *Super Mario Bros 3* – and no, spoilers, we never did crack it, though we came bloody close a couple of times. Nor, as we both got older, was there any attempt to stop us from smoking in his bedroom, beyond one complaint when his mother misread the smell of Marlboro Reds as weed.

Logically, they must have purchased the VHS tapes for him. Did they not know what an 18 certificate was, or did they just not care? They surely can't have seen the movies themselves... Right?

Anyway.

Freddie was *obsessed* with the movie series. Sure, watched them over and over; yes, could quote verbatim; but I'm talking 'stole kitchen knives from his mum in an ultimately abortive attempt to actually make his own Freddy glove' levels of obsession. I want to be clear – he never completed the project, and, as far as I know, never hurt anybody. Still. Blimey.

This is all an unforgivably longwinded way of saying these movies are indelibly linked in my mind with Freddie, that house, those sleepovers; watching the movies over and over.

I watched them out of order, too, of that I'm certain. Like, maybe he didn't have the first movie straight away? I feel like 3 came first, 3 then 4 then 2. I remember being flummoxed by the first movie when I eventually got to it – Krueger seemed oddly reduced in terms of his powers; Tina's murder was incredibly graphic, but there was really no way anyone would misinterpret it as a suicide, the way the deaths in *Dream Warriors* were. And he just wasn't as much of a presence – the wisecracks were mostly absent, the majority of his 'lines' actually just that (admittedly legendarily creepy) chuckle, and though I wouldn't have had the language for this last, he wasn't, for the most part, positioned in the camera shots like the movie icon he would become by the third and fourth films. It was, looking back, maybe my first encounter with a sort of temporal displacement; everybody who knew the franchise agreed the first movie was clearly the best, and I was utterly flummoxed by it.

Because, better how? The effects work improved movie by movie, as effects work is wont to do; even the film most consider to be the weakest entry in the franchise, Part Five (*The Dream Child*, and for the record, I think it's actually pretty good, or at least underrated) had the incredible motorbike transformation scene. *Dream Warriors* had Freddy's head stretching out of the top of a TV, antenna standing up from the top of his scalp like, well, antenna; it had a drug addicts' needle tracks opening and closing, thirsting for the spike; and, in what is for my money one of the most outright gnarly close-up-of-a-wound shots in horror cinema, it has a kid being turned into a puppet *because Freddy has sliced open his arms and legs and is now using his veins and arteries as strings to walk him about.* It's not that the first movie doesn't have its moments, of course; especially the full body burn in the basement and Freddy's final appearance, slicing his way through the stretched-out bedsheets, intent on finally ending Nancy for good. But there's nothing the first movie does, effects-wise, that later entries won't comprehensively top.

And then there was the crucial matter of body count.

It was trivially obvious to early-teen me that a major measure of quality must surely be the number of gruesome kills that occur in a given horror movie. I mean, that's just good common sense, right? And in this regard, the debut simply doesn't measure up at all, bringing in a paltry four deaths – only one more than *The Dream Child*, which, now I think of it, is probably why I had that movie ranked as the weakest outing of all, motorbike o' death notwithstanding. Hell, even the 'let's-pretend-it-never-happened' second entry, *Freddy's Revenge*, managed five canonical deaths, though I remember earnestly discussing with a friend the high likelihood, if not outright certainty, that there had to be a significant additional death toll associated with Krueger's appearance at the swimming pool, as, having finally asserted control over Jesse, climbing out of the lad like a snake shedding skin, he stood, fire lighting the air behind him as he held his arms wide and proclaimed "You're all my children now!"

In this regard, the third and fourth movies were clearly the cream of the crop, boasting a mighty six kills each; and really, at that point the argument came down to which of the movies had the more stylish deaths.

Except, no, it's more complicated than that, isn't it? Because if we're talking in terms of raw effects extravaganza across the two movies then I think you'd be hard-pushed to say *Dream Warriors* (3) has anything to match the cockroach transformation in *The Dream Master* (4); honestly that fucking sequence is off the hook, what with the meaty ripping sound her arms make when they drop off, the slurping noise as her face is torn away from the goo on the floor, revealing the insect head behind, and the climax, in which we catch a glimpse of Freddy's giant eye, at which point the scene flips, and Krueger is shown staring into the cardboard Roach Motel grinning. Add in the by-now expert delivery of the punchline ("You can check in, but you can't check out!") followed by the fist closing, the last of the transformed girl running through his scarred fingers as a flowing tide of yellow snot/slime/pus, and yeah, it's a stomach turner for the ages.

But on the flip side, while that particular punchline definitely lands, elsewhere shit in *The Dream Master* is starting to get juuuuuuust a little goofy. Whilst I personally think the 'Soul pizza' gag lands on just the right side, mainly due to the detail of the screaming children's faces that are uncanny replications of recognizable victims, plus the utterly gross crack/squelch noise they make when Freddy spears one with a blade before eating it, elsewhere the silly/scary line is getting stomped all over – yes, Freddy claw cutting through the water to resemble the Jaws fin, I *am* looking at you, see me after class.

See, it's not that *Dream Warriors* doesn't have punchlines. *Dream Warriors* has many brilliant punchlines – "Feeling a little tongue-tied?", "Sorry, kid; I don't believe in fairy tales!" and the absolutely incomparable "Welcome to prime-time, bitch!" but, well, let's take that last as representative. Is it funny? It absolutely is, full of trademark Freddy cruelty, mocking his self-harming, fame-seeking victim before dispatching her by driving her face through a CRT television screen in a shower of glass and sparks. But, as you've probably intuited even if you haven't had the scene indelibly printed upon your memory by endless VHS rewatches, it's also gruesome and terrifying. The image of the girl's body suspended above the floor, feet dangling, face hidden in the guts of the TV as smoke from the explosion stains the wall the set is hanging from... it's a brilliant, grotesque tableau that's funny and shocking and scary all at once – not least because, hilariously, her death is treated as a suicide.

I want to be clear: I loved *The Dream Master* and *Dream Warriors* very, very much; and you know what, full disclosure, I fucking adored *Freddy's Dead* too, when it came out. Part of what this essay is teaching me is how scattershot and – let's be charitable – eclectic my criteria were concerning what made a horror movie 'good', back in the ancient land of twelve to fourteen years of age. But I did definitely slightly prefer *Dream Warriors*, and I think this point about the humour teases out why. When I did a movie-by-movie blog series for Gingernuts on the franchise (still available on the site, knock yourself out: gingernutsofhorror.com/my-life-in-horror), I was frustrated by how no movie in the franchise ever felt like quite the full package; how it took them until *The Dream Master* to really *get* Freddy as an icon, and yet, paradoxically, by doing so, they started to lose the menace from the first three movies. And though I wouldn't have been able to articulate it in those terms, I think that's why I gave the edge to *Dream Warriors*, all those years ago.

And I think the best illustration of the difference comes in comparing the two finales.

Dream Warriors runs a duel confrontation, with Nancy's father, teaming up with a doctor from the asylum the children are resident in, doing battle with Freddy in stop-motion skeleton form (no, really), while the kids try and Judo throw the fact they're in a dream to give *them* powers to fight Freddy in the dream world, with varying success. Are the effects hokey? Sure they are – in the case of the skeleton, delightfully so; even as a kid it felt like a throwback. But narratively it *works*; there's threat and tension at both ends, but also, Freddy can only be in one place at once, so the pincer movement keeps him hopping. Plus, there's a method to the madness; Freddy's mum (no, sorry, we don't have time for that particular Watney's Party Can O' Worms) has let the gang know that Freddy's ability to continue to haunt and hunt the living is because he was never given a proper burial. So, the kids fight Freddy in the dream realm while the grown-ups try and put things right with shovels, holy water and a crucifix. When they succeed, Dream!Freddy is consumed by light, burning through from the holy artefacts attached to his skeleton, and away he goes. It's maybe just a touch abrupt, and, again, nobody's idea of world-class special effects, but narratively, it's enormously satisfying, making sense on its own terms, and in the context of the first two movies.

And then there's *The Dream Master*.

On the VHS copy Freddie had, there was a ten-minute 'making of' short, where the director talked about how Freddy had never been given a proper send-off in any of the films, and they wanted to fix that this time, really make his death something spectacular.

Well, they sure managed that.

In the finale of *The Dream Master*, the souls of all the children he's consumed – souls that, he made clear in the previous movie, are making him more powerful – regain agency, whilst still housed within his flesh.

And they literally rip him apart.

It's awesome.

The flesh of his chest and stomach ripples and writhes and stretches as the souls try and push their way out of him. Small arms burst from his chest and back and start tearing at him. It's super gross and super satisfying, and probably my favourite Freddy death in the whole series.

But.

Look, there's no polite way to say it; the triggering event is shite. Total bobbins. If you know, you know. If not – are you really ready for this? – after four movies of Freddy shredding, it turns out (according to a nursery rhyme that only turns up in this movie, just to be clear) that the way you defeat the demon who can murder you in your sleep, *via your dreams,* is… show him his reflection.

And. I mean. Just. Fuck. Off.

It bugged me even as a kid (though, to be scrupulously honest, nowhere near as much as it bugs me as a grown-arsed adult). The thing about the burial in *Dream Warriors* was it really *did* make sense, at least in as much as it fit in with the established mythos; Freddy was a child murderer who had been executed by the parents of Elm Street who then covered up their crime, after all, and although the first movie doesn't get into it, the idea that he wasn't given a proper burial was implicit the whole time.

Again, one of the things that bugged me about the series on a rewatch was the fact that it never felt like they managed to land a genuine gold-plated banger of an Elm Street movie. Something always felt just a bit *off,* whether it was the fact that the first movie didn't yet grasp what Freddy was, the second movie's gonzo approach to the mythology (though, to be clear, on the revisit, that entry went up leaps and bounds in my estimation), some of the acting and writing choices in the third movie, or, from four on, the way the Freddy wisecracks became the point rather than the cherry on the fear sundae. It's one of the best ideas for a horror movie franchise anybody ever had, and yet they never really managed to make an outright classic, in my humble opinion.

But oh, my dears, my young teenage heart thrilled so. For years, these movies were the gold standard of Horror, for me; at least until *Hellraiser* came along, this was the definition of cinematic nightmare made glorious technicolour.

And, unlike with *The Lost Boys* (as we discussed back in Volume I), I do not begrudge my teenage self this crush.

My friendship with Freddie may not have survived first contact with the wider world, but Krueger, warts and all, will, I suspect, always be a Mount Rushmore icon in my horror imagination.

SURRENDER TO ME

CANDYMAN

This one loomed large in my childhood. At the time of the film's release, I was 14 years old, and while I didn't see it until at least a couple of years later, when it finally broadcast on UK TV (my video recording of the broadcast started 30 seconds or so late and missed the title card, though it still captured much of that beautiful overhead traffic shot), the premise of the legend at the centre of the movie was electric playground gossip. I don't know how many of the kids had actually seen the film, but *everyone* was talking about it; and specifically talking about the 'say his name five times' thing.

Like, it was an obsession; who had claimed to have done it, whether or not they believed they'd *really* done it, who'd chickened out, who would *never* even *think* about doing it; on and on the conversation went, for what felt like weeks. And this may be false memory, but my recollection is that the legend wasn't immediately connected to a film.

The legend came to me first.

I have a lot to say about this film, and not all of it straightforwardly positive, but it's worth starting there; this is a piece of storytelling that was staggeringly successful at what it set out to do. A story about the perpetuation of urban legend in Chicago that itself became a delicious piece of playground gossip and goosebumps as far afield as North Devon, England. I don't know a horror writer worth their salt that doesn't dream of creating something with that kind of reach and impact.

And at its core, that's about simplicity, right? The trappings don't really matter; whether it happened to a friend of a friend, a relative of a relative, boy or girl; no, all that matters is someone staring into a mirror… and saying his name five times, and then… and then…

It hits every archetype you want this kind of urban legend to hit; gruesome murder, sure, ferocious monster with a hook for a freakin' hand, check... but the best bit, of course, is the *invitation*. Say his name five times! Why would anyone...? And yet, once you've heard it, especially as a kid, how can you not at least think about it? You look in the mirror every day, your own youthful, immortal face looking back at you. You're rational on the surface, maybe even aggressively so, depending on your temperament... or maybe you're superstitious and ashamed of that, wanting to prove something... or maybe you're just curious, desperate to know if any of it, the supernatural, is *real*...

I've talked before about how horror is often small-c conservative, and really, this boiled-down horror story archetype is as clear a demonstration of that tendency, the clarity perhaps exacerbated by the purity of the distillation.

Because in the legend of the Candyman, he isn't some maniac that follows you home, or stalks you in the street, or even kills you in your dreams.

In the legend of the Candyman, you summon your doom.

This is one of the darkest, most incendiary concepts in all of horror, maybe *the* darkest, one that lurks in the depths of many of the most outright disturbing works in the genre; the notion that victims are complicit in their undoing. *Exquisite Corpse* (see Chapter 36), features a particularly visceral, erm, execution of this core concept.

Sorry.

This is not new territory for Clive Barker (on whose source material *Candyman* is based) of course. *Hellraiser* (see Volume I) is an exemplar of the form in many ways – "The box. You opened it. We came." and so on. But even there, the picture is complicated; nobody in the first movie actually knows the consequences of opening the box, after all. Frank may have been chronically unwise, but that's hardly an eviscerating offence, and Kirsty is entirely innocent.

Candyman, on the other hand, is pure death drive in action. Consider the opening telling of the story. The movie, all about stories and storytelling, starts with our hero, Helen, being told the story, but then dissolves to a flashback/dramatisation as the voice-over continues. In it, 'good girl' with 'good' boyfriend has decided that tonight, she's going to shag 'bad boy'. This is *classic* teenage Sex And Danger territory, a narrative that could play out any number of ways, from porn to romance to crime to horror, or pretty much any combination of the above. I'd argue it naturally skews slightly horror, because at core she's breaking taboos – fidelity, chastity, and valuing libido over heart – and we know how small c-conservative horror feels about Women Who Enjoy Fucking, but I recognise other avenues are possible.

And then they're in the bathroom, in front of the mirror, and she's in her white bra, and they're both fully panting, and then she tells him the story, and dares him to do the thing.

Sex and death, baby. Sex and death and teenagers.

There's a nice twist here, too; one that might not leap out on first viewing, but a significant moment, I think. The narrator tells us that having said the name four times together, and then sending the horn dog boy downstairs to await a 'surprise', the girl says Candyman's name the final time on her own (at which point, we're treated to the first of several brief but brilliantly executed, erm, executions).

And the thought that might fairly occur at that point is this: how does anyone know that she said his name a final time, given her extreme deadness?

It reminds me of the great urban legend about how, if you have a falling dream, and you don't wake up before you hit the ground, you die in real life. It's brilliant because most of us have had falling dreams, and almost all of us have been woken up *by* the dream, the sensation of falling causing us to start awake (that sensation in turn often caused by some form of snoring or apnoea that's preventing proper breathing). But I've never spoken to anyone who has had a falling dream where they've hit the ground.

So. You know. Maybe.

Like all great supernatural premises (including the biggest one of all, religion) it's by its nature unfalsifiable. We'll only ever know for sure it's true if we *have* that falling dream, land, and die. Or not.

Same principle applies here – assuming any part of the story is true, if the girl died, there's no way of knowing what caused it, because she was alone when it happened. Interestingly, the moment is repeated later in the film, when Helen and her friend Bernadette look into her apartment's bathroom mirror and say his name in unison; Bernadette chickens out, and Helen alone makes the final intonation.

The movie is implicitly about religion in another way, too; it's about belief. According to the man himself, Candyman is a legend, an urban myth, a 'whisper in the classroom' and so forth. Belief sustains him, and when Helen takes actions that challenge his existence (in the eyes of his... followers? Congregation? We'll come back to that part, because it's complex and messy and problematic) he is 'obliged to come'; to reassert the myth and expand the legend, using Helen to do so.

I always find stories about stories to be dicey affairs, personally. I always feel there's a non-trivial risk that they can puncture the entire enterprise. Suspension of disbelief is a tricksy, nebulous phrase that likely obscures as much, if not more, than it illuminates. Nonetheless, one of the things I come to fiction for is immersion, absorption; I want to be taken into another world, or another part of this world, and see it as clearly as I can through the eyes of someone else. And if, in the course of telling me a story in that way, you start banging on about storytelling, you run the risk, I think, of exposing the wires that show me how the effect is done. I don't mind a 'making of' documentary, but it's not a substitute for watching the actual movie, and I certainly don't want to sit down expecting one and getting the other.

All that said, done well, it's brilliant; the much-maligned *Last Action Hero* does a bang-up job of interrogating the logic of Action Movie Land, using arguably the biggest action star of all time to do it, and King's work is no worse for the many, many writers who often serve as heroes or protagonists in his stories.

And I think *Candyman* does it about as well as it's possible to do.

It does so by leaning all the way in. The lead characters are academics, researching urban legends. They are sceptics, in other words; but also bright and inquisitive people. This means they can voice every objection the audience will have to the premise, of course; but for my money, the cleverer part is that when things *do* start getting actually hinky – when they locate an actual, real-world murder that has been ascribed to the urban legend – their reactions of unease transmit to us very clearly. They are the experts, after all. If they can't explain it...

That said, the movie is playing an interesting game here, because the opening monologue of the film is from Candyman, extolling the virtue of myth as the camera slowly zooms into a swarm of bees. We *know* the rationalists are wrong, that *Candyman* is real, because he told us so at the beginning. In this respect, we're converts, believers, watching a tale of the faithless as they stumble around in their blindness.

This is ballsy stuff, because it inverts the standard horror trope of 'what if it's not real?' that is usually the staple of this kind of narrative; a series of escalating spooky events, any one of which could have a rational explanation but which cumulatively wear down the protagonist until they are not sure what's real and what isn't – at which point either a monster or explanation presents itself. *Jacob's Ladder* does this about as well as it's ever been done, IMO. But *Candyman*, like *Hellraiser*, is doing something quite different.

That should make the first half of the narrative suffer, really. We should be frustrated by the investigation Helen and Bernadette undertake, knowing as they cannot that they are stalking a legend, not the gang leader who has taken the trappings of the myth to spread fear and intimidation. But I didn't find it to play out that way; instead, I found those scenes were infused with a sense of fatalistic dread that heightened the tension, rather than dissipated it. The sure and certain knowledge that it was all going to turn horribly to shit at some point created for me an almost sickening tension; akin to the classic thriller scenes like the climax of *Silence of the Lambs*, as Clarice moves blindly through the darkened cellar, stalked by the killer we know is right behind her.

It works, is what I'm trying to say, at least for me. Helen working out how the killer may have entered the victim's apartment (a genuinely creepy-as-fuck notion that behind the bathroom cabinet mirror is a crawl space to the apartment next door: way to make sure no-one who lives in a tower block ever sleeps again, assholes), and the extended field trip to Cabrini Green drip with tension, as Helen explores the murder scene, and the space the killer must have come from. Even her epically unwise solo return to the Green that eventually leads to her assault and mugging somehow works; at least partly down to some great performances from all concerned, and another story-within-a-story that is brief but incredibly gory.

All that said, it's interesting to reflect on, because even as the film textually removes doubt from the moment of the opening monologue that this is a supernatural tale, you could still read the whole movie as Helen's psychosis. Sure, there's no apparent root cause for her to go kill-crazy, but I like the idea that to the outside world, she is someone who researched one too many gruesome stories and became obsessed enough to start acting them out via a series of psychotic breaks. Even the moments where Helen appears to be hypnotised by Candyman fit into that, seeming to suggest her mind slipping from reality (the first occasion, when she finds herself back in the Green, a severed dog head lying in a pool of blood next to a meat cleaver, is another gore-ridden tour de force of performance, direction, and effects).

Though that brings us on to the vexed topic of race.

So, let's start by sounding two claxons – white guy over here, talking about race; and also, white Brit talking about US race relations. Chances I say something unintentionally dumb, fairly high. Fair warning, though if/when I fuck up, please let me know – it's the only way I'll learn.

See, Candyman is black. And Helen is a white woman.

That matters, textually, for two reasons; one involves Candyman's origin story, and the other Helen's exploitation of her white privilege (and, sure, class privilege also) to first investigate The Green, and later, to help bring down a gang leader operating in the tower – about which the movie is explicit, by the way, I'm not reading that in. Helen fully calls out how gross it is that it takes a white middle-class woman getting assaulted before the cops get involved (the older black cop does point out that it's *because* she's not from the Green that she feels safe pressing charges – if she'd had to live in the same tower as the man's accomplices, she'd have had a powerful incentive for keeping her mouth shut). So in that sense, it feels like the movie understands it's playing the white saviour trope, grounding it in the reality of the extreme poverty of the Chicago projects.

When Helen and Bernadette, who is black, first visit Cabrini Green, they dress in smart clothes, and in doing so convince the gang that runs the tower that they are cops. In this moment, they are obviously playing on class privilege as well as Helen's race; but again, the movie is later explicit that Helen's whiteness is part of the equation.

But then we have the origin story for Candyman, and there, race is also a critical factor.

It turns out that, according to legend, Candyman was a black man who lived in the city at the turn of the century. He fell in love with a white woman. They had a love affair but were eventually discovered, at which point the white menfolk tortured and murdered him, before scattering his ashes where Cabrini Green now stands.

The racist fear of a black man and a white woman is deeply ingrained; it's a pivotal image in the KKK-approving film *Birth of a Nation*, and has been referenced by Ice T, Public Enemy, and many others. Making such a relationship pivotal to the origin story of our titular monster makes sense, and follows a long tradition of including real-life horrors within wider supernatural narratives.

But it does also mean that the central plot of the movie revolves around a white woman being stalked by a physically imposing black man.

And it's a seduction of a kind, albeit one with frankly rapey overtones. Candyman appears to have a hypnotic power over Helen, causing her to black out and wake up in strange places. In the finale, he commands her to surrender to him, as the price for allowing a baby to live, and when Helen acquiesces, he appears to sexually assault her with his hook.

This is utterly incendiary subject matter, combining one of the most powerful racist tropes with, at best, ambiguity around sexual consent. And really, I'm being gross by giving it that much leeway; there's no difference in form between what happens to Helen and what happens to any victim of a date rape drug, or anyone who has been forced to have sex due to intimidation or threat of violence. It's fucking vile.

It does also highlight the unanswered mystery at the heart of the story; why does Candyman do what he does? Why does he kill?

Or, outside of the events of this movie, does he kill at all? After all, in his opening monologue and later in the film he claims to be a rumour, to not actually 'be'. So one reading is that he *doesn't* kill, but instead becomes attached to murders committed in the area by virtue of the legend. Until Helen solves a 'Candyman' murder, putting the myth in doubt.

So in one sense, his motives are clear; by killing and framing Helen for the murders before bringing her back to the Green to die, he can reignite the legend. But the question underlying that is why kill at all, and to its great credit, the movie leaves that question to the imagination of its audience, not providing any answers.

What the film does imply, however, is that the ability to become a legend is there for anyone, under the right circumstances. And so it is that when Helen does surrender, only to find herself in the bonfire with Candyman and the baby, she is able, through no small suffering on her own part, to supplant the Candyman image and become a legendary monster in her own right (in a for-the-ages closing scene when her weeping ex-husband says her name five times into the mirror).

Still, for all that it's clear that the movie is aware of the valences of its subject matter, I still found some of the handling of race... difficult, especially in the final scenes when the residents of the Green congregate to burn the bonfire, seemingly knowing it contains the Candyman, and later show up en masse at Helen's funeral, to drop his hook into her grave. It felt uncomfortable to me, this group of almost exclusively black people enacting such odd, monolithic group behaviour, and it's one of the few moments where I feel like the storytelling comes just a little loose: are they under some form of mass hypnosis? Is the bonfire an annual Green tradition, part of the legend? Absent that, it came across to me a little odd – an irrational group behaviour that seemed to render the Green residents 'other', when the movie had elsewhere taken such pains to humanise those characters.

Still and all, I think *Candyman* holds up exceptionally well, as a horror story with an underpinning as traditional as the form that manages to make a unique film experience. And it spawned its own urban legend that fired childhood imagination.

No mean feat.

ENTERTAIN US

NEVERMIND

It seems impossible that I was eleven years old – and yet, it seems most likely. Surely no older than twelve.

We've previously discussed – at arguably too much length – the transformative power that Guns N' Roses had on my young mind. There'll never be a part of me that doesn't want to be the singer in a long-haired rock and roll band. I've had enough experience of being in a band by now to know it was never, ever going to be a viable career path for me, but still, I've tasted the zone often enough; that sweet, sweet moment when the wall of perfect noise surrounds you, when the part of you that is you is both amplified and totally subsumed by the living moment of vibration in the air; the moment where The Living Now becomes All, and you are fully present in an instance of pure expression. It's a drug, of course, a rush they can't touch you for. The Disciples of Gonzo are unlikely to ever play again, and I miss it, and them, already. We made a good noise, in our day.

As for writing, it's just always been something I knew I could do. There's no way to say that without sounding arrogant, and I apologise for that – and, to be clear, I'm not actually saying, even now, it's something I can do particularly well, necessarily, only that it always felt like a natural avenue of expression – but it's undoubtedly one of my biggest regrets that I didn't go much harder, much sooner on writing. It's very clear to me that if I'd started writing twenty years ago, or even ten, instead of five... well, I'd have five to fifteen years more experience, and that couldn't fail to be helpful. But, so it goes, we are where we are, and damn if the journey isn't fun. Regret? Sure, but nothing more work won't cure.

But there was another love, one I've rarely spoken about. We touched on it briefly back when I was laying out The Ballad Of Scott (see Volume I). And yet, from the ages of ten to eighteen or nineteen, it was, ostensibly, My Calling – the profession that was to dominate my existence, the art I was committed to. I've mentioned before that I failed BTEC in Performing Arts (yes, I actually managed that); given my oft-expressed proclivities, you might fairly have assumed that was in the music strand.

Whereas, in point of fact, it was Theatre.

People often say they feel like they haven't really grown up; that they feel, inside, perpetually stuck in their late teens or early twenties. I can relate to that in a lot of ways. To this day, the movies and music of my youth resonate with me on a bone-deep level (as this eight year, two book project is clear testament to). I will absolutely make a complete idiot out of myself at any wedding disco where 'Sweet Child O' Mine' is played, for example, because I have air guitar game that can rarely be matched. But I have to say that this part feels utterly alien to me now. I know, intellectually, that I did it, that I was kinda in love with it (or, at least, with performing in front of an audience)… but there's no resonance there at all anymore. Tell me you've got a pub rock band looking for a frontman, I do believe I'd be there in a second (as long as it was reasonably local), but tell me you're putting an am-dram production of Hamlet together, and there's not so much as a flicker.

It's possible that doing the music turned out to be the cure, as I think about it. It was always what I *really* wanted, anyway, and it was only a combination of crippling low self-esteem, pretty low raw talent, and a couple of incredibly toxic people who I trusted telling me I was dreadful at singing that kept me from trying it. Theatre felt safer. It wasn't really you on stage, after all, it was the character. You got to disappear for a little while, and bathe in the rapt attention of being someone else. Plus it was storytelling. I've always had a thing for storytelling.

Still, the fact remains – from the age of ten to the age of nineteen, I was always attached to some stage production or other. In panto, I played the genie of the ring (the green makeup took hours to wash off, and made the Coke I drank smell of farts), and Prince John in *Robin Hood*. That was properly brilliant. The Sheriff was the comedy villain, who did all the slapstick and stupidity, but I was the straight-up, flint-eyed villain. There was a moment in the final scene where I marched in, back of stage to front, coldly cutting down the good guys' scheme and seemingly killing the happy ending. The boos and hisses were loud enough to rattle my fillings. Fantastic.

At college, I played one of the teachers in *Spring Awakening*, Prof. Strychnine, behind a heavy, cod-Comedia mask. I played one of the shepherds in an abridged version of the NT's mystery plays (learning the Yorkshire accent was a job of months, mimicry never being a particular strong suit of mine – again, in retrospect, a pretty worrying gap in the skill set for someone aspiring to act). Even better, in the first act, I got to play Isaac, and was almost-sacrificed every night, to stunned silence. Good times. I also played a psychopathic killer in a play I co-wrote with two other students. *Growing Pains* was a one-night-only production. I'd love to see the script now. I remember it fondly.

But before all of that, there was *A Midsummer Night's Dream*.

So, there were two youth theatre groups running out of this arts centre. There was a juniors group, which ran 10-13 year olds, and then there were the teenagers. The teenagers got all the good parts, of course – often, in fact, all the speaking parts. The kids, we just fit around whatever was going on.

And for *Midsummer Night's Dream*, that meant fairies.

Goth fairies, I feel I should add. Oberon was played by Brian, an impossibly tall pale goth with jet-black hair down to his arse. He strode about the theatre like he owned the place, and indeed all of creation besides. I worshipped him. Titania was impossibly beautiful, also pale, and black haired. And we of Oberon's train were made up in the image of our king – faces painted white, with black and silver work around the eyes, hair sprayed black, torn black jeans and T-shirts (any visible skin beneath the holes also painted white – we were a professional outfit).

We looked fucking awesome, is what I'm trying to say. Best faeries ever.

And I got to drive the tree.

I have no idea how it happened, at this distance. Obviously, none of us had speaking parts, but we were instructed to react to what was going on when we were on stage, becoming part of the psychodrama between Oberon and Titania. My suspicion is that I gave good react. Regardless, the upgrade was pretty sweet; we had a tree that was spray-painted silver and mounted on wheels, and my job was to move it around the stage at certain points, to simulate being in a different part of the forest, and also the effect of the fairies' interactions on the lovers. The practical upshot of which being that I was on stage *a lot.* I remember getting a note, about two or three weeks from curtains up, where the director praised me for, at one point, coming out from behind the tree and jumping up and down in delight as the lovers fought. I can't think of a clearer testament to how much respect I had for our director that I still feel a surge of pride at the memory. You'd better believe I did the move at least once every night of the run. Sometimes twice.

My memory is that rehearsals were every weekend, for three months. What I am certain of is that we were all expected to attend every rehearsal, without exception, and missing even one was grounds to be removed, unless we were actually ill. I have no idea if the rule was enforced, but I do know that I never missed a single one.

It paid dividends in two ways – neither, sad to say, involving the installation of anything resembling a work ethic on your humble correspondent. Both payoffs had the same root, which was that as a consequence of my attendance, by the time the play went on, and for several months afterwards, I could recite the entire play, from cover to cover, word for word, without hesitation, deviation, or repetition. Eleven-year-old brains are like that, I guess; or at least, mine was. I retained enough of the play that when we came to study it at school when I was 13, I could cruise through the lessons paying basically zero attention and still scored an A for the work for that year. Yes, I am counting that as dividend one, and no, I clearly wasn't kidding about the work ethic.

The second major benefit came about because of an encore performance.

We did a four-night run. It was very well received, even though we had to abandon one performance right at the end due to a fire alarm – a garment had been thrown over one of the bulbs surrounding a mirror backstage, and the smoke had triggered the premature evacuation. It went down so well (the play, not the fire alarm) that we got invited to put on a performance at a local school. I remember the dimensions of the performance space were narrower than the stage at the theatre, which meant I had to work on my tree blocking to make sure I didn't overshoot my marks. Hey, us tree fairies are serious business. Shrubbery doesn't drive itself.

Anyway, *that* went well enough that we were invited back to the home theatre for a command performance of a Final Night. This was basically unheard of, and we were absolutely thrilled.

And then Peter Quince got ill.

She was the sister of a friend of mine, so I was often around her house. I'd seen her the night before, and she'd said to me that I might have to step in if she didn't recover. I'd laughed it off, then spent the entire walk back to my house running through her part in my head (or, knowing me, probably out loud).

Just in case.

I walked from school to the theatre the following day, a 20-minute stroll, entering the premises around three thirty.

"What does your uniform look like?" The director asked, in place of a hello.

"Erm, it's black…" I began.

"Take your coat off, let me have a look."

I did.

"Do you have a tie?"

For reasons passing understanding, I did. I had a purple clip-on bow tie. Not part of the uniform. I think… I *think* I had it in my bag because I'd worn it for a stage magician act I'd done earlier in the year and never taken it out again, but who the fuck knows why eleven/twelve-year-old boys do anything. Either way, I had it, and I put it on.

"Yes, it could work… you'll need a jacket. And a clipboard."

"So… what's going on?"

"Peter Quince is ill. You'll be playing the part tonight. The other mechanicals are upstairs. We'll be rehearsing in ten minutes."

And here and now, decades after the fact, I can be honest; I pretended to be nervous, but in truth, I was absolutely thrilled.

And honoured, of course. This was a promotion from the kiddie league to the teenagers, and it happened with absolutely no hesitation. I was in, and I was in because the director knew I could do it. She was right, of course, but that doesn't mean I didn't feel a kind of pride and confidence and acceptance I have rarely felt as strongly or clearly since. Looking back, I can't help but wonder if most of my devotion to acting for the following six to eight years didn't have it's root in that one simple moment; a feeling of belonging, a feeling of a challenge that I knew I could meet that others could not. As buzzes go, friends and neighbours, I gotta tell you, it's elusive to find, and very, very tough to beat.

The rehearsals went like a charm. I had the script on a clipboard that I was to use as a prompt, but I didn't need it. The other cast members mouthed every single word I was supposed to be saying whenever I made eye contact, and I didn't need that either, but I did appreciate it. I even got a mention in the local paper review, and they damn near spelt my name right. It was, and I can't find a more apt word, in spite of its troublingly confrontational implications, a fucking triumph, and it gives me joy to recall to this very day.

Funny, how something as simple as knowing you can do something well can feel so transformationally good. Damn if there isn't a lesson in there somewhere.

And if you've come this far and are wondering why on earth this is a My Life In Horror chapter, as opposed to a My Life In Nostalgia For Childhood Glories, I hear you, and here's why; there was a party in the theatre to celebrate the last night of the show, and at that party, I got drunk for the first time in my life.

I stole the beer, I remember that. There was a crate of possibly-stout that had been left under the bar. It came in a glass bottle with one of those rubber corks attached to a metal contraption you had to pop open. When I did so, it foamed out and splashed everywhere. It also tasted, to my twelve-year-old palate, almost undrinkably bitter.

Keyword there; almost.

I *think* I took two bottles under the bleachers and drank them there. I don't *think* I drank them openly. I feel like someone – even a group of Devon teenagers, mostly themselves also underage and drinking, though not as underage as me – might have said something. I do remember – later, once I was definitely drunk – confessing my state to at least one of them. His girlfriend thought I was joking, but he, after looking into my eyes gravely for a few seconds, declared with a friendly grin that I was. I can also remember the surge of pride and validation I felt in that moment.

It gets fragmentary from there. There was a guy who ran the sound effects, who played the 'Sweet Child O' Mine' riff on the keyboard, to demonstrate a specific sound, and I remember a rush of recognition and joy at that. Later, that same guy, incredibly drunk, would film drunk me rambling and swearing incoherently. He was drunk enough that he dropped the camera at one point. Years later, I bumped into him again, and he told me he still had the tapes, but I never saw them. I still can't tell if I hope that footage is still out there or not, at this point. Part of me would love to see it. Another part… wouldn't.

Later, I remember a drunken not-quite-row with one of the older girls, concerning the bi-or-homosexuality of Freddie Mercury, and the weirdly apposite nature of the lyrics to 'Bohemian Rhapsody', given the cause of his death. I was arguing against his being gay, not out of homophobia, to be clear, but rather because of a visceral distrust of the tabloid press who had run the stories. So, I was being an idiot, but at least a well-meaning one.

Was someone running the lights, or were they on some kind of auto-pilot? I don't know. What I do know is that they were flashing more or less in time with the music, and the stage itself was empty – everyone was congregating around the sound desk, or copping off in the bleachers. The stage was mine.

And when 'Smells Like Teen Spirit' came on, I took it.

Now, just a refresher for those of you not down on your early 90s musical tribal allegiance. I was a Guns N' Roses kid in '91. And that means that… well, okay, it means I was definitely twelve when all this happened, because 'Teen Spirit' came out in '91. In point of fact, I'd just turned thirteen. So, okay, I was thirteen. Fine. The point is, GnR was my band, which meant I wasn't allowed to like Nirvana, from a purely legal standpoint. Grunge was The Enemy, y'see, and as I've previously mentioned, one that claimed many former friends from the rocker tribe over the course of that summer and autumn. I mean, full disclosure, I actually did have a copy of *Nevermind* on cassette that one of my mum's cooler friends had recorded for me – the same cool friend who would later take me to my first rock show, The Pixies at Exeter Uni, so pretty fucking cool – and sure, I'd listened to it, but…

Well, here's the thing; while I could freely admit *Nevermind* had many of the qualities I'd come to find desirable, even admirable, in music – namely, that it was ear-splittingly loud – something about it didn't connect with me. I think in retrospect, my issue was with the nihilism. I love me some angry tunes – then, now, always – but there's a coldness at the heart of *Nevermind*, I always think; a darkness that's more despair than anger, like the anger is a symptom rather than the focal expression. And while I appreciated it some then, and appreciate it a great deal now, it doesn't speak to me, doesn't resonate with my soul. I am angry, of course – perpetually so. But I find that anger to be life-affirming. In my anger with injustice, I am reminded that justice can exist, that better ways are possible, that we, collectively, deserve better, and that sometimes, via an expression of collective will and outrage and struggle, we can achieve better. I am angry, but I also believe in change-for-the-better, and in the transformative power of anger to help facilitate that change.

And the anger of *Nevermind* is absent that. The anger of *Nevermind* is an ill-fitting mask for desolation, hopelessness. *Appetite For Destruction* (vile misogyny, snarling misanthropy and all) felt like a call to arms, a battered grin that said it could take every punch you could throw and would spit blood back in your eye and just keep grinning. And maybe that's projection, *probably* that's projection, but it's how it made me feel, how it still makes me feel, and *Nevermind*… doesn't. *Nevermind* is a howl of pain into an all-consuming void.

And as 'Teen Spirit' started playing in the theatre, my drunken teenage brain started firing a new synoptic pattern, and – suddenly – I got it. And I danced, flinging my head around, the last (the first?) of the mad moshers, alone on the stage where I'd taken what would prove to be my finest moment in theatre, and one of my most straightforwardly good days ever, and I spun and headbanged, letting the guitar riff fling me across the stage. I danced like nobody was watching, and probably nobody was. I felt through the booze haze the turn of that song, that band, and I danced not because I wanted to but because I had to, to express something I had no language for but felt right down to my bones.

Alcohol is a shit drug. It's a depressant, and an irritant; it makes us dumber, and angrier, and clumsier, and really, as a species, let's face it, those are not qualities that we are well served by exacerbating. It's telling that we use this substance so freely at our moments of greatest triumph; indeed that our very celebrations involve profound overuse of a depressant; it's almost as though we feel the need to punish ourselves for feeling joy.

I still drink. Often in moderation, occasionally to excess. I love whiskey, with the kind of passion I normally reserve for gaming, and like gaming, it's something in my life that can be healthy, and can be... not. It does bring me pleasure, on occasion. And truth be told, as I've gotten older, I've found the numbness and relative stupidity comforting, in a way I doubt young me could begin to comprehend.

Still, I think back on that moment, that day, from time to time. My biggest stage moment ever. My first drunk. And connecting to Nirvana on a level that had hitherto eluded me. And I can't help but feel – and I'm kidding, but I'm not – that God is a terrible, terrible hack.

Because there's no way, as a writer, I could get away with making that shit up, is there?

DON'T THEY KNOW THE RULES?

BODYCOUNT

Content note: discussions of racism, which includes use of racial slurs.

It's 13th June 2017. And, accompanied by my dear friends Justin, Duncan and Rob, as well as my stepson, I'm inside my favourite music venue in the country (at least since they tore down The Astoria; yes, still bitter, thanks for checking), Brixton Academy, London.

We've had a beer and some grub in a nearby bar, and, T-shirt acquired, we're positioning ourselves in a good spot; centre stage, far enough back to hopefully not get caught in the initial crush, but plenty close enough to soak up the considerable atmosphere.

And, sure, the boy and I had seen them just the previous weekend, as part of probably my favourite Download 3-day weekend ever, and they had been Mighty… but this was Brixton fucking Academy, and the crowd was, as I believe the kids used to say, lit. And as well as Prophets Of Rage had gone down in front of the Download crowd (very, very well indeed), the intimacy of this show, a feeling like we were in on the ground floor of what was sure to become a world-beating colossus of hip-hop/metal supergroupery, promised something truly *epic*.

So, we're in the pit, and getting ready for some moderately serious jumping up and down action, and the reception that greets DJ Lord is raucous and rapturous. He acknowledges the crowd, and with an obligatory 'Make some noise!' (we do), he starts doing his thing.

And 90 seconds in, a guitar riff comes rolling out the speakers…

And suddenly it's, fuck, mid to late 90s and I'm an angry young teen, and I'm browsing The Ghost's moderately sizable cassette tape collection, and I notice the black-on-red script, gothic style, single word.

I pull it out, look at the cover. The image is so dark it's hard to make out, but I can just about see a painting of a bare-chested, muscular, angry-looking black man, with a gun in his belt, and that same word – band or album name? – half on either side of him, in two columns.

"Is this any good?"

He looks up. "Yeah, it's good. Heavy. It's Ice T, but it's metal."

Huh.

I know *of* Ice T, of course; even in whitebread North Devon, we've heard of Ice T. I will have known very little about the man, and what I did 'know' was likely playground bullshit, potentially even filtered through second-hand tabloid panic, laundered by schoolkids too dumb to even know that's what they were doing, absorbed by me, also too dumb to know better. Still, the name carried weight, cache. All I really knew was Ice T was Cool, and a Bad Ass. Despite the seismic influence of Rage Against the Machine, I still wasn't connecting with hip-hop in a wider sense; screaming guitars still basically owned my soul, and with the depth of my passion and the shallowness of my pockets, I didn't really have any way to explore other genres if I'd wanted to.

Still...

Ice T.

And Metal.

Interesting.

It opens with something that I now know as a standard of hip hop albums, but which at the time was deliciously alien to me; a skit. Ice T gets a gun from Mooseman (bass player in the band, we learn in the following track), goes over to a policeman, asks him for help changing a flat tyre, then shoots him.

The track is called 'Smoked Pork'.

A guitar starts chugging. A siren wails. A voice says the name. Another voice yells "YEAH, MOTHERFUCKER!". A second guitar joins. The drums roll in.

"BODYCOUNT!!"

Over a riff and chant (hypnotic, repetition, bodycount, bodycount), we hear the sounds of a car chase; police sirens, squealing tyres, gunfire popping off. The guitars are *immense*. As they drop into the second riff (still no sign of anything so dull as a verse or chorus) guitarist Ernie C shreds a wild flurry of notes out into a wailing bend that gives me chills.

I have no idea what's going on. It sounds like someone wrote a song to recreate the feeling of playing GTA; like, fuck verses, fuck choruses, just pure riff and attitude, get it.

I do. By the time Ice T has introduced the band and taken us back into the... verse? First riff? I am sold. It's fucking glorious. "BODYCOUNT, MOTHERFUCKER!" I yell, then and now, joining in with Ice T as the song ends.

And, you know, sure, back then I couldn't really say there was nothing like it, because I was a teenager, fucking *everything* was new to me; I had no idea what musical innovation really sounded like. I didn't have the terms of reference. I liked how RATM had made me feel, I liked how Bodycount was making me feel.... But I also liked how GnR and WASP made me feel, and I'd never heard anything like them, either.

But coming back to *Bodycount* after thirty years... man, there really wasn't anything *quite* like this, was there?

Sure, as noted above, the constant interjections – 'Opera', 'Now Sports', 'A Statistic' – mirror hip hop 'skits' (though there's not much in terms of humour, here), but there's also the fact that there are no less than three tunes named after the band (the album opens with the one/two punch 'Bodycount's In The House' and 'Bodycount', with 'Bodycount Anthem' towards the end of side 2), which, what?

Then there's the, uh, eccentric approach to song structure. So, in addition to the opener, whose lyrics consist entirely of the word Bodycount repeated a lot, the band being introduced like at a live show, and the phrase 'Bodycount's in the house!', we have 'Bodycount', with a long spoken-word intro over a gently picked guitar riff, before, for the first time on the album, we get into something that resembles a verse/chorus structure. And even there, after the second verse, we get a drum solo into chorus into an extended guitar solo. And I want to be clear; it's not that it's bad. It is not bad. It's pretty fucking awesome, combining a punk inventiveness and energy with metal musicality, and all the muscle of both, with the continued vibe of a live show ("Yo, Beatmaster V! Take these motherfuckers to South Central!").

It's a pure adrenaline shot, and in many ways it's almost an ideal of metal, shedding the flab the genre is not infrequently known for, but preserving the musicianship. And this persists – 'There Goes The Neighborhood', 'Evil Dick' and 'Momma's Gotta Die Tonight' have similarly gonzo structures, and 'KKK Bitch' has spoken intros to each verse, setting up the scene.

And sure, coming back after 30 years, it's not flawless. 'Bowels Of The Devil' is a metal/hardcore riff for the ages, but the lyric is pretty basic, and the chorus punchline (*And you don't want to die there! / They call it going out the back door!*) only really lands the first time. Similarly, 'Voodoo' chugs along perfectly serviceably, but there just isn't enough *there* there in the lyric to really sustain the song. And I'm never going to be a fan of anti-drugs ballads like 'The Winner Loses'; the sincerity is there, and the directness is admirable (opening line: *My friend's addicted to cocaine* lets you know what you're in for), but it's a genre that basically always bugs me. Like, I don't even dig 'She Talks To Angels', you know?

Elsewhere, though, hearing the album is throwing open all these doors of memory; reconnecting me with a very teenage sense of rage at the state of the world that never entirely left, and seems to be resurging with some force as I approach the midway point of my fourth decade on this planet, given, well, *gestures at the absolute state of the world*. But remembering that sad, angry, scared, lonely teenage boy, listening to this album at stupid volumes, I guess there are two things I really have to get into: the anti-racism, and the misogyny.

Let's start with the anti-racism. As I may have mentioned before, I spent most of my childhood in one of the whitest areas of the country, if not the planet. In my entire school career, there was exactly one Asian kid, and zero teachers of colour – and that includes school and college. What flows from that? Well, I was raised leftie, and I knew discrimination was Wrong. And I think my mum's feminism, especially, gave me a leg up, purely in terms of a 'people have the right to do what they want, and love who they love' mentality. At the same time, the absence of any chance for first-hand experience with anyone not-white led to a shy awkwardness, when I finally made it to London. I fucking loved the multiculturalism of that city – hell, still do – but I carried a mortal dread of saying or doing something stupid out of the ignorance I knew I carried, and, yeah, that took a bit of time to process.

And that was compounded by the fact that the shared ignorance of my young white peers (alongside, in some cases, some good old-fashioned bigotry) meant there *was* a lot of racism around me in Devon: at school, at college, and in society in general. Random examples float into memory: the bizarre piece of graffiti on a wooden locker at college, where someone had written across the dark door in tippex the phrase 'Ja Rasta Fart'; the late 20s guy who, as part of a wider conversation about whether or not jealousy was innate to the human condition or a social construct, calmly asserted to me that he believed white and black people had evolved entirely separately; the apparently nice eccentric older gentleman who wandered around town barefoot, and was always up for a chat, who, upon hearing I was moving to London, frowned and said "Why would you want to do that? It's full of wogs!".

And the endless jokes about black people.

And I just can't. And I don't need to. You've heard them, one way or another, and I can see no value in rehashing them here, devoid as they are of any scintilla of merit, as harmful as I now know them to be, as shameful as it is to recall now how I would listen, and God help me, sometimes even repeat these... I mean, jokes are meant to be funny, and they aren't, so, I don't even know what to say. I was young, I was dumb, I was surrounded by assholes, and I am deeply ashamed, and that's kind of it, really.

I also, and I do want to note this, did know it was wrong.

I say that not to excuse, incidentally, rather the reverse. What kind of person, even a kid, goes along with something they know is wrong, harmful, for... what? Some kind of shitty awful badge of 'cool' or 'edgy'? Some imbecilic and not remotely thought through 'commitment' to 'free speech'? Repeating lies I knew were harmful to impress people I didn't even like?

Jesus, what a wretch.

But that knowing it was wrong, that *did* matter.

Because when Bodycount came along, they were ready as fuck for my dumb white ass. And they had some shit to tell me.

'There Goes The Neighbourhood' is the riff DJ Lord hit that sent me spinning down the memory hole, even as I joined the crowd in a roar of approval. Jesus, that riff. And then the title, delivered staccato as the drums crash in, and *then* that piledriver verse riff as Ice T just rips the lid off. Earlier, on 'The Real Problem', he'd spoken about the fear of white kids liking a black artist; on this track, he takes that up to eleven, directly addressing racism in rock by ventriloquising the meathead position. He's dropped n-bombs throughout the record, but here it's different. Here, he's voicing the ugliness, the fear, the hate.

And, I mean, by this point, the start of side two, he's completely won me over. This is a fucking awesome metal album, with a bluntness and brutality I've seldom experienced but always been looking for, and a (mostly) righteous fury that I feel as my own, despite the chasms of life experience and culture that divide us (and, fucking hell, isn't that the point of music, of art, when you get down to it? Aren't we all reaching out for that, either as creators or audience?). And if you want to call bullshit on a dorky white teenager in North Devon finding music written by a black man from LA relatable, I of course can't really argue... but it doesn't change how I felt, or how I feel now, as I listen back to the album.

I *do* feel a connection. And hearing 'There Goes The Neighbourhood', especially the breakdown when Ice T announces *We're here / we ain't going nowhere / we're moving right next door to you / Bodycount, motherfucker!*, man, my teenage fist is punching the air in mute agreement.

And by taking on the stupid, racist position in the verses, the moral vacuum of that stance was revealed to me on a visceral level, in a way that no amount of well-meaning teaching about 'we're all the same' could ever manage. Like, no disrespect intended to those teachers (well... maybe a bit) but this, *this* was precision-engineered to reach a kid like me – a white metal dork who knew racism was wrong... but maybe didn't really understand why on a level beyond the intellectual, not having had occasion to see the impact up close, first hand.

And then here's Ice T, who, having kicked my arse for an entire side of punk-metal of variable quality but undeniable energy, gets right up in my fucking face and over the best riff on an album with an abundance of face-melters, says, in effect, 'whose side are you on?'

And the correct answer on this issue, then and now; your side, Ice T. I'm with you. And I can't unsay the things I said as a child, but I can – I could, I did – commit to talking less bullshit and more truth, from that point on. And it did mark a moment for me, a before-and-after, both in terms of how I'd behave and what behaviour I'd tolerate in the people close to me. Looking back, *Bodycount* was the moment I first grasped that anti-racism was a verb, not a noun – not something you are, but something you either do, or do not.

Man, it's really tempting to end things there. But, well, there is the small matter of the album's cartoonishly awful misogyny.

Now, as we'll be discussing in chapters past and future, (see Volume I, and Chapter 31 in this volume), this isn't an issue particular to Ice T, or hip hop, or metal. It does, however, feature prominently in all those forms, and as uplifting as the anti-racism message of Bodycount is, if I'm being honest, I do also have to reckon with the comfort zone that the likes of Guns N' Roses had given me for misogynistic art.

Because I mean, fucking hell.

Women, on this album, exist exclusively as objects of lust, or as pains in the ass, and that's it. 'Voodoo' features a woman with a voodoo doll fucking up Ice T just, you know, because, and 'Evil Dick' features a sequence that is toe-curling even by 'Rocket Queen' standards. And sure, that last is clearly a tongue-in-cheek riff on, as the *Oprah* intro phrases it, 'male promiscuity'; still, it's not exactly *not* a celebration of fucking whoever you want. And to be clear, as long as there's enthusiastic consent, fine, but… well, I just think it's not ideal if half the population is reduced entirely to their potential appeal as sexual partners, as opposed to being, you know, fully functional human beings.

And the two tracks where this tendency becomes most apparent and egregious are where the two themes collide: 'KKK Bitch' and 'Mama's Gotta Die Tonight'.

'KKK Bitch' has some of the feel of a skit, given the aforementioned spoken intros to each verse, and sure, the story of Ice T dating the daughter of a KKK Grand Wizard is, I mean, if you're not already grinning or even laughing at the concept, I dunno what to tell you. And it is, transparently, a gag, to be clear – right down to the third verse intro where Ice T says ...*it really don't matter, if you from mars and you got a pussy, we will fuck you, and you know that's all we tryin' to say...*

And I can't tell you if that's a funny line on the page, but in the context of a song where Ice T is touring southern states with Bodycount and shagging all the white women whose racist boyfriends can't satisfy them, the way he delivers it… look, I'll own that it still makes me grin.

At the same time, the 'woman as object' trope is all over the song: Ice T is 'using' the daughter to get to her dad, the song even has him getting turned on and having angry sex with her as her old man delivers a racist speech. And she has no appreciable personality or agency of her own, she exists purely to worship Ice T sexually, and...

Like, I get it, I get it, I get it. She's not real. None of it is real. It's a story, a goof, a joke, and the punchline is racists are awful. And teenage me is looking at adult me with total confusion, but like...

Well, the problem, teenage me, and Ice T, for that matter, I guess, is this: you didn't dig those other jokes that denied humanity and agency to a whole segment of the population. And at this point, I honestly can't tell if I'm an alien or I'm missing something that's blindingly obvious to everyone else, but, like, misogyny has a bodycount, too, and violence against women is an endemic and ongoing crime against humanity, and obviously, fuck playing oppression Olympics, and fuck whoever even first coined that hateful phrase, but...

I grin, sure, but the grin doesn't sit easy. And sometimes I listen, and sometimes, I skip. And I don't have any answers, and I'm not saying the song shouldn't exist or that you shouldn't listen to it or shouldn't enjoy it. I'm just saying I think 'There Goes The Neighbourhood' does it all way better, and doesn't leave an unpleasant aftertaste.

And then there's 'Momma's Gotta Die Tonight'.

And this one's way tougher for me, because I really fucking like this song. I like it because it comes on like a horror movie, I like it because it's about anti-racism as a verb, I like it because the core conceit is you really need to fuck off racists in your life, no matter who they are, because racism is Actually Evil. And as we've already rehearsed at painful length, that was a message I very much needed to hear, when I first heard it, and the internalisation of that message measurably improved my quality of life.

On the other hand, it's a song about murdering a woman and chopping her up.

*Yeah, but a **racist** woman,* I know, teenage me, I did catch that bit *I learned my momma was an evil woman / She hated black people, Mexicans...* on and on, yup, racism wrong, racists bad, got it. Still, tho... at a certain point, it's hard not to notice that there's at least a subtheme of the album, and it's not 'women are awesome'. And no, nobody is obliged to put out art that does that, of course not, but... It's not just me, is it?

Like, music; at least the music I really love, the stuff that goes down deep and really matters, has always had a liberatory quality; and I know that sounds both corny and laughably subjective, and it is both those things, but it's also how I feel. And, as with much of the horror literature I love, there's a specific liberatory quality to laying bare dark truths: ugly impulses, unworthy thoughts, dangerous, unpleasant beliefs, vomiting them up and really poking about in the chunks and drool, see what's what. There's a purging, but also a reckoning – and let's face it, we vomit for a reason, right? If your body is trying that hard to get rid of something in your stomach, you're probably better off rid.

And viewed through that lens, and given the utterly pervasive nature of misogynistic patriarchy, the literal and metaphorical stranglehold it has over women and men alike, there's a case to be made that art that doesn't at least reflect that to some degree isn't being honest (well, *my* kind of art, anyway – I guess utopians get to imagine what humans look like without this poison coursing through every interaction, and good luck to them). And Ice T is an artist, and I can't see into his soul any more than I can into anyone else's.

Still, I can't get away from the lack of challenge. Bodycount, a band of black musicians that Ice T knew would primarily appeal to a white audience, comes right the fuck at racism from the off, understanding that the vast majority of metalheads would embrace the attitude and be moved in the right direction as a result. Bodycount was throwing the *best* party, and the only price of entry was to reject racism.

And, again, just to be crystal clear, fucking good show.

But there's nothing here, or, really, in most of the music I love, from that era to this, that challenges the poisons of misogyny or patriarchy. Sure, in grunge, the outright misogyny is mainly absent, and of course, that's not nothing, but nor is it doing what BC was doing here with racism.

And I think that's a damn shame.

Not – one more time – because patriarchy was or is Ice-T's problem to solve. But because when I see and hear so much of how men still behave, in the year of our Lord 2022, I feel like a fucking alien, and I just wish some artist had done for them what Ice T did for my dumb teenage racist self.

Still. 30 years on, *Bodycount* still packs a punch, and I'm grateful to have had it in my life.

PS: Prophets Of Rage absolutely killed it. But that's a story for another day. And, indeed, project. :)

I'M THE TYRANNY OF EVIL MEN

PULP FICTION

There's a lot I don't know.
I knew the director by reputation. His first movie had been infamous, with That Scene the topic of delighted playground gossip and exaggeration, but I'm pretty sure, at this point, I hadn't seen it. For a horror kid I could be oddly squeamish, and the notion of a straight-up torture scene in a movie triggered my squeam.
So I'm pretty sure this movie was my first experience with this director.
What I can remember is that I bought it on VHS without ever having seen it.
That was a pretty serious commitment, by the way. It was a recent release, so it will have cost £10 brand new, and back then, a tenner was a tenner – four packets of fags, or two bottles of cider from the local pub that would serve anyone who could see over the bar plus one packet of fags. Big money.
And I remember interrogating my dad about it over the phone, who'd said it was both brilliant and horrible, and also brilliant. And then, well, there's that goddamn poster, right? Surely one of the great pieces of static image advertising of all time: the book cover, the gun, the burning cigarette, and that beautiful pale face framed by that exquisite black bob.
And, obviously, the title itself, promising thrills and chills in equal measure.

169

I wasn't eighteen. But somehow I bought it anyway, and in this particular instance, I can confirm Mia's proposition – sometimes, it *is* more exciting when you don't have permission.

There's a phenomenon I've observed with the truly great crime cinema and TV, which is that, particularly on a first viewing, they are incredibly, almost unbearably tense. I think back to my first viewing of *Goodfellas, Casino, Sopranos, Deadwood* (yes, *Deadwood* is a crime show, don't @ me), and the common thread of the experience is a screaming, desperate fear that imbues pretty much every scene. Because these are violent men, with volcanic tempers, and the spectre of that anger, and that capacity for violence, haunts every fucking scene they're in; I can never relax on a first viewing, because, bluntly, I'm always having to mentally bolster myself for things kicking off in a major, mortal way in pretty much every scene. It makes for a viewing experience both thrilling and exhausting, a kind of low-key adrenaline high that lasts for the couple of hours the movie runs. I find crime novels the same, and as I think on it more, that's probably the reason I absorb crime fiction so voraciously but reread so rarely; once I know how it pans out, and where the explosions are going to happen, that particular part of the experience is gone.

And with this movie, given the reputation of both this title and the director, and my otherwise total absence of information (we're pre-internet here; I'm almost certain I've seen only the poster, no clips, no trailer, probably not a cast list – what, exactly am I doing here? Flying on instinct, I guess), when I first put the tape in and hit play, I imagine even the piracy warning notice made me jump.

All of which is a borderline unforgivably long-winded way of saying I was *psyched.*

And within approximately two minutes of the movie starting, I was plain blown away.

I'm second-guessing the setup now, because my memory is that actually, I did know Tim Roth, and there's a limited number of places that could have been, with *Reservoir Dogs* being the most likely contender. *Rosencrantz and Guildenstern*, maybe? Regardless, I knew/thought of him as cool, and this guy… wasn't. He clearly hadn't shaven for a day or two, his skin and teeth were both bad. And his girlfriend… something was off about his girlfriend. I mean, now, with my almost 43 years of watching movies, I could point you to half a dozen things QT is doing in this sequence, from camera positioning to script to sound design and on and on, to create and build that sense of tension. But in the moment, at 15 or 16 years old, all I know is that, despite the kookiness of the two characters, I am freaking the fuck out long before the gun hits the table with a startlingly percussive noise, and HunnyBunny yells "ANY OF YOU FUCKING PRICKS MOVE, AND I'LL EXECUTE EVERY MOTHERFUCKING LAST ONE OF YOU!!!"

The freeze-frame on her rage-filled yelling face before she's finished speaking, coupled with the title card, and *that* guitar line kicking in... I get echoes of that first-time thrill every time I watch it (hell, I'm getting a ghost of an echo of the thrill just recalling it now), but that first time... it felt like whole sections of my brain being permanently rearranged, just plain picked up and put down again somewhere else.

And then, of course, we cut away, and now it's two immaculately suited, unbearably cool-looking gangsters sitting in a car talking about the 'little differences' in McDonald's restaurants across Europe, every single line of which now feels like a weird kind of movie nerd scripture; like Python, lines that you can quote endlessly, and that your fellow tribe members will immediately fall into with you. Part of that's the rhythm of the writing, of course ("You know what they call a Quarterpounder with Cheese in Paris?" "They don't call it a QuarterPounder with Cheese?" "Nah, man, they got the metric system, they don't know what the fuck a QuarterPounder is." it's exquisite, no?), part of it is how funny it is (the punchline of "I dunno, I didn't go to Burger King" tells us so much about Vince and the hilarious limits of his 'American abroad' bit) but, again, what I think it's easy to miss with the passage of time and the curse of the familiar is just how jarring and tense it was, alongside what had just happened and what was about to happen – this inane-yet-somehow-brilliant conversation is casually interrupted by a POV car boot shot where, in the same casual tones as they discuss international cuisine, they bemoan not having 'shotguns for this deal'.

The film does this time and time again, at the micro and macro level, the fractured time structure setting up tensions, laying down strands – think about the casual confrontation between Travolta and Willis in the bar, Travolta's dripping contempt for the aging boxer; we never find out why Vince is so contemptuous of Butch, but his petty unpleasantness is paid off in spectacular fashion in the Gold Watch portion of proceedings. Similarly, the movie rather ruthlessly exploited my 15-year-old racist face blindness such that I was convinced I'd found an actual flaw in the storytelling first time out, with Jules appearing in a scene with Vincent *after* he'd decided to leave The Life; of course, it's not, it's the barman from the earlier scene who has apparently been promoted to enforcer in Jules' absence, and given a cool new suit into the bargain.

I'm forcibly reminded – don't laugh, or at least not yet – of the chapter I wrote about *Gremlins* (see Volume I). There, as here, the subsequent viewings render the whole as a brilliantly crafted, rollicking black crime comedy, really; with thrills and spills aplenty, sure, as the name implies, but ultimately a slice of entertainment. And, you know, sure, of course it is.

Now.

But... then? That first time?

The Gold Watch sequence is the obvious one; if you hadn't been spoiled, the unbearably slow-motion release of The Gimp was, well, pretty much unbearable, and I think even knowing what Butch is going to find when curiosity drives him, katana in hand, back to that basement, there's still a kind of sick shock value to proceedings, the impact of which, for me, hasn't really faded with rewatching.

But it's Mia's overdose scene, for me, that serves as an exemplar – maybe *the* exemplar – of the 'first as horror, second as comedy 'effect.

Because it is *hysterical. Pulp Fiction* is back in rotation on the Sky Movie channels right now, and consequently, I'll often find myself watching 20 or 30 minutes of it before going to bed of an evening, and if I happen to tune in anywhere around Jack Rabbit Slim's (another scene which on a first viewing felt almost terrifying, the social bear traps Vince is surrounded by and the potential lethality of falling into one of them, my God), I know I'm strapped in until I see pale, sweaty, dishevelled Travolta blowing a kiss. And I know I'll be laughing like a drain pretty much the whole time. Travolta's dead-eyed, remorseless fixation, and the way it explodes into raw panic during the confrontation on the lawn, Eric Stoltz just losing his shit as every heroin dealer's worst nightmare crashes into his garage and threatens to die in his living room, the escalating fury and utter pettiness of his interactions with his wife (exacerbated by her, through no fault of her own, being about a minute behind the conversation for most of it), the fixation on pointless detail ("a little black medical book!" "A fucking felt pen! A fucking fat magic marker!"), all while crime boss Marcellus Wallace's wife twitches her way to heroin-induced oblivion... look, it's not high art, exactly... but it's not exactly *not* high art, either. I've seen it I don't know how many times at this point, and like all truly great comedy, I find it at least as funny now – if not more so, knowing every single beat and every single piece of dialogue – as I did the first time.

Or rather, and this is the point, as I did *the second time*.

Because the first time, honestly? This was one of the most shit-your-pants scary bits of cinema I had encountered to date.

I was *invested,* that's the thing. Like I suspect 80% of the male audience, I was half in love with Mia Wallace by this point, and I desperately wanted her to be ok. And, you know, Vincent is clearly a gangster and somewhat of a bad dude... but he's also goofy and charming and clearly also half in love with Mia, and it's already clear that the likely consequences for him if this goes all the way south are going to be Old Testament Biblical. And all the actors in the scene sell it magnificently; a lot of the second time viewing comedy comes from how everyone in the scene is just about out of their minds with fear about what's going on, and about what may or may not happen in the next ninety seconds. But first time? Nah, mate. First time, I was a bundle of raw anxiety, proper fear sweat on, absolutely no fucking idea what was about to happen.

It was brilliant.

One of the themes that comes up again and again in the chapters of these books is the similarities between horror and comedy (applies to erotica as well, I guess, though that's not really my area); tension and release, set up and punchline, stress and catharsis (even if, in horror, the catharsis is a gut punch rather than a smile). But I think *Pulp Fiction* exemplifies something else, something more complex: sometimes, it's horror the first time and comedy the second, *because the second time through, you know the punchline is a punchline, not a gutpunch.*

I don't know exactly what to do with this information, and it almost can't be an original observation, at this point. That said, I remain incredibly grateful to *Pulp Fiction* for delivering such a hand grenade of a movie, at a time and place where I'd simply never seen anything remotely like it. It changed the way I think about story, and like all great traumatising art, it has since become a comfort space – a go-to film where the dialogue and performances wrap around me like a warm blanket, and, for a couple of hours, take me away completely to another time and place; a place where horrible things happen, sure… but also a place where I know how it's all going to shake out; freeing me to enjoy the horror of the absurdity of, well, people and circumstance.

And given our current state of play, as a species, I'd strongly advise you to take your joy wherever you can find it.

EL EYE VEE, EE ARE PEE, DOUBLE OH EL

CRACKER

Back when I was bleeding my useless heart over crimes committed by the Thatcher era police forces of West Yorkshire (See Volume I), I mentioned in passing that as a child, I called myself a Liverpool supporter purely because in the one football match I had seen, they'd beaten Barnsley 2 – 0. I also mentioned that it was literally just something to say to answer a question boys would sometimes ask me, and beyond that I cared not a jot. I *also* claimed in that article that I basically didn't know anything about Hillsborough as an event until the time of writing that chapter.

And you're just going to have to take my word for it that, at the time I wrote that, I believed it.

But it's total horseshit. Because one of my all-time favourite moments of TV horror occurs smack bang in the middle of a story in which the events of Hillsborough are intricately and inextricably woven.

Wikipedia informs me it is October, 1994. I am, therefore, 16 years old. And I think, though I cannot be certain, that as it's the 17th October, I watch this particular episode of television at my father's house, during the October half term week.

Cracker was a show that loomed enormous in my teenage brain. My memory is that I either wasn't allowed to watch the first series, or possibly had just missed it first time round. I *think* the first story I saw was the season one finale, maybe as an omnibus repeat prior to the season 2 premiere. Except that can't be right, because I have a distinct memory of talking to my dad, either over the phone or face to face, about the characters in 'To Say I Love You'. So maybe I just missed the first story in the series, 'The Mad Woman in the Attic', and was on board by the second story of Season 1. That feels right, actually.

Certainly, 'One Day A Lemming Will Fly' had a gigantic impact on me. I videoed it off the telly, either on broadcast or the later omnibus broadcast, and I could quote whole chunks of that thing verbatim by the time I got to sixth form college, especially the monologue Fitz delivers to the hapless school teacher to talk him down from the ledge, which contains the episode title – a moment that culminates in Fitz apparently talking himself into jumping, making Mr. Cassidy pull *him* back from the edge, incredulously calling him a 'crazy bastard'.

It's an absolute tour de force of a scene, in a two-part story not short on such moments. It's also a ballsy-as-hell story for several reasons, not least of which is that Fitz monumentally fucks the entire investigation up in pretty much the worst possible way. Bear in mind that up to now the show, over two stories and five episodes, has built this guy up as forensic psychology's answer to Sherlock Holmes (except, as I'm slowly working out in my Patreon-exclusive podcast on the subject of Mr. Holmes with dear friends Jack Graham and Daniel Harper, it turns out Holmes might have been a proto-forensic psychologist, actually). Sure, Fitz is an alcoholic, gambling addict, chain-smoking manipulative womaniser and emotional rapist, but by golly he gets the job done, and when ethical-but-inevitably-compromised young DI Bilborough (played with painfully sincere realism and angst by the mighty Christopher Eccleston, forever my Doctor) is up against it, of course he, against his better judgement, calls in The Bastard, and The Bastard gets it done.

When 'One Day A Lemming Will Fly' begins, Fitz has already managed to identify a man who has been murdering women in train carriages, in the process exonerating the prime suspect, a chap who had been at the scene of the first murder but had amnesia. From there, he's drawn into investigating a murder where, in a crime scene investigation worthy of The Great Detective, he finds several clues the police have missed that allow him to put together a profile of a male/female couple working together to kill. The final episode of *that* story is an absolute doozy, with Fitz interrogating the woman while her other half closes in on her parents, leading to an epic fear-sweat finale, as Fitz goes in to negotiate with the incensed boyfriend as he holds the women's parents hostage in a house filling with flammable gas.

So, sure, we're only three stories in, but the pattern has been set; whilst in the first story, Fitz's ability to 'crack' a suspect is limited by having the wrong suspect on ice, the show goes out of its way to show that while the cops had the wrong guy in custody, Fitz's assessment of the actual killers' psychology is note-perfect, and the scene in Episode Three of 'To Say I Love You', where he desperately tries to break down the killer's partner, is one of those top-drawer-scripts-meets-world-class-performers moments that keep us coming back to telly as a medium, frankly.

So, having established that Fitz indeed Has The Goods, and is clearly streets ahead of the cops he works with in terms of intelligence and insight, when a school child is found murdered (initially suicide is suspected, as the child is found hanging, but the postmortem confirms foul play) and a school teacher ends up in the frame, we think we know where this is headed.

There's also an incredibly poignant scene in this story, one that throws Fitz and his bullshit into (apparent) relief. Once the murder has been confirmed, Fitz spends some time, alongside DI Penhaligan (a young female detective Fitz flirts with outrageously throughout the season, despite being twice her age, married, and, well, Fitz), counselling the family over their loss. Through a series of crossfades, we hear both parents talking through the inevitable feelings of guilt and grief as they try and come to terms with what's happened. And Fitz is just brilliant; attentive, asking questions respectfully, skilfully drawing them out, and then, in a closing monologue, talking them through the reality of guilt as a step in the grieving process; and one that, with time, will pass, leaving grief alone in its place. "Grief is good. Grief is your friend. It allows you to mourn. Allows you to remember." He says this to their stricken faces, and you see them believe him, hesitantly, but definitely.

And it's brilliant, and *he's* brilliant, and you find yourself thinking 'well, hey, look, say what you like about this chap, that was A Good Thing he did there'.

And then, if you're anything like me, it occurs to you, somewhere on your fourth or fifth rewatch, that... well, yeah, he did the Good

Thing, sure, but also, Penhaligon, the object of his flirty lust for the entire season, was there too, and when he later propositions her, and she, even later, accepts the proposition, you (okay, I) can't help but wonder if Fitz hadn't calculated the impact of seeing him do that kind of work up close would have on her. And I mean, let's face it, it's Fitz, so *of course he had*.

Anyhow, when Fitz zooms in on the prime suspect – the aforementioned down-from-the-ledge school teacher – we kind of assume he's right, and that the remainder of the story will be focused on the long, slow wearing down of the clearly guilt-ridden suicidal man. And after he attempts suicide again (this time by gassing himself), and *then* after the grieving father and his rather perfomatively enraged friend try to murder the teacher by attacking his house with an actual wrecking ball (and yes, that is every bit as surprising and awesome as it sounds) sure enough, Fitz, Mr. Cassidy, and DI Beck (the detective Fitz, in an utterly characteristic display of vicious belittlement, describes as 'a man who can solve a Sun crossword in under two weeks') are ensconced in a hotel room for 'protective custody' – the police station has been targeted by vigilantes, following Grieving Dad's Wrecking Ball Escapade, making it unsafe for the actual murder suspect to be held there.

What follows is a sustained single scene of dialogue – between Fitz, Beck, and Cassidy – that is, in a quiet and unshowy way, as brilliant and layered as you're likely to see. It starts with Fitz apparently ignoring Cassidy and going after DI Beck's homophobia, describing a scenario wherein Beck took on performative, aggressive gay-hating at school, beating the boy he secretly had feelings for. Beck is incensed, angrily denouncing Fitz as 'sick' and guilty of projection – 'because you look inside and see something sick, something twisted, you think we've all felt it. Well, we haven't! Some of us are normal!'.

But it's a blind, misdirection; the *real* target is apparently-closeted Cassidy (confirmed in Fitz's mind as such, and by extension the audience, in the earlier scene where Fitz tells Cassidy's girlfriend Cassidy is gay and she's he's beard, news she takes with shock but seems to believe). And over the next – what, ten? Fifteen, even? – minutes of dialogue, Fitz wears him down, finding every chink in Cassidy's psychological armour and applying expert pressure and manipulation. It takes forever – Cassidy denying, Fitz pushing, angle after angle, Beck gradually stunned into silence as he realises what's *really* going on. Every actor in the scene absolutely rocks it, and the near-sexual pleasure on Coltrane's face as Fitz realises Cassidy is *finally* on the hook, needing only a promise to 'share his pain' in order to confess, is stomach churning.

But, you know, it's okay, because he's *right*. Cassidy did it, and Fitz, unpleasant, manipulative bastard though he undoubtedly is, has gotten his man.

Only he hasn't.

In a gut punch twist in the final five minutes, Cassidy summons Fitz to his cell (Fitz already showing impatience, boredom, his promise to share the pain already ringing hollow, The Thing You Say To Get What You Want) and tells the truth. He *didn't* kill Tim. He felt guilt, because Tim fancied him, and because he'd visited Cassidy and Cassidy had turned him away, and it was that guilt that had set off Fitz's spidey sense. Cassidy tells Fitz, you said you'd share my pain. Well, now you're going to. Because when Tim's killer strikes again, you'll feel what I felt – that you had a hand in it, could have prevented it, if only you'd acted differently.

Fitz shits the bed, button-hooking DCI Bilborough just before he goes in front of the press, demanding he not announce Cassidy's confession, swearing that he'll quit. Bilborough goes out to the podium, blinking in the harsh TV lights, hesitates… and then announces in a curt message that a suspect has been arrested and charged.

Fitz walks out, and goes home to his wife and kids, letting the answering machine catch an angry call from Penhaligon at the airport, realising that Fitz has stood her up.

I'm almost certain the show was intended to run one season only; or, at least, that it was *prepared* to only run one. The arc of these seven episodes of television is, after all, absolutely perfect, and the end note – Fitz quitting the cops and returning to the family unit, Penhaligon let down, Bilborough forging on alone – rounds the whole thing off brilliantly. At the same time, I'd imagine that once the word of mouth got out (looking at the viewing figures via Wikipedia, a hell of a lot of people jumped on for the second story, as I had, and every single damn one of them stuck around for the rest of the season, word clearly having gotten out that this was a special one) a second season quickly became inevitable.

And before we actually get to what I thought, when I started this, was the point of the essay, namely the final five minutes of Episode 2 of Season 2 of Cracker, I need to make what is almost certainly a deeply unsurprising if still shameful confession: at 17 I basically hero-worshipped Fitz.

I wasn't a big drinker, but as we've already discussed (see Chapter 13), I smoked with all the pathological evangelism of a newly minted Bill Hicks fan, and where Fitz was overweight, I was skinny and short and with long hair and a pretty big chip on my shoulder. And here was a man who used his brain to get whatever the fuck he wanted out of whoever he wanted to get it out of, who lived for instant gratification and fuck any and all consequences. A man who, without even trying, half drunk, could argue his way around anyone; outsmart, outthink, and leave them, rhetorically, bleeding from a thousand perfectly placed cuts.

And let's just put our finger on the really toxic part, and make it squirm, the little bastard; he could get away with all of this bullshit *because he was smart and charismatic.* Not handsome, not really, but magnetic, through sheer force of personality and will. But above all, because he was the best at his job, the thing he put his mind to. That meant he was needed, and, because he was needed, he could get away with any old shit, basically.

And yeah, of course, because he was white, and male, and middle class.

And at 17, I am ashamed to recall, that was a power fantasy I found *incredibly* attractive. I can rationalise why I did, understand the root powerlessness I felt, the slowly dawning realisation that in the real world, or at any rate the corner of it I inhabited, my smarts, such as they were, were not only not a magic bullet, but a kind of curse; the ability to understand the depth of the hole I and my peers were in better than almost all of them, alongside the understanding/belief that I had no power at all to change things.

And sure, that's true, but it doesn't change the fact that Fitz was/is a deeply toxic man, and my love for that character was/is very troubling and not at all to my credit.

Here be demons. And the ghost, of course.

Still, I *was* hooked, which brings us, 2000 words in, to where we started: October 1994, Season 2 of Cracker, and a story entitled 'To Be

A Somebody'. Because, yes, this is a show that's demonstrated that it can, amongst many other very cool things, subvert expectations, pull the rug in quite spectacular fashion. But this is a matter I have given entirely too much thought to, and I don't think a TV show has *ever* done to me what Season 2, Episode 2 of Cracker did; a moment of shock so profound I feel the echoes of it even now, some… fuck, some 25 years after the event, sweet fucking Jesus I am *old*, goddamn.

Anyhow. The setup is pretty simple. Albie, played by one of my favourite screen psycho actors, Robert Carlisle, already frayed and worn down by a tough manual labour job, divorce, and PTSD from surviving the Hillsborough disaster, finally goes off the deep end shortly after burying the father he's been caring for as the latter was dying of cancer. The final catalysing event is desperately trivial; the local corner shop owner refuses to accept underpayment for… I want to say a chocolate bar, something like that. Albie is 5 or 10p short, and 'I'll bring it over later' provokes a calm, polite, but clear refusal.

So Albie goes back to his room, shaves his head, takes his father's bayonet, goes back to the corner shop and hurls racist abuse at the shop keeper before stabbing him to death.

And, I mean, talk about a redundant sentence, but it's shocking and horrible. The scene really sits in the gut, indigestible. Because Albie as set up is sympathetic, even pitiable; but at the same time, his explosion of racist violence isn't merely wildly disproportionate to the shopkeeper's offence, it's an obscenity that, for me at least, erases any sympathy that may have built with him to that point. And in retrospect, I'm far from convinced by it as a psychological response to his circumstances. 2022 me has some very pointed things to say about how a depiction of racism as something that is generated spontaneously in response to trauma is kind of dangerous bullshit, to the degree that it erases how racism permeates white culture, and kinda-sorta makes excuses for it.

But it's October 1994, and there's every chance that 17-year-old me thought it was Pretty Good, Actually – assuming he thought about it at all, which, you know, let's be real, probably not.

Albie leaves some numbers at the scene – 9615489.

And Fitz… doesn't get called in. Still raw about the bust up over Cassidy at the end of the previous season, DI Bilborough brings in a different forensic psychologist to profile the killer. Fitz, facing pretty serious money problems due to his insane gambling habits, and pressure from his justifiably irate missus, keeps hitting up Penhaligon (who is righteously furious about being stood up for a dirty fortnight away by a man twice her age) about the case. There's a wonderful moment where Fitz gives her the kind of profile she can expect from the guy they've hired ('and when he does say that, that's how you'll know he's a prick!') and when she visits the scene with the new guy, she is, indeed, able to finish his description based on what Fitz told her.

Sidebar (and I swear, I'm getting there, but good man, this show): there's two delicious ironies here. Firstly, Albie is so furious about the profile given of him by the new police psychologist that is then leaked to the press that he hunts him down and murders him, all but guaranteeing that Fitz will be brought back into the investigation. And secondly, the profile ends up being, like, 90% accurate; white working class, male, 30s, football fan. The scene later where Fitz delivers this description, having Done The Work, is hilarious.

We're really getting to it, I promise, but look, this is one of the things the show does at a level I've rarely seen before or since; it's as much about the relationships between the characters as it is about the cases they are investigating. Indeed, the courses of the investigations are directly impacted by those relationships, for good and ill. In some ways, it's soap opera elevated to high art (so... just opera, then? Without the singing, obv).

Case in damn point: Fitz is back, but the team dynamic is utterly borked. Billborough is still sore with him over Cassidy (not helped by Fitz making even-for-him tasteless references to gas chambers and ovens, in response to Billborough's admittedly morally bankrupt 'following orders' defence of the prosecution). Penhaligon is still furious with him for being stood up. And as for DI Beck.... well, Beck has *always* hated Fitz, for all the reasons you'd expect – he's several orders of magnitude smarter than Beck, and he wastes no opportunity to wield that enormous intellect like a blunt instrument to bludgeon Beck, and belittle him. And there's a lot to belittle: Beck is a detestable person, not merely not bright but with a kind of wilful, proud ignorance that comes from a lifetime of profound insecurity marinated in toxic masculinity (which, by end of the season, will explode in the most powerful, awful fashion, with the events of this episode marking the tipping point). Add in Beck's actually justified contempt for Fitz's continued unsubtle attempts to get into the knickers of a woman half his age (but/and/also who Beck almost certainly fancies himself, adding salt to the wound) and... but I mean, just look at all that. The complex interweaving, the psychological depth and interplay, the sheer fucking *dynamism* of it all, constantly in flux, colliding, spinning off.

All this, plus a murder investigation. This fucking show.

Anyhow. The psychologist is murdered, Fitz is rehired, and gives, hilariously, basically the same profile, except he intuits no prior history of violence or hooliganism (which, again, yes, *Cracker* is explicitly about psychologically unusual limit cases, but, really?) and the coppers start going door to door in Albie's neighbourhood. DI Beck, of course, knocks on Albie's door. He notes the shaved head, and the white working classness. Albie, thinking fast, claims that his baldness is due to undertaking chemotherapy, and uses his dead father's appointment letters as proof. My memory is that the same drawer also contains the bayonet, just in case Beck doesn't fall for it.

But Beck, of course, falls for it.

My memory is that Beck has some family history with cancer that makes him overreact, but also, well, let's face it, the man is a gullible chump at the best of times. His guilt reaction as he switches from mean investigating cop to so-sorry-let-me-put-out-my-smoke is priceless, but also weirdly heartbreaking; Beck is a callous man, a really questionable copper, not above witness intimidation (and, you suspect, brutality, if he could get away with it) but he's also credulous enough to be manipulated by a pretty desperate ruse. And it's that shred of humanity that leads him to make a mistake that, by the end of the episode, will have lethal consequences.

I can't remember exactly how it plays out, at this distance, only that Albie lays a trap for Bilborough, and that Fitz, Beck et al become aware of it in HQ as Bilborough is approaching the house.

And, like, we've seen this one before, right? It's the classic thriller nailbiter, where the Goodie walks into peril, the audience aware of the Lurking Baddie, HQ trying to get through. The signal normally arrives Just In Time, the Goodie able to anticipate the attack, deflect it enough to be safe, with the Baddie escaping, maybe injured, to set up Part 3 as the net closes in, followed by Fitz doing his thing in the interview.

And *Cracker* looks you right in the eyes and says, not this time, baby.

I can still remember the visceral shock that ran through me as Albie stabbed Bilborough in the gut – memory suggests over total silence. I remember sitting bolt upright, and if I didn't swear, it's probably because I'd temporarily forgotten how to speak. Chris Eccleston. The fucking DI. Episode 2 of the season. And he is crawling, bleeding, turning pale, giving a fucking dying man's statement over the radio ("I know what a defence attorney will try and do with this... I'm lucid... I'm scared, yeah, I don't wanna die...") while Fitz, Penhaligan, and most of all, an utterly stricken DI Beck listen, helplessly...

And, like, the beauty of *Cracker* is that everyone is kind of a prick, to some degree or another, and Bilborough was no exception – he was, at times, quite blatantly sexist towards Penhaligon, his ambition sometimes clouded his better judgement, and he wasn't shy of using Beck for some pretty close-to-the-line bullshit if he thought it'd help his case. So, hero? Nah. But *human,* and clearly striving to do good, to be good, in a job where that's basically impossible, and here he is, bleeding out in the street in the fucking second episode of the first three-parter of the season, and I am profoundly shocked, both by the textual and metatextual implications.

The entire rest of the show pivots around this moment, by the way; Beck's spiral into self-destruction, the fallout of which will profoundly damage everyone else in the show, is triggered by this explosive moment. Nothing is ever the same. The show is permanently scarred by the passing of DI Bilborough.

And so was I. Like some of my very favourite stories, I realise, as I am working my way through the second, final part of this project, it's this moment of profound transgression – as shocking to me as the death of Jason Todd (see Volume I), or for that matter the climax of *Casino* (see Chapter 29) – that lodges the deepest, sends the largest ripples.

As a moment of TV drama, it's rarely been equalled, and for my money never surpassed.

This. Fucking. Show.

I WASN'T BORN WITH ENOUGH MIDDLE FINGERS

MARILYN MANSON

Here there would have been an essay about Marilyn Manson, and specifically his album *Antichrist Superstar*. That essay is still available on Gingernuts Of Horror, if you want to read it:

gingernutsofhorror.com/my-life-in-horror/my-life-in-horror-i-wasnt-born-with-enough-middle-fingers.

I just no longer feel comfortable charging people any money at all to read me saying nice things about the art of Marilyn Manson. Because Marilyn Manson turned out to be a gigantic fuckhead. So, fuck Marilyn Manson.
Here are the contact details for a group that supports survivors of domestic abuse. Please give generously because, and I really can't emphasise this enough, fuck Marilyn Manson. Thank you.

thepixelproject.net

And in conclusion: fuck Marilyn Manson. Fuck him forever.

IF ONLY THERE IS SOMETHING WE COULD HAVE DONE

XCOM

It's 1997. Or 1998. I am 17, or 18, or 19. It doesn't matter. Nothing much really matters.

My life revolves around precious little. In theory, I am at college, but really, I'm just existing; claiming Jobseekers Allowance whilst aggressively not studying or looking for work.

I don't drink. I don't smoke anything stronger than Boar's Head rolling tobacco, at least not very often. Can't afford it, no other reason. I don't eat well, but I eat often enough, the poverty diet of noodles and chips and Brian Ford's breaded Beef Cutlets.

I am miserable, but there are chinks of light. I have a small but tight-knit social group, and we have a regular roleplaying game (see Volume I). And, of course, there's the music – music that speaks to me (see previous entry, alas), and later, music that saves me (see Volume I).

And there is also addiction.

I sometimes think, as I reflect upon my life, that I have in general been very fortunate in the addictions I have been drawn to. Whilst compulsive behaviour is almost by definition not healthy, and while a side effect of my various obsessions has been persistent issues with sleep deprivation and exhaustion, and the occasional psychological issues such tiredness can bring, it's very rare they've been destructive beyond the time sink factor. Poker held me for about 3 years, but while I sunk many hundreds of hours into the game, I was good enough to break even over that period. Ultimately, while I wasn't quite good enough to make money at it, it at least only cost me time. I know that it cost – and still costs – a lot of other people a lot more.

Similarly, my obsessions with various pieces of pop culture seem to have done little harm – in the cases of *Doctor Who* and horror fiction, they've led to some amazing friendships, and of course the enormous privilege of writing a monthly column for the biggest independent horror review site in Europe. In Stephen King's *IT*, adult Eddie (always my favourite, bless you Eddie) talks about how the secret of life is to find the little bastard who lives in your head, fucking everything up, and get your hands around the little bastard, and then…. Don't choke him out, but put the fucker to work. I'm not going to claim to have fully mastered this advice – or, indeed, that I don't still have the issues that I am working through, and the odd wobble, as we've previously discussed – but I've certainly found that turning that compulsion towards getting words on a page has done a pretty spectacular job of replacing a still-entirely-absent work ethic. 'I don't know where you find the time!' people often remark. I normally make some joke about sleep being for the weak.

It's not really a joke.

Anyway.

There is one other item that keeps me going during this 1997/98 period. It's a 384 PC, ancient even then, a hand me down from a university that's upgraded the student PC lab. It's a gift from The Ghost. Of course. Ostensibly for study, and for writing – even back then, writing feels like something I should be doing, though my output is pitiful in both scale and content, only happening when the mental pressure feels so strong that I literally can't help but get something down, and I know how that sounds, but I was there and it's how it was.

But really I only cared about it because it could run games. Not many. Not *Doom*, much less *Quake*, which was just coming out around then. But it could run *Wolfenstein 3D* just fine.

More importantly – all-consumingly important – it could run *UFO: Enemy Unknown*.

UFO – later rebranded *XCOM* – is, in your humble correspondent's opinion, one of the greatest PC strategy games of all time – maybe the greatest. The premise is simple: aliens make first contact with Earth, and they are not friendly. The player takes on the role of commander of the hastily assembled XCOM team – an international military project established with the explicit goal of combatting and eventually defeating the alien threat.

To do this, the player is given a base, some interceptor aircraft for shooting down UFOs, and a small army of soldiers for assaulting the downed ships and killing any remaining aliens. The player will also end up building laboratories for researching the alien artefacts that are recovered from the crash sites (and hiring the scientists to work in those labs), and workshops and engineers will be employed to manufacture more of these items once they've been researched.

So it's a combination of strategic base/resource management (funds are limited, as are alien materials, which cannot be synthesised and must instead be recovered from sites), and a hyper-tense turn-based combat game, where you sneak your soldiers around a procedurally generated map, with the geography very loosely based on where the UFO crashed on the planet, and try very hard to kill a better armed, tougher opponent.

This is, I think, the core of the genius of *XCOM*. One aspect of game design that I am really coming to appreciate as I get older is that of balance. The deck building game *Legendary* is a perfect example of this – it's essentially a cooperative game where you work with the other players to beat a villain and their scheme – and the genius of *Legendary* is you usually win... and it's usually really, really close. You normally feel like you just squeaked it, just got it put away in time. *Pandemic* is another excellent boardgame example of this.

And in *XCOM*, you basically always feel like you're on the back foot, up against it, struggling to hold ground. Every combat mission feels like it could end in disaster (and it often does), you never have enough money to do all the things you need to do, and if you screw up missions (and you do, frequently), you lose funding from those countries in subsequent months, further putting the squeeze on your options – indeed, one of the main ways you can lose the game is by having enough countries leave the project that you're no longer funded. Additionally, your soldiers improve with each mission, becoming more effective, but that very effectiveness leads you to end up putting them into more and more dangerous positions.

And most of all, there are the aliens.

They get smarter, for starters – or, at least, it feels like they do. They certainly get tougher – there's more of them per spaceship, and there are a *lot* of species, each with their own weaponry, movement, threat. The first few months are a near constant exercise of perpetual what-the-fuck-*now* as you round the corner of some farmhouse or gas station and see a reaper or cyberdisk – or one of the aliens starts flying, or one of your troops suddenly falls under enemy control and starts shooting his compatriots.

And the game fucks you over in other ways. Example: your scientists inform you that in order for the research to *really* progress, you'll need to capture one of the aliens alive. And in order to do *that*, you'll need to use a stun prod – which as the name implies has no range at all, meaning that you need to be adjacent to the aliens to use it. So now, you're taking your most experienced troops (with the most movement and health) and giving them a weapon they can only use at point blank range, and running them up to aliens to zap them, hoping it works.

It doesn't always.

It's an exercise in sadism, is what I'm trying to say. The game delights in finding new ways to punch the player in the face. Oh look, now the aliens are sending huge super-tough forces into cities to murder civilians, and if you don't try and stop them the country will leave the project, but if you go you can't use any of your explosive weapons without killing civilians yourself. Oh, look, the alien UFOs are tougher now and can shoot down your interceptors. Oh, look, they've figured out where your base is and are attacking it. Oh look, you lost. Again.

It's punishing even on the lower difficulty settings, and on anything from 'normal' up, it's downright vicious. And holy shit it's a *slog*. An average winning game will have engaged in well over 50 combat missions, each taking around an hour to complete. You will have researched huge numbers of items and tech. You will have – somehow – taken out one of the giant UFOs *and* captured its commander alive – or assaulted an alien base on earth and somehow captured the leader from there, instead. *Then* you'll have built a new ship that can take your soldiers to Mars, where you will finally assault the alien base there and – if you're lucky – destroy the huge beating heart at the centre of that base and win the game.

IF ONLY THERE IS SOMETHING WE COULD HAVE DONE

I loved it. I loved it because it was so fucking hard. I loved it because it was such a fucking slog. I loved it because it was a series of repetitive tasks with endless slight variation, constantly escalating challenge. I loved it because even when you'd played it through once, it took so fucking long that you'd forgotten the tech tree and had to guess at how best to assign research all over again.

Most of all, I loved it because I could become absorbed in it. By it. The world around me, the crowded, dirty bedroom filled with black bin bags and stinking of cigarette ash, and the house outside the room with the dodgy electrics and mouldy shared bathroom and filthy kitchen, and the town outside the house that was rapidly becoming the limits of my imagination and understanding, a town full of callous indifference at best and a kind of dull-minded sadism at worst, a town/world that seemed pretty well personally tailored to grind me into a fine powder and scatter me to the wind, never to be seen again... it all went away. And so did I.

I'm not saying it wasn't fun. But my abiding memory isn't of fun, exactly. It's more of a blankness, where all the challenges are abstract; a space where there is still complexity and difficulty and unfairness, but where all that can be overcome by rigorous application of understanding.

Addicts talk about this a lot – the blankness that lies at the core of it, at the bottom – doing the thing so hard and so long that everything else vanishes. And I still think there is, or can be, a therapeutic value to that, at least in theory. No-one can spend 24/7 inside their own head, after all. The human mind is kind of the opposite of a safe space.

But it was absolutely a compulsion, too. I'd lose days to the game, playing until I couldn't keep my eyes open, sleeping for 12 hours, waking up, shoving some food down my throat, and then straight back to it. Whilst I was nominally attending college, the need to attend the odd class held it in check a bit, but once I'd given up the pretence of ever passing anything, there was also nothing to keep me from turning on, loading the latest save game, and dropping all the way out.

And – newsflash – I'm not cured. Not even close. Because it's now 2018, and I am 40 years old, and over the last few weeks, I've lost hours – hours of sleep, hours of potentially productive writing time, hours I can ill afford – playing the PlayStation 3 iteration of *XCOM*, in the name of beating the Ironman Classic version of the game – a particularly sadistic setting where the game saves after every decision, overwriting the previous one, so you can't simply reload if you fuck up. It took me over 30 attempts to finally beat it, and more late nights than I am prepared to admit. All for a couple of PlayStation 3 trophies that mean absolutely nothing to anyone that isn't me, and the ability to be able to say 'I beat *XCOM* on Iron Man mode, classic difficulty'.

Quite early on in this writing thing, I remember talking to a mate about how I was struggling with balancing PS3 time and writing time. My rationalisation for the time I spent playing was that it was when I was too tired to write.

Well, guess what? That was bullshit.

Turns out, if I am awake enough to game, I am awake enough to write. Right now, I am fucking exhausted, and half cut on my second beer of the evening, and in less than two hours I've gotten over 2000 words out of my recent relapse into *XCOM* addiction.

The truth is, I can *always* fucking write. And the next truth is, when I do it, I always end up feeling better – much better than I end up feeling after a three-week *XCOM* binge. And as a bonus, I have something to show for it at the end; something that might bring other people some kind of pleasure.

And yet.

I still feel the pull of it. The platinum trophy. The two sequels. *XCOM* is a near-perfect game, in both the original version and the recent remake, and a part of me wants to shut this down, right now, and just go and fire up the PS3 and play until I can't see straight.

It's absolutely a compulsion. It's absolutely an addiction.

And as much as my life is, thankfully, transformed from that time in 1997 and 1998, when I was adrift and essentially alone in my own skull, afraid and terrified and desperate to just disappear, it's clear to me now that part of me lives there still. And that part of me is still terrified, and adrift, and uncomprehending of the life I've built for myself. Still expecting it to all come crashing down, and leave me back in a single room in a deathtrap house, with no money, no hope, and no future.

That part of me will always see play, not as a pleasant diversion, but an escape, a lifeline. A welcome isolation, a blessed cell.

And I rather suspect that I am no more done with *XCOM* than *XCOM* is done with me.

Postscript: This is the essay I struggled with the most, during the process of making the conversion from blog post to book. My initial instinct was to scrap the whole thing, do a ground-up rewrite, taking into account everything I now know about ADHD, how it works, and how, despite only very recently being formally diagnosed, it's an issue I've been wrestling with my whole life.

But then I realised, actually, no. This piece has significant value as originally written, because *this is what ADHD looks and feels like, from the inside, when you don't know what it is.*

So. This is what it is, and now I know, and so do you. And if you find what you've just read resonates – if, as the kids used to say, it seems like Highly Relatable Content – maybe look into ADHD symptoms, diagnosis, and coping mechanisms.

For myself, whilst reading this back was in some ways low-key enraging – how did I not know? How did no one else know? – there's also a blessed relief. Not, to be clear, because the issues are any less of a challenge – I've just spent too much of the morning I was supposed to be using to edit this manuscript on a new mobile game, for fuck's sake, issues persist – but because at least I know *why.* And knowing these persistent issues are not a result of moral failing or laziness, or being 'scatterbrained' or disorganised, but are instead part of having a brain that doesn't work the same as other people… it's a fucking relief, I gotta tell you. The guilt that suffuses the piece you've just read… Well, okay, it's not gone, because sometimes I still let people or myself down and that still sucks.

But it's less. Less crushing, less all-consuming; properly situated. And I'm a better and happier person for it.

So. You know.

KING KILLER
BIG WHEELER CAT PEELER

THE GREAT MILENKO

So. The fucking ghost is back, I'm sorry to say. This record came out in '97, and I have no idea how he came by it – must have been through his Uni connections, I suppose – and I must have made a cassette copy, because I can picture the CD he had, and I didn't have a CD player back then.

Anyway.

As previously discussed, '97 wasn't a good year for me. '98 was worse; that was when the wheels actually fell off. But '97 was the guy with no chute halfway between the plane and the ground, saying 'so far, so good'. My friend group and I are in the death trap house where we will play many hours of *Werewolf* (see Volume I), and, as we've just discussed, I will play many hours of *XCOM* as I aggressively ignore the fact that I'm failing college, and that merely having some level of talent at acting isn't going to mean shit in a world where I simply cannot get my arse out of bed with anything resembling a regular pattern.

So there's a good chance that this was the first outright hip-hop album I ever owned. Rage Against the Machine had forcibly disabused me of the notion that rapping was a somehow inferior form of expression ('they only talk because they can't sing' is something I almost certainly said at some point, because, yeah, I was that kind of ignorant dumbshit kid) but I still needed loud guitars to engage my gut before the rest of me would be willing to come along for the ride. And, sure, the *Judgement Night* soundtrack punched another hole in the armour; still, tho, we're pairing hip-hop artists off with metal acts, so it's not exactly taking me over the cliff. And, look, true, this record features Alice Cooper, Slash and (I literally learned ten minutes ago, thanks to a Google search) Steve fucking Jones guesting on various tracks. So maybe that makes it the perfect bridge.

Regardless, the fact remains; looking at the Public Enemy, NWA, Ghostface Killah, and yes, sure, Eminem CDs on my shelf, there's a non-trivial chance none of them end up there if I hadn't first been exposed to Insane Clown Posse's *The Great Milenko*.

How did it appeal to me? Let me count the ways. Let's start with the intro – a skit that starts with rednecks in a bar, putting on a country record for 'a shindig', only for the record to slow, before bleeding into an Alice Cooper monologue that sets out the stall of who – what – The Great Milenko is. It's pure horror hype bullshit ('The unleashing of the fourth joker's card! The Necromaster!'), and it might as well have been precision engineered for my late teen brain.

See, as we'll cover in more detail in the penultimate chapter of this book, I was at this point notionally still in training as a student of magic. And an album that set up its protagonists as magicians (albeit clearly cartoonish, carny magicians) had a deep appeal. One phrase I'd been given to conjure with at this point (yeah, sorry about that) was 'hiding in plain sight', and I think it's possible teenage me half-believed ICP might just be doing something like that: setting up the exaggerated sense of magical carnage to hide a kernel of Actual Real Shit. Which, not to jump ahead, but of course they were, though their particular kernel – Born Again Christianity – was something I'd already found wanting (if you want to know what was going on for me on that subject, I'd recommend checking out my debut novel, *GodBomb!*).

If fact, fuck it, let's deal with this now: how on earth did nobody notice ICP were Born Again? Viewed through the lens of hindsight, it's kind of embarrassingly obvious; for all that they dress the idea up in terms of Shangri La and Juggalos at a never-ending live show/ party, it's clear that the final song is about heaven and hell. ICP and everyone else with 'clown love' (carefully described as multiracial, plus redneck truck drivers, implying an interesting class distinction we may return to) having a good old post-death time, while the 'greedy skank motherfuckers' burn forever. Sure, 'free money, and mad bitches non-stop' doesn't sound exactly Biblical... but for white trash hip hop heaven? Sure, why not?

And when you start looking at some of the other songs, it's striking how many of them run as pretty straight-up morality plays. The obvious ground zero for this is 'Halls Of Illusions', where a Cypress Hill tinged beat bleeds into a shredding chorus from Slash, as a series of men are shown visions of their families living happy, pleasant lives, only to be dropped back into a violent, squalid reality, created by their misdeeds (before being slaughtered by our faithful narrator). But elsewhere, 'How Many Times?' lays out a litany of modern misery about the human condition (with an admittedly off-beam dig at being taught science in school that feels like a precursor to their infamous 'magnets? Fuckin how do they work?' moment), and 'Under the Moon' feels like an Old Testament rumination on the hollowness of violent revenge. Now, with that last, you might fairly ask how that squares with the rest of the gleeful horrorcore slaughter of nasty people; I'd answer that 'Under the Moon' doesn't feature any supernatural elements or characters, so it feels like a slice of 'realism', dropped in an album that is constantly swinging between genuine portrayals of deprivation and desperation alongside EC Comics level blood, guts, and humour. In other words, vengeance belongs to God (or at least, in the case of this album, God's agent, The Great Milenko), not man. And 'Piggie Pie' has a vengeful wolf taking out a series of worthy targets – a racist redneck, a sadistic judge, and in the final verse a very, very rich man. Yes, the album does equate obscene wealth with The Devil.

And I think that last begins to signpost how they got away with it.

Because I did find myself wondering, as a kid. The final one-two of 'Just Like That' and 'Pass Me By' clearly pointed at a belief in an afterlife predicated on your behaviour when alive. And though some of the subject matter of 'Pass Me By' fits the same mold as their earlier celebrations of The (Juggalo) Life – Faygo root beer, women with a bit of meat on their bones who like shagging Clowns, hip-hop being awesome and Elvis sucking – there's a shift in tone, both in the beat (which samples an evangelical preacher talking about 'mansions above' over an insistent piano) and in the voices of the performers. Throughout the album, Shaggy 2 Dope and Violent J (yes, really, that's what they're called) have yelled, shrieked, snarled, voices constantly under some physical or emotional strain, an audible representation of

Insane Clown energy... and in the last song, it all shifts, their tones lower, become calmer, working in an entirely human register. There's a sincerity that comes from letting the act go... and sure, it's in part an energy juxtaposition with the penultimate track, a man so frantically engaged in the concerns of the present that he doesn't realise he's hurtling towards his own end until it's past him. But it felt like there was something more at play; like this was something that actually meant something to them, some deeper truth they actually believed in.

So, sure, I picked at it. But they disguised themselves so well.

Not so much with the misogyny or violence; even at that age, I'd known enough born agains to understand neither of those particular issues were seen as in any way a barrier to entry, especially as the violence was always either directed at 'worthy' targets, or presented as a symptom of poverty (though I remember having doubts even back then about the random claims that ICP had ever been involved in armed robbery – it seemed a bit 'stolen valour' then and seems even more so now). No, it was partly the class dimension, I think; the constant identification with the suffering of poverty, alongside a surprising willingness to blame rich people for the suffering, that felt very at odds with the materialism present so often elsewhere in hip hop. And the constant positive references to voodoo and 'dark magic' felt hard to square with even a relatively mild Christian doctrine.

But it was mainly because they seemed to hate evangelical preachers.

The track 'Hellaluja' is a shotgun aimed right at the heart of prosperity gospel preaching. And throughout the song ICP aim, reload and fire over and over again. And they do not miss.

Their outrage is palpable, their fury audible with each spit lyric. The framing device for the song is a preacher delivering a cheesy healing ceremony, imploring the crowd to give 'the first portion of their income' before bringing on a disabled boy and promising that 'for just $6000 we can heal this boy!'. This skit interrupts the song at a couple of points, including at the end of the second verse with an absolutely outrageous phone call ("People, that was the Lord! Today, he will heal this boy for just $5000!"), each interruption demonstrating the hypocrisy the verses excoriate. It's the opposite of subtle, with ICP bringing a full-bore contempt for the subject that I found, and find, admirable.

We had a local born-again sect in the town I was living at the time, and they'd infrequently witnessed myself and my friends. I'd also had occasion while living in a halfway house for people at risk of homelessness to read some of their 'literature', left there by one of the residents, who was in a faith-based recovery from drugs and alcohol addiction. Of that read, I have retained only an emotional impression; a rising tide of incredulity and disgust, with an undercurrent of fear – just how crazy were these people, and how many of them were out there? The only concrete articles I can remember any detail of were both op-ed style pieces (though I suspect the whole magazine ran along similar lines), one explaining that capitalism could only work if it ran alongside a Christian society (which, erm, okay) and, I shit you not, a piece justifying private jets for preachers, on the basis that precious souls might be lost if said priest was too fatigued from an inferior form of travel to offer the correct words of spiritual comfort at the crucial moment.

Yeah, really.

So 'Hellaluja' hit hard.

And, really, it kinda still does. It's absolutely excoriating about spiritual conmen and the role they have to play in reinforcing poverty, by soliciting payments from those who can least afford it (the snarling bridge captures this best, with a menacing *pass the collection plate!* cut alongside *Show me how you give, I'll tell you how you live!*). And, knowing what I know now, it's fascinating to revisit and realise the rage comes not from a generalised disdain for the religion as a whole, but rather the fury of a couple of believers at the commodification of faith for evil ends.

And look, here's the thing; ICP are pretty much universally discussed and described in critical circles as a punchline. Sure, there was that moment of insanity when the FBI actually classified Juggalos as a criminal gang, but I think it's telling that this was mainly met with howls of derision rather than outrage from the wider music community – because, seriously, *ICP fans*? Even before their spiritual coming out, the band was treated as a punchline; contemporary reviews of *The Great Milenko* were excoriating, and Eminem's brutal, homophobic skit mocking them on one of the best-selling hip hop albums of all time, *The Marshall Mathers LP* (see Chapter 31) pretty much buried the band in terms of pop culture relevance (oddly, a fate not accorded to Kid Rock's infinitely worse album from the same year, *Devil Without a*

Cause (see Chapter 30) which is still inexplicably listed as 'important' somehow). Tellingly, that spreads even to your humble correspondent; despite loving *The Great Milenko* on release, and appreciating it a huge amount on a contemporary revisit, I can't report any especial desire to engage with their more recent work. I remember playing *MMLP* to a friend of mine who'd encountered *Milenko* the same time as I did, and, despite that friend overall not being a hip hop fan, and certainly not being in any way as enamoured by Eminem as I was, nevertheless sadly concluded That Sketch was the most effective nail in the ICP coffin imaginable. Not to jump ahead, but Slim Shady as a character shares enough characteristics with the ICP Juggalo aesthetic that the Wicked Clowns can't help but be harmed by the comparison. It's not that ICP are bad MCs; *The Great Milenko* is competent-to-good horrorcore hip hop, and it also has a genuine sense of humour, plus some class-based righteous anger that's surprisingly well targeted. It's just, you know, it's Eminem; one of the finest natural talents hip-hop has ever produced. It's not a remotely fair fight.

That said, this isn't exactly Limp Bizkit vs. Rage Against the Machine, either. For starters, ICP are legit contemporaries of Eminem, if not antecedents; the root of their entire beef was when a young Marshall Mathers added ICP as 'possible' guest stars at a party he was organising, which unsurprisingly pissed off ICP, and there's really no way to spin that to make Eminem the good guy in that situation (though it's fair to say as the beef evolved that ICP probably took things a bit too far with the diss tracks).

Whereas Limp Bizkit feel like something the record industry dreamed up – 'what if Rage Against the Machine but without all the messy politics?' – ICP have remained absolutely committed to a bit that has been mercilessly mocked from the moment of inception onward, and it's hard not to find that kind of admirable. Similarly, their relationship with their fan base remains strong; mutual solidarity of the mutually despised and mocked that, you guys, I just don't have it in me to disrespect. I remember hearing some stand-up comedian laughing about Juggalos as "the 'Uncle Harry ain't going to bad-touch me no more!' gang" and thinking, you know what, my smug dude, so fucking what if they are?

Because ICP, I have (re)discovered, actually meant a lot to me at the time they came along. The love affair may have been relatively short-lived, and their place supplanted by rappers with undeniably superior technical proficiency, but they spoke to me at a time I was sliding into a pretty dark place. They spoke with adolescent humour and rage about real-life concerns; there are differences between post-industrial collapse Detroit and North Devon... but there are similarities, too. This is an album written by men who understand the claustrophobia of poverty, and the crawling, sweaty feeling of shrinking horizons, door after door slamming shut. They understand dark humour as a response to horror, the powerless fantasy of supernatural retribution against the rich and powerful at whose whims we suffer, bleed, starve.

And here we are in 2022, and I am sad to report that doesn't feel less relevant. My own personal circumstances may have improved almost beyond comprehension, but the big picture is bleaker than it's ever been, the arc of descent clear and still accelerating, and for much the same reasons: an insane pursuit of wealth, a machine of appetite into which our bodies and the futures of our children are being fed, pulped, burned. We're ruled by a tiny number of sociopaths with unimaginable power and influence, and they absolutely don't consider anybody actually reading this as real, as you and I understand the term. And no, ICP's *The Great Milenko* doesn't exactly articulate that... but it doesn't exactly *not* articulate it. The targets of the album's fury – racist rednecks, corrupt, evil judges, prosperity gospel grifters and, above all, very, very rich people – are all either the problem or enablers of the likely terminal cancer currently afflicting our species. And, I mean, I really, really love Eminem, I do, and we'll get into it... but there's really nothing in his body of work that comes close to this, in terms of identifying unapologetically with an underclass and against the oppressors. And let's not forget that the reason this album obtained notoriety in the first place was because of a backlash from Christian groups that led to the label pulling the release at the last minute. Unquestionably, that controversy helped sell more records, but that wasn't inevitable. This is an album that spoke truth to power, and power hit back.

And while we're on the subject; yes, it's true that this album contains misogyny, of the type that appears as baked into hip-hop as it is rock 'n' roll, but frankly it's a lot less vicious than in many other artists. And unless I've missed something on my recent relistens, there's not a single even tacit bit of homophobia, which is, sad to say, itself kinda noticeable in the context of the general milieu. If that doesn't strike you as anywhere near good enough, I'm not going to argue with you; but it's not nothing, either.

You know, it's genuinely gleeful to discover, after writing so many of these essays, that the process of My Life In Horror is still capable of surprising me. I knew I'd be writing about this album, and honestly, I was dreading it, certain that it'd be, at best, a *Headless Children* moment, and at worst, another *Lost Boys* disaster (as discussed in Volume I). Instead, I find myself, improbably, in the opposite position; not merely defending but damn near evangelising for a piece of work that was despised at the time, and has been basically reviled ever since, by a group that has near-universally become a synonym for embarrassingly bad music.

I knew *The Great Milenko* had been an important album for me when it came out. I could never have predicted that, in 2022, it would still be important.

But it is.

And it fucking rocks.

FAIRNESS WOULD BE TO RIP YOUR INSIDES OUT AND HANG YOU FROM A TREE

SCREAM

So. It's Halloween, 1997. The town in which I am living in benefit poverty while slowly but surely failing college has a cinema, praise Milenko; one screen, old school seating; the place vibed theatre, though I have no idea if it ever was. It was a genuinely beautiful building and space. There was even an old-school Ice Cream Lady who appeared at the front of the stage in between the trailers and the main event, just in case you had a sudden craving for a comically overpriced choc ice or Calippo to go with your movie of choice.

Being poor, I didn't go very often; I did catch the *Star Wars* special editions there (and loved them, especially the first two, which I'd only ever seen on TV in pan and scan before; I know the CG in the new scenes has not aged well, but it blew my tiny mind at the time). And I discovered later that *Spawn* was maybe the worst first date movie ever (we bailed after 30 minutes and went for burgers).

But it was Halloween. And it was Wes Craven. And, do you know, despite being a childhood fan of the *Elm Streets*, *Hellraisers*, and related concerns, I'd never actually seen an 18-certificate horror movie at the cinema?

Plus, I mean, just look at that poster (the version, to be clear, preserved in my head, though I can't find an exact version of it on a Google image search, so, you know, whatever) The white space, the blood red writing at the bottom, spelling out the single word title below the face of the transcendently beautiful Drew Barrymore, eyes wide with fright, hand mostly covering her mouth (and also blood red lipstick), features fading into the white background.

I-fucking-conic.

And so I settled into my seat, probably not with popcorn, given the tight budget, and as the lights dimmed and the movie certificate and title appeared on screen, I felt an honest-to-God gut thrill; after endless years of VCR, here was, finally, horror as intended: twenty feet high and ninety wide.

It was time for *Scream*.

And, you know, I am aware that *The Blair Witch Project* was about to set new levels in terms of marketing hype and misdirection – hell, by 97, they may have already started with the websites that would cause such a sensation in the run-up to release. But I gotta say, whichever genius asshole put Drew on the posters did an absolute number on me.

She was a star, is the thing. Probably about as big as she ever got, in 97. So of course it made perfect sense that she'd be the star of Wes Craven's massive slasher movie. And when the film opens with her and her creepy phone call, I am absolutely delighted and thrilled, but not remotely scared. I appreciate it, of course – no fucking about, we're in, archetypical, young woman, home alone, creepy man on the phone, a sense of building dread... better yet, both the creep and the woman seem to know it; the conversation revolves around scary movies, and my memory is that I guffawed when Drew's character talks about how much she liked the first Elm Street, but not so much the sequels. I know I was hip to the joke, and, at age 19, almost insufferable in my smug pride at getting it. I mean, what a delight, they're banging on about *Friday the 13th*, there's a superb gut-drop as Drew realises she's being watched, and then the reveal of the bloody boyfriend on the patio, bravo, good people, bravo. Most excellent entertainment.

And I think I picked up on the role reversal – the boyfriend in peril rather than the girlfriend – and if so, no doubt nodded in similarly smug approval. And when the chap does get eviscerated, it felt suitably bloody and shocking (though interestingly far less so on a rewatch). And when Ghostface finally made his entrance, I was suitably thrilled, envisaging a frantic tussle, then escape for our heroine. I even remember wondering if the whole movie was going to be some real-time stasher/stalker a la *Halloween*, with Drew legging it across town, pursued by a relentless knife-wielding maniac (who would, naturally, dispatch several innocent bystanders along the way).

And do you know what? That would probably have been a fun movie.

But Wes Craven, the magnificent bastard, had quite different plans.

I can still remember the visceral shock when Drew Barrymore was stabbed. I remember, just like a living cliche, sitting bolt upright in my seat, eyes wide. No fucking way. No fucking way is this happening.

And her crawl! The movie teases us one final time, oh, sure, look, there's rescue, just out of reach, but she'll get there, okay, this is like the *Halloween* opening, we've got a 5 years later caption coming any second, Drew looking all haunted and hardened by her near brush with death. And she can't scream. That's the final brilliant touch. Her lung appears to have collapsed, she can only whisper, and it's not enough, and then, just like that, she's murdered, and we are off to the fucking races.

And I know I've just spent a thousand words on the opening five minutes, but in my defence, it's pretty clear I've never gotten over it. And it's a good microcosm for the film as a whole – a horror movie that's about horror movies; or, to be more specific, a slasher movie that's *also* about slasher movies. Like my beloved *RoboCop*, *Scream* manages to be both of genre and commenting on genre; and, sure, these days pretty much every single show and movie has some moment of wry self-reflection. But in '97 it was a lot less common, and I would argue it's very rare indeed that a horror movie does it this blatantly *and* this well.

The kids *know* they're in a slasher movie. They talk about it constantly, the way kids would; sure, in the famous 'rules of a horror movie' scene, with a teenage Jamie Lee Curtis having a spectacularly bad pumpkin day in the background, but elsewhere, too. In the video store, they're picking each other apart, looking for suspects, and there's a level of casual cruelty that felt painfully real to me, watching it as the last of my own teenage months bled away.

The adults, interestingly, don't, for the most part. Courtney Cox's reporter is obsessed with the murders, but she thinks she's the star of a movie about a plucky reporter who lands The Big Scoop (hilariously, she doesn't seem to much care what the scoop is, as long as she lands it). As for the cops, they fall into a proud tradition of Wes Craven police going all the way back to *Last House on the Left*: they're hilariously inept and totally fucking useless. Which, given recent events in the US, I'd say is hard to argue with as the best-case scenario, honestly.

And as for Henry Winkler...

It's a goddamn genius piece of casting. I recently found out it happened at the last minute; that the part was written after filming started when the filmmakers realised that after the opening, they didn't have another murder happen until they hit the second half of the script, and they, I think correctly, assumed this might raise some eyebrows with the audience. So Winkler's part was written, cast and shot pretty damn fast. And it's a great example to me of the magical power of cinema as a storytelling medium, because I genuinely can't conceive of *Scream* without his presence. Taking the ultimate icon of teen cool and turning him into a stick-up-his-ass high school principal – the ultimate teen cop, if you can dig it – should have earned everyone involved in the decision-making process awards and bonuses. It works brilliantly. Winkler chews the scenery, a take-no-prisoners hard ass for the ages, coming over so ludicrously angry at one point he becomes a semi-plausible red herring himself... right up to the point where he's murdered in one of the finest it's-behind-you jump scares in slasher history, complete with an *Elm Street* reference that almost certainly made me punch the air in the cinema (it sure did on the rewatch).

There are few, if any, weak links in the cast, to be fair; sure, David Arquette's character is a goof off, but again, this is Wes Craven and cops – he's supposed to be. Neve Campbell grabs the lead with both hands, managing to make naturalistic-yet-self-aware look easy. Rose McGowan is superb as her best friend (and scores my favourite death of the film, a spectacularly over-the-top encounter with the dog flap on the garage door).

And then there are the killers.

Skeet Ulrich is great as Billy Loomis. He has a tricky part to play, as the red-herring-that-isn't boyfriend, and he does a good job throughout the movie hitting the pivot points. In particular, his seduction of Campbell's Sidney towards the end is perfectly pitched, making his 'murder' and final reveal a superb twist moment, at a point where such twists are landing thick and fast.

But, hoo, boy, Matthew Lillard.

Lillard's Stew is brilliant because he's demented from the off, gurning and cracking gross in every single scene, right out there hiding in plain sight... and yet he does hide, and I remember the visceral shock I got when he was revealed as one of the killers. And from the moment he is revealed, he just opens up the crazy can and spills it all over everywhere; a scenery-chewing for the ages that manages to be both laugh-out-loud funny and genuinely unnerving all at once.

It's another microcosm of what the film does so well, actually – he and Billy trade pseudo justifications (Billy blames Sidney's mother sleeping with his father for causing their marriage to fail and is therefore enacting revenge; Stew, hilariously, claims to just be easily led) and it's both a commentary on the arbitrary nature of slasher villain motivation and an expression of it, at the same time. And, again, it absolutely *is* funny, but Stew in particular is also absolutely creepy as fuck, especially when the scheme takes a turn for the seriously deranged and he allows Billy to stab him as part of the plan to ultimately frame Sid. The blood helps; we've been treated to 'corn syrup' effect blood when Billy was fake-stabbed, and the filmmakers ensure the rest of the blood spilt in the scene is of a different shade and consistency, and it's absolute genius because, even in a scene that is highlighting and pointing out artificiality, it manages to play that against the viewer, subconsciously selling you on the 'real' blood by showing it differently, and I'm sorry, but that's genuinely clever filmmaking.

It's interesting to look back at Craven's grimy, deeply disturbing debut, *Last House on the Left* (as, indeed, I did in Volume I). The hype text for the poster there reminded you, if you were feeling faint, to repeat to yourself 'It's only a movie'. *Scream* spends its entire runtime yelling at you that it's a movie too; using the conventions, naming them, playing with them, having characters call out the cliches, and then finding ways to subvert them, play with them, spin-off them. And yet – at least for 19-year-old me – in doing so it didn't in any way sell the horror short; rather, it uses that awareness to play with the audience, confound expectations, and deliver something brilliant and funny and scary all at once.

Wes Craven was a massive part of my childhood horror experience. And as much as my revisit to Elm Street for this project wasn't the unqualified delight I'd hoped for, I was forcibly reminded of how strong the core concept of those movies was, and how mind-melting some of the effects work was.

When Wes Craven passed away, there was a lot of commentary among horror fans on social media about the man and his legacy. It's absolutely true that many of his movies didn't live up to the high tide marks of his best work, but I have to say I felt some people overcompensated for that a bit, in some of the critiques they offered. Like, *Last House on the Left* may not be to your taste – it sure wasn't to mine – but it's kind of hard to deny the baseline awful power parts of that movie have to shock you in ways cinema rarely does (and you could make a case that *The Hills Have Eyes* delivers similar levels of shock with less issues relating to storytelling, and I'd certainly entertain such an argument). And caveats duly noted for *A Nightmare on Elm Street*, it defined an entire decade of horror cinema, and remains one of the best ideas for a horror movie anybody has ever had.

So it seems fitting that I'm wrapping up my coverage of Craven's work with *Scream*. Because, like *Last House on the Left* and *Elm Street* before it, *Scream* set the standard and conversation in horror cinema for the next decade, for better and worse.

And with all due respect to the critics, that means Wes Craven was responsible for making one of the most important horror movies of the decade for three decades in a row.

We should all fail so well.

Alleged Adulthood (16+)

THAT'S YOUR SHADOW ON THE WALL

NATURAL BORN KILLERS

This one was on and off the list a lot. Right up to the last couple of months of the project, I was leaning towards not covering it. Truthfully, if I hadn't noticed I was heading towards writing not one but three essays about white hip-hop artists from Detroit as the online finale, and realised it'd be best to break that run up, lest I test your already superhuman patience with my bullshit entirely past breaking point, you might not be reading this at all.

And a big part of the problem is that I can't do the usual pack drill with regards to when, where, how old I was. None of it. Did I see it? Yes, yes I did, on a small screen, sometime in my late teens/early twenties. Did it peel the top of my skull back and take a loving shit over my brain? Well, now you mention it, yes, it did.

And yet.

The fucking rep this movie had, too. I mean, *Reservoir Dogs* had a rep, and so did *Pulp Fiction*, but this bad boy was next level; like, 'banned' from a video release (yes, it's more complicated than that, but that's what I understood at the time) next level. It also ran into a couple of very UK-centred shitstorms, which, okay, yeah, I guess we do need to get into that, don't we.

Okay.

So. In the UK, in 1993, a two-year-old boy was abducted from a shopping centre in broad daylight, taken to a second location, tortured and murdered. His horribly damaged body was discovered two days later on a nearby railway line.

The perpetrators were charged eight days later. They were two ten-year-old boys.

Yeah.

Now, a lot of people had an awful lot to say about what could possibly have caused this kind of unfathomably awful crime. And, because we have a uniquely vicious, virulent and stupid right-wing tabloid press tradition in the UK, every single aspect of the perps' lives was poured over in obscene detail.

And it turned out they'd probably watched a few horror movies.

The main focus of ire was, and I shit you not, *Child's Play 3*, as there seemed some certainty that the boys had seen it, perhaps even owned a copy. Point is, it kicked off a weird and thankfully short-lived second 'video nasty' type scare, with all the attendant moral panic bullshit. You're a horror fan, you know the drill by now: corruption of innocence, sick, depraved Hollywood, monkey see, monkey do. Won't Somebody Think Of The Children?

So when *Natural Born Killers* found itself up before the BBFC in the summer of 1994, the tabloid press went into full-on Ban This Sick Filth mode, and some nonsense reporting about possible copycat killings in the states led to a delay in certification. Ultimately, the movie (cut by 3 minutes to achieve a US R rating) was given an 18 certificate and made it to cinemas, but the miasma of controversy was well established.

And look, I've talked about this before, but truthfully I'm kind of a wimp when it comes to 'extreme' cinema. *Last House on the Left* did permanent damage (as discussed in Volume I), I've never seen *The Texas Chainsaw Massacre*, and I'm pretty confident I'll go through my entire life without ever watching a *Saw* movie. Some of that is a basic squeamishness about blood and guts, sure… But I think there's more to it. I think that certain movies have a reputation for me that, itself, has become a kind of psychological barrier to entry.

And I think, for me, thanks to the sheer volume of tabloid panic (exacerbated when the movie's proposed VHS release date coincided with the Dunblane massacre, leading the distributors to unilaterally decide to 'ban' the movie until 2001, despite securing an 18 certification for home release), *Natural Born Killers* became one of those movies.

Which, when you consider what many of the obsessions are that drive the movie, is pretty fucking funny, really.

I don't think I caught the Channel 5 broadcast, shown while the movie was still in limbo in terms of a home viewing release. For one thing, Channel 5 was a dicey proposition in North Devon at that time. For another, I suspect that rep just made me steer clear. So I think – and it really is just a guess, but – I *think* I must have bought it on DVD, when it finally came out in 2001. Which, logically, must be because I'd by then become familiar enough with Oliver Stone's other work (especially *JFK*, which hit me with the force of revelation in my late teens) that my desire for more work from this man was enough to override my previous fears.

I was finally ready. Or so I thought.

It's frustrating, not being able to do what I usually do, and reconstruct the shock of that first viewing. On the other hand, this is a movie that I've seen many, many times, and yet its power to shock me has barely diminished at all; indeed, there are ways in which I find it even more disturbing now than I did as a young man.

The sheer *ferocity* of it, is what lingers the most. Sure, the violence, both the overtly, hyper-stylized opening diner massacre and the later gruelling and gruesome prison riot scenes. Both sequences have, in their own way, left their marks on me, on my imagination. But also, one of the things the movie does, with its shifting modes of storytelling, kaleidoscopic soundtrack and dizzying use of different film stocks, is present the viewer with an interrogation of the form itself; the movie, especially through the first half, appears to be in a state of constant transformation, creating moods, inhabiting genres, only for those states to collapse upon themselves, as if they're unable to bear the weight of the story they're trying to tell (or, perhaps, the rage of the characters the movie is concerned with). We shift from hyper-stylised action movie to oversaturated colour to sit-com (complete with monstrous laugh track), and in between, these collages of film and sound, as Mickey and Mallory's Cadillac appears to be travelling through some portal between worlds, haunted by monsters and black and white streets.

Never mind the action on screen, the very editing itself, the soundtrack, the lighting, it's all fucking furious, and it wants you to know it.

Because, sure, the film is about violence. Mickey and Mallory are both products of violent childhoods, escaping via the nihilism of a shotgun barrel pointed at anyone that gets in their way. Similarly, the deeply fucked-up cop pursuing them is also a product of childhood trauma. Violence perpetuates violence throughout the movie, including, in the second half, the mass violence of the carceral state. I don't think the movie revels in the violence, exactly (and the accusation that it celebrates it is not just fatuous but Actually Wrong, IMO), but it sure doesn't pull away from it, either.

Still, that's not all it's about.

The story goes that as the film was being made, Stone realised the movie could be much more than a straight-up fucked-up crime thriller about two mass murderers. At some point in the process, Stone started to realise it was about America, and more specifically, how America saw itself, down the lens of a TV camera. As with 2021's *Don't Look Up*, *NBK* is absolutely excoriating in its treatment of the media, and the venal race-to-the-bottom of ratings über *alles*.

And that tendency is given flesh in the person of Robert Downey Jr, giving for my money a career-best performance as the slug that walks like a man, Wayne Gayle.

He is magnificent. A surface smarm/charm that is almost instantly obliterated by his monstrous ego, Gayle quickly takes the movie over from about the one-third mark; as soon as he appears, the story of Mickey and Mallory starts to warp in his hands, footage of the pair replaced by actors shot from salacious angles, and full of artless cuts and inserts. It's ballsy as hell, when you think about it, given just how gonzo the filmmaking has been thus far; almost as if Stone is winking at us as he says 'of course, this can be absolutely dreadful, if you don't know exactly what you're doing'. And yet, does Gayle have his own dark, awful attraction? Sure he does. He's so awful, you can't take your eyes off him. You are – I am – both disgusted and delighted by my disgust. Every time I feel he can sink no lower, Gayle plumbs yet further depths of narcissism. He's the perfect avatar for the worst that infotainment represents.

I mean, is it any wonder the press weren't thrilled with this one?

They're still at it, by the way; a recent Google search showed that on the 25th anniversary, *The Guardian* ran a piece saying the movie failed because it ultimately blamed the media for Mickey and Mallory's violence. Yeah, somebody got paid to write that. Given what we've already discussed about how the film portrays violence as a cyclical, generational phenomenon, it's hard not to take such a poor misreading as deliberate; in that respect, I guess you have to give Stone credit that more than 25 years later, the movie is still making media types sore enough that they feel defensive.

Because, no, obviously, the media isn't to blame for the violence.

What the media – specifically, the news media – is guilty of, is the sensationalised *coverage* of the violence (If It Bleeds, It Leads), turning murderers into celebrities, trials into circuses, and, often, matters of scientific fact and political reality into matters of opinion and topics of 'debate' or 'controversy'.

Seen through that lens, the fact the *NBK* predates the establishment of Fox News by two whole years gives the movie an aura of eerie prescience. The utterly amoral, value-free rendering of 'reality' as entertainment is a poison that, in 2022, feels likely to be terminal, as we continue to 'both sides' ourselves off the cliff of climate apocalypse, and the flapping gums whose only job is to keep us informed of what's actually going on shake their heads, shrug, and say 'gosh, it's complicated, isn't it?'

It's not that *NBK* predicts that, exactly; it's that in the movie, you can see the contours of the trends that will lead us there, the swirling black hole of cultural vacuity. You can almost feel the rough beast of Murdoch's poisonous News Station child slouching into place.

I think that's what I mean when I say I found it more disturbing on a rewatch than I did as a young man. Back then, sure, it seemed bad, but, well, a) it was America, they're all nuts, everybody knows that, and, relatedly, b) It Couldn't Happen Here. Back then it was the violence that got to me, the electric confrontation between Gayle and Mickey, and the teeth-grinding tension of the jailbreak – which, to be fair, is no less raw and darkly thrilling as it was on first viewing.

But now?

Shit. Now it's 2022, and it *is* happening here, and it's happening everywhere, and I just don't know anymore. The anger of this film used to sing to me; it used to light me up, helped me feel like less of an alien. Because, on some level, based as it was in emergent trends and then-current concerns, it felt like satire, still: overblown, caricatured. It has some serious things to say, but it still felt like a warning.

Now? Shit. Now it feels like a prophecy of something it's become too late to fix.

And a world in which *Natural Born Killers* no longer feels like an exaggeration is a scary fucking place to be.

WE WILL BURY YOU

CONFESSIONS OF A RELUCTANT BARMAN

Between December 1998 and December 1999, I worked in a pub in the east end of London, as a barman. It was my first 'real' job – I'd done short term leafleting for a second-hand book shop back in Devon, but otherwise, paid employment was alien to me – and given my (lack of) educational qualifications, this kind of work was as high as I felt I could safely set my sights.

I can still remember the rush of excitement I felt after being told I'd secured the position straight at the end of my ten-minute interview for the job. It kind of hurts my heart to recall. Such joy. A clearer measure of how subterranean my self-esteem had sunk, that this felt like a step up, somehow, is hard to imagine. God's a bit on the nose sometimes, I think, don't you?

Anyway.

I learned a lot that year. Having fled to London based on an understanding that to stay in Devon was to begin, at the age of 20, the business of dying (inevitably, it was music that proved key in reaching this realisation), this was, initially, where I landed.

And, you know, at first I was excited. I thought bar work could be fun, and would help fund the stand-up comedy career I fondly imagined I'd be able to start any day now, just by turning up at an open mic night, opening my mouth and being funny. Not that I was doing anything as grand as working on material, you understand – or for that matter, finding out the location of a single open mic night in the city. What was the hurry? I was 20, and I was out of Devon. All things were possible, and there was no rush. Anyway, probably the bar work would help provide material.

On that last point, I was certainly correct in general terms, though the genre would not end up being comedy. Suffice it to say that *The Debt*, short story 'Valentine's Day', and the protagonist from *Lifeline* would not exist in anything like the form they do now if it hadn't been for the experiences I had working this job. It was a year of my life I'll never get back, mostly spent in boredom, with occasional side forays into despair and the odd shot of fear for my physical safety (and on one occasion, for my life) – but I'm also not sure I'd trade it. Like so many of the artistic traumas I've documented in this series, I learned so much, for good and ill, about myself and my fellow man, about the hells that people construct for themselves, partly through circumstances and partly through outlook – and most of all, perhaps, just how dark and bleak and joyless 'normal' can get.

It started with the staff, actually. The landlord was an oddly charmless man – a Tory who smoked Marlboro Reds and was a big fan of Peter Hitchens (then writing in *The Express*, copies of which the pub carried for free, as part of a deal with the chain). His marriage seemed permanently strained, with sniping and often mean spirited sarcasm the order of the day, and yet neither seemed to show any signs of actually rethinking the arrangement. To me, they seemed more like squabbling siblings than a husband and wife, and I found their mutual antagonism mystifying.

He was also a man who would look for marginal edges wherever he could. Realising I didn't understand the difference between being on a salary or an hourly rate, he put me on salary for Christmas, and then proceeded to load me up with 6-day weeks, all for a flat rate weekly wage. Then, come January, he informed me by phone that he was unhappy with my performance and might need to let me go, before pushing me onto an hourly rate and reducing my hours (which he could do easily, January being a very quiet month in the trade). He similarly wasn't below purchasing stolen goods – specifically, food items stolen by a white van driver (from his employer) who drank regularly in the public bar – and selling them as special menu items in the restaurant attached to the pub. He'd also occasionally throw temper tantrums when someone was late or off sick – sudden, rage-filled outbursts that would come and pass like summer lightning. I remember describing him to a friend as having a 'hands off' approach to management – to which she responded "sounds more like the 'fuck off' school, to me".

But he was a walk in the park compared to Loz.

Loz came from Brighton, worked the bar, and lived in the pub. I never got a 100% clear story on his background, but he'd apparently left under a cloud involving drugs and possibly owed money. He was a bit older than me – I'd guess mid to late 20s – and he'd treated me with laughing contempt and hostility from our first encounter – literally, as he'd spat laughter and turned his head when we first shook hands at our introduction. He proceeded to order me about, giving me cleaning jobs he didn't want to do under the guise of 'training', and then not actually explaining how they were to be done, meaning I ended up getting grief for not doing them 'properly'. That particular hazing didn't last long – once I'd actually had the tasks explained to me, doing them was easy enough – but there was an underlying low-level hostility throughout my time there, which bubbled under for months before, inevitably, exploding.

It came to a head when he started stealing. By this point, we'd both been banished to the 'Public Bar' area of the pub, which was mainly frequented by the hardcore drinkers who lived on the local council estate – Loz, for his general incompetence and frequently hostility to other staff, me as punishment, I suppose. Traffic in the bar was light enough that there was never more than one member of staff required, so we worked lone shifts. I can't speak for Loz, but it suited me just fine – I got a lot of reading and smoking done.

The only problem was, we shared a till, and around the same time that Loz started showing up for his shift cataclysmically stoned, money started going missing from that till. He was canny enough to make sure it only happened when he and I shared a shift. The first time, it got written up as a mistake, but the second time, we were both called in by the covering manager (the landlord was on holiday). I knew that for the shift in question I'd had at most half a dozen till interactions – the bar was dead from 12-6pm, when the workers would come in on their way home for a swift pint or six – and I knew damn well I'd not made any mistakes, let alone a £10 one. Loz, on the other hand, clearly still high, admitted he had made a £10 mistake, and so we were asked to pay back half the missing £20 each, to cover the till shortfall.

In other words, I had just put £10 – the best part of three hours wages, in these pre-minimum wage days – into Loz's pocket.

I was raging. I remember – oh to be 20 again – putting together a mix tape made up mainly of tracks from Metallica's *Load* and *Reload* albums (with a smattering of the more aggressive *Garage Inc.* punk covers) which I listened to on the way to work every day, keying myself up for a confrontation. We'd moved to separate tills following the last incident, and we only saw each other at shift swap over, but I knew that it was only a matter of time before some confrontation happened – not least because I'd categorically decided I was done taking his shit, and I knew he wouldn't be able to resist dishing more out, sooner or later.

It was only a week or two later that it happened. Some guy had come around calling for Loz (the later gossip was it was someone Loz owed money to, but I never got that 100% confirmed) and I'd knocked on his door, as requested, to no response. Later he came at me raging, threatening violence if I ever went to his room again. I made it clear I was not going to pass on any more messages (the phrase 'not your fucking errand boy' may have been used) and also made it clear I wanted nothing more to do with him. This in front of a small handful of customers in the early afternoon – the lunchtime drinkers, I seem to recall.

That evening, as we had the 6pm handover, I was heading towards the urinal, when Loz called to me from the bar, from under a dark glower, "See you later".

I paused, at the toilet door, just like in a bad western. Then I turned and, with a shit eating grin, and my heart pounding so hard in my ears that I could barely hear my own voice, said "Take care of yourself, Loz!"

I said it loud.

With just a little extra swagger, feeling the eyes of the dozen or so regulars on me, I walked into the toilet. I can recall the adrenaline, but also an odd kind of ultrahigh, elevated calm. I felt ready for whatever was going to happen, and sure I was better prepared than Loz was even capable of being.

I heard the door bang open just as I was starting to piss. He was yelling about what I'd said, and how I'd been off with him, and when he grabbed my shoulder to turn me around, I was calm enough to consider carefully whether or not to keep urinating and piss on his shoes or not. I opted for not, and tucked myself away as he continued shouting, flushed and angry.

I was calm, arms loosely by my side, Not listening to his words, focussed only on his eyes, and his shoulders, waiting for movement. I had adopted back then (thanks to The Ghost, as I think of it – and we'll get to that in a lot more detail, before we're done, alas) what seems to me now a suicidal code of conduct when it came to violence, and the first rule was to never throw the first punch. It was partly about moral high ground, and partly because I believed it wasn't possible to swing a blow without also making yourself vulnerable to a counter strike; and indeed, I had in the past had some success with just such a move.

So I waited, calmly, not backing down but not hitting his go button either, and eventually he made his move.

He was lethally quick. If he'd actually swung a fist with any kind of power, I'd likely still be out cold. But my confusing solid-but-not-aggressive stance had made him unsure, so instead he grabbed me around the waist – to push me back into the trough urinal, maybe. I was standing in a good, stable stance, so his efforts didn't have much result.

We grappled for a second or two, my arm around his neck, his around my waist. I remember that the initial shock of his sheer speed had worn off, and I was just wondering if I could allow one of his pushes to bring his head into contact with the hand dryer behind me, when a regular who'd clearly realised what was going on came in and separated us.

I'll never forget that moment. The man held us apart, and I looked into Loz's flush face and furious eyes. I looked at him, and he looked at me. Into my eyes. And his expression dropped from fury into something else... and he just said, very quietly, "Oh".

It went to the replacement manager, and the regulars denied seeing anything – one word against another, nothing further to be done. Loz got a telling off, and after that, he really did leave me alone. I came out of the experience with a little more self-respect, and a feeling like I could handle myself okay, if I had to – at least against a bully like Loz.

That was the first lesson in confrontation that I learned in that job. The second would come not from a member of staff, but a customer. The only real negative result of my confrontation with Loz was an aversion to Fahrenheit – the aftershave he wore – which was all over my hands after the fight, and the smell of which to this day sours my stomach.

The next one would teach me a little of what it feels like to face mortal terror at the hands of another.

2

It wasn't all bad.

God knows why I feel the need to say that, given how long ago it was and how banal an observation it is, but still. Aside from Loz and the landlord, most of the rest of the staff were kind and decent people, working shit jobs with stoicism and humour. Though I stayed in touch with no-one after I left, principally because I was a mobile phone holdout and therefore didn't have the easy ritual of swapping numbers on my last day, I do find my mind turning to them, sometimes. I hope they're well, happy, and in better employment circumstances.

Anyhow.

One of the side effects of my relegation to the Public Bar ("see what you can make of it" said the landlord, as though he were a millionaire granting his wayward son a start-up business with which to prove his mettle, and I had to resist a quite powerful urge to reply "I think I'll make soup") was an exposure to the Public Bar customers. It was here I learned the obvious yet obscured truth about pubs – they make most of their money from alcoholics, functioning or otherwise.

It was only years later that I learned one of the core responsibilities of a barman is to cut people off if they've had enough. As in, it's a legal requirement of holding a licence. And yet, not once did this information make it to me via my training on the job, and not once did I see my boss, or any other staff member, exercise this responsibility. Not once in a year. And before you start speculating about whether or not it was just an especially lucky year, with no customers reaching a level of intoxication necessary to be cut off, I'll save you some time by confirming that on one occasion during my term of employment, a patron of the Sports Bar literally drank himself to death one night, keeling over and expiring just outside the premises. Thankfully I wasn't working in that bar on that evening – though I did have to deal with some of the fallout, as some of the Sports Bar regulars decided to spend the rest of the evening in a bar that hadn't just had a corpse outside, so they could finish their pints without unpleasant thoughts intruding overly.

But for the most part, the Public Bar attracted the hardcore alcoholics; partly because the Sports Bar had a nominal dress code, but mainly because – and I am not making this up – lager was 2p a pint cheaper in the Public Bar; perhaps in apology for the shabbier decor and faint smell of decay.

The clientele was exclusively over 30, with the mean age comfortably over 50 (even allowing for the aging effects of drink, which for most of the regulars was considerable), overwhelmingly white (there was one Asian regular, and one bus driver of Indian descent, and zero black people) and male. Only two women frequented the bar on anything like a regular basis – one was the wife of one of the regulars, who would always order her pint in two half glasses because it looked 'more ladylike', and Dot, the wife of Paul, an Irishman drinking his way through throat cancer. Paul drank in there every day until he passed, and Dot would always join him on Sundays. After Paul died, she came once more, on the day of his funeral, and then I never saw her again.

As I think of it, Miss 'two half-pint glasses' also stopped coming, after her husband got barred for calling the landlord's wife a sour-faced cunt. So after that it was, except for behind the bar, pretty much a woman-free zone.

Which meant that I got a crash course in a kind of masculinity that even a childhood going to school with the sons of farmers had left me woefully unprepared for.

I cannot now recall the context of the first time I heard a woman referred to as 'it'. I recall the feelings vividly – a deep confusion, followed by a dawning understanding as the context made the meaning clear, a surge of rebellion at the very notion, and then a kind of awed horror. I remember waiting for someone to laugh, to acknowledge the transgression, render it a joke. But no. Women, especially in any kind of sexual context, were 'it'. I'd fuck it. I'd leave home for it. Look at the state of it.

I was raised mainly by my mother, and she's a feminist, and I'm a long way from being a good feminist myself, but I was still genuinely shocked – and as improbable as it may sound, the shock didn't really diminish with familiarity. I would wince inwardly any time the word was used, as it was frequently, especially when Countdown came on the TV – Carol Vorderman being quite the object of desire for these ageing alcoholic men, hitting their third or fourth pint at 4 o'clock in the afternoon.

And, I mean, I've given this entirely too much thought, but of course it's also an insight into just how rock bottom the self-esteem of these men were, that they could only comprehend people they desired as objects, that dehumanisation was the only way they could relate to sex and sexuality. It's desperately sad. It's also just monstrous and despicable and skin crawlingly awful to be around – especially when it's assumed that because you are also male, this must therefore be how you think, too.

And then there was the curiously specific anti-black racism. Which... you know what, let's do this one via case study.

Let's talk about Trev.

Trev was a white van driver and regular of the Public Bar. Trev was a gregarious, friendly type – always a smile for the other patrons, always chatty, quick with a joke. He had charm. He also had access to amazing food, which he stole from his employers at every available opportunity.

The way the theft would work was childishly simple: he'd drive to the posh eateries and upscale supermarkets in central London – places that had the kind of clientele that would consider Waitrose to be slumming it – and phone in the delivery. Sometimes they'd open up the back and he'd unload the pallets. Other times, if they were especially busy, they'd ask him to post the order form through the letterbox or pigeonhole and leave the delivery by the loading door. On those occasions, the slip would go through the letterbox, and the produce would go down to the local market, where it would be transferred over to stallholders in exchange for good, hard cash – except for the odd giant pork pie, or rack of scotch eggs, which would make their way down to the Public Bar for a feast.

For a while, when I first joined, he was also robbing to order – a pint would get you a dozen frozen servings of potted shrimp in butter, just nuke for 2 minutes and eat out of the tub – but that was curtailed after stock checking became more regular. He would often regale us with stories about how his boss (who, in Trev's telling of it, had an outrageously plummy RP English accent) would bemoan the loss of a delivery, Trev indignantly claiming that he'd warned 'em about leaving it out there, and how his boss would always say "of course, Trev, I don't blame you".

And, you know, I laughed too.

Trev also raised money for a local charity that specialised in helping people with severe mental disabilities. He would explain that he couldn't put into words how it made him feel, when the people he'd raised money for called him a good person – a phrase he knew was not an accurate description of him, but that he loved to hear, anyway.

Trev was also the most racist human being I've ever met, and was engaged in a sexual relationship with his widowed neighbour that was at best one sided and manipulative, but was more likely, based on his telling of it, actually outright abusive.

I find I am unable to stomach extended retellings of anecdotes on either subject, so I will give you just one, and ask that you trust me when I say this is not cherry picked for outstanding awfulness, particularly – it's merely the first one that comes to mind.

In this story he described simply how a friend of his had lived in South Africa during apartheid – and how this friend would, when drunk, load up a truck with a few like-minded friends and some firearms, and drive through the townships taking random pot shots at the black population. He would always conclude this story – which he told many times – by turning to his interlocutor with a charming grin and saying "now THAT sounds like a perfect evening, to me".

So, yeah. That was Trev.

Trev was also a serious alcoholic.

He drank too much as a matter of course. But every now and then, he'd go on big, two- or three-day benders. He'd drive up – yes, in his white van, so far over the legal limit he'd be close to internal organ failure – and come in and drink for hours, then leave and go home and drink more and come back again. I remember vividly one occasion where he asked me to sign his payment slip for him, as he'd paid by card. I refused – I had exactly that much sense of self, but no more – and he scrawled an x. Which I then processed, and gave him his beer and cashback, and watched him drive off at the end of the evening.

My moral failings – let me count the ways.

The excuses are true, but ring hollow – I was young, ignorant, scared, desperate for employment and, most of all, basically clueless about practically everything. All true, all useless, as I think back on how I smiled at and laughed with this man, and I burn with shame. I never laughed at his racism, never joined in or offered the tacit (or often explicit) moral support many others did – but fucking hell, what kind of pathetic bullshit is that, in the light of day, 20 years removed? He was a vile man, an evil man, and I enabled his self-destruction and risked the lives and welfare of others, and listened to stories of abuse and did nothing but pull him another fucking pint.

I wanted to say all this. It's important. It's important I own my own complicity, confess my own weaknesses. The shame I feel I deserve to feel.

It's also important context, because it was on one of those three-day benders that Trev brought in front of me a man who, I believe, intended to hospitalise me, and who I also believe had the capacity to kill me outright.

Trev gave that man a lift, and watched from his van as the man berated me, as I sat outside the locked up pub on a cold autumn night, and wondered if my cab was going to arrive before this guy beat the ever-loving shit out of me.

He just watched.

3

So, then.

It's late Autumn, 1999. The confrontation between Loz and I happened over the summer, and things have been quiet since. I still mainly work the Public Bar, though at weekends I'm back in the Saloon, and much as I still hate the place… no, actually, there's no turn happening at the end of that statement – I still hate the place.

And a couple of nights before, I met Ben.

I've changed names throughout this trilogy to protect the guilty, but in Ben's case, I can't remember his name, so for all I know, he really is called Ben. Anyhow, if you've read my novella *Lifeline* (currently available as part of my novella collection, *Breaking Point*), you already know what Ben looks like – he's a white skinhead, early- to mid-twenties, slightly above average height, slightly above average pitched voice, single silver hoop earring, black puffer jacket, combats, army trousers.

He was related to one of the regulars – one of the few decent ones, a painter named Tom. Tom was his uncle.

Anyway.

He'd made his first appearance in the Public Bar earlier that week, and he put me on edge almost immediately. He was loud. He was, on the surface, gregarious, but there was a performative strut and swagger that was unsettling. It was an old man boozer, with old and well-respected hierarchies, and he sauntered in like he owned the place. We were regaled with graphic details of a recent sexual encounter where he'd performed oral sex on a woman (something he talked about doing a lot, for some reason) before having sex with her, only to later find a soiled tampon on the floor that she had removed just before the act. "I fucked it, I went down on it, it seemed alright to me!" was the grinning punchline. In fairness to the old boys, they didn't seem terribly impressed.

It's like that old gag about how you think someone is Satan, then the real deal turns up, and you realise the guy you were so scared of was just the guy who goes down to the corner shop to buy Satan a pack of cigarettes. Within about five seconds of meeting this guy, Loz was relegated in my mind instantly to annoyance.

This was threat.

He took an instant dislike to me, as he would shortly make explicit; mostly on the basis of how I looked. That, and refusing to gamble with him for a pint over a hand of... see, I can't remember the name of the card game, only that you were dealt thirteen cards and had to make three card brag hands and play them in descending order of strength. I actually already knew how to play, but had feigned ignorance because I didn't want to – which meant he'd felt obliged to teach me. We'd ended up splitting the hand, two tricks each. I'd felt the need to loudly proclaim as we started that there was no wager on it – partly because I wanted witnesses in case he won and cut up rough, partly just because of the intensity he brought to creating his hands just plain made me nervous.

He started in on my personal appearance not long after. The hair, obviously. The earring too – and again, credit where it's due, the regulars were not standing for it. When he said, of my earring "Bit faffy, innit? Want more a plain hoop around this manor, right?" I can clearly remember one of them calmly replying "not really – it's all a matter of personal style, innit?"

I remember smiling at that. Which may have been a mistake.

He made immediate friends with Loz and Trev. Obviously. And I'm pretty sure what followed was on Day 3 of Trev's Epic Bender – the same one that led to him signing for his purchase and cashback with an x, and me meekly handing his money over.

It's cold and dark outside the pub. One of the many shitty things about working in a pub in London in 1999 is that by the time the kicking out has all been kicked, and the glasses cleaned and drip trays polished and stored, the buses have stopped running for the night, and the taxis are rammed. And if, like me, you have a shitty boss who lives on the premises and wants to go to bed as soon as the last ashtray is wiped clean, you find yourself sat outside a locked up, lights-out pub, in the cold, waiting for a cab that could take anything from 30 minutes to an hour to arrive.

And this evening, the door has hardly shut behind me, and I've barely had time to settle on one of the outside benches, zipping up my coat and plunging my hands into my pockets for warmth, when Ben comes around the corner, arm in arm with a girl.

I smile a greeting, but my stomach is already tightening. It goes into freefall as he opens with "What's all this about complaining about me behind my back to my family?"

It's a perplexing opening gambit, and I stumble partway through a reply when he cuts me off with "Don't give me that! My uncle's been giving me earache about calling you a poof! I don't even remember calling you a poof!"

"I don't, either…"

"…then why is he saying you did? Are you calling him a liar?"

"No…"

"Are you calling *me* a liar?"

"Of course not…"

"Then why did you say it?"

"I didn't…"

"Look I don't even remember saying it, right? I don't even remember calling you a poof, right? But I'll say it now, yeah? You're a poof! Alright?"

I shrug, honestly perplexed, as well as miserable. I do know it's supposed to be an insult, but it just… isn't, for me. Probably just as well, in retrospect.

"He ain't a poof" his lady friend pipes up, looking me up and down with sleepy eyes and smiling.

He turns to her, eyes rolling. "No, I know he ain't…"

"You can tell. Tell just by looking at him!" (and I have to admit to the fact that, in the moment, with all the terror I was starting to feel, I found that assertion curiously gratifying, though with a gun to my head I couldn't pick apart why, exactly).

"I *know* he ain't, but I'm just sayin'... look, don't worry about it..." He turns back to me "Are you gonna be here for a bit?"

"I mean, I'm waiting for my cab..." *which can turn up any second now, really,* I think, frantically but with no real hope.

"I'm just gonna..." he points at the girl, and mimes wanking – I can't tell if she sees or not, cares or not – "...we'll finish this after, okay?"

"Sure," I say, with as little sincerity as I think I've ever felt.

"Good."

And then he's gone.

And in retrospect, so should I have been, but here's the thing: no mobile phone. Limited funds. The nearest bus stop is a ten minute walk, and if I have missed the last one of the evening, it's more like 30 minutes to get to the high street, and again, no phone, so no cab, and it's fucking cold, and here, now, I know someone is coming to find me – I imagine being out walking the street when he sees me again, chasing me down...

So I sit and I wait and I smoke and I hope that a vehicle is going to pull in. And eventually, one does.

Trev's white van.

He's sat behind the wheel, and as the door opens, the dome light hits his face, and he looks like a corpse. I don't really have time to absorb this, though, because as the door slams shut again and the light goes out, Ben is striding across the carpark towards me, yelling "I've just had a fucking 'nother one come up to me!" and it's obviously pure bullshit, and worse, he knows I know it and doesn't fucking care, and there's something about his eyes and demeanor that tells me he's wired on something but I don't have enough experience to know what, but I know there's shit out there that'll make you angry and pain immune, and he's clearly a well skilled scrapper in any case, no Loz, this is the real deal, and I think about what I know about self defence, and I look at this guy, and I realize I am probably good and fucked.

I buckle in. Try and go cold. It's an effort.

He stands over me, leaning forward, telling me he can't 'ave it, all these relatives, why go behind his back, I'll call you a poof now, to your face, what you gonna do about it?

I offer him a cigarette. I say I will do nothing.

He takes it. I light it for him. He tells me he wants to hurt me.

To beat me. He delights in describing 'smashing my skull into pieces', and his voice distorts with emotion before he can finish saying it. What colour were his eyes? I can't remember, I want to say brown, but... I can't remember. I do remember looking up at the van, straight into Trev's corpse face. No help there. Back to Ben's angry scowl, angry eyes. Getting angrier. I drop my cigarette butt and grind it out with my boot, making sure that my knee is ideally placed for a groin shot, but I look again at his frame, his fluid, easy motions, into his something-not-right eyes, and with a tired, sinking dismay, I realise that such a shot is very unlikely to work.

See, there's something worse than bullies. That's what I learned that night. Bullies are horrible, of course, and they inflict misery, but (as we discussed earlier, see Chapter 9) most bullies, fundamentally, don't actually want a fight – they want to deliver a beating, exert dominance. I'm not saying that wasn't also the case with Ben – it transparently was, he sweated insecure, need-to-prove alpha – but with him there was also, underneath, a base, feverish love of violence for its own sake.

He stared me down and smoked my smoke, and I stared back because I knew if he was going to go, his eyes would tell me at least a little before he went, or his shoulders would, which were in my peripheral vision. His repetition loops were getting shorter, more angry – he had me trapped rhetorically, between calling either him or his family a liar, or admitting to talking behind his back, and he'd made it clear either conclusion would lead to violence, and I remember an awful drowsiness starting to settle, a distance, a numbness. I knew it was happening, could feel it – like being hypnotised by the world's angriest man – but I could do nothing about it. Everything was draining away, including my basic focus, and at some point, mid rant, I groaned and said "What do you want from me?"

His nostrils flared at that, and he leaned closer, scowling. "The fuck you talkin' bout? I don't want nothin' from you, man! Nothin'! I'm just tellin' you, I'm going to break your fuckin' skull into pieces *(or did he mean two pieces?)*! Talkin' about me to my family like that!" He leaned forward, slapping my jacket with the back of his hand, and I was too numb to flinch, as the final barrier began to crumble. "You may be able to handle yourself, I dunno... nah, you might," he said as I laughed a hollow laugh "...but I promise you, I will fucking break you!"

I didn't say, *I don't want to fight you.* I didn't say, *I'm not going to fight you.* I thought both, but said neither, thinking them dangerous. He leaned forward again, tapped me again, a little harder, said something else. I could feel him winding up, the spring inside now lethally tight, my whole sense of self pulling away and away...

The headlights from the cab almost blinded me as it pulled in. I jumped, grabbed my shoulder bag, mumbled 'that's my cab', and not-quite ran. My last image of him was turning away from me, face half in bright light from the van headlights, the other in black shadow, furious, and then his back as he strode towards Trev's van. I told the cab driver my destination, leaned back in my seat, and waited for the shakes to come.

I didn't have to wait for long.

Postscript: I went back the next day and worked the 12-6pm shift. It feels crazy to write that, but it's the truth. I phoned in and – again, I can't believe it, and I did it, but – asked the asshole landlord if I should stay home, and he insisted I shouldn't, and I believed him, as though he ever for one second had my best interests at heart.

And Loz and Trev were apologetic, in their own ways, and uncle Tom told me if it ever happened again, to tell Ben that Uncle Tom Said No – as though something similar hadn't caused the whole fucking mess in the first place.

I never saw Ben again. Not awake, anyway.

And autumn turned to winter, and I kept working, and the Public Bar got emptier and emptier on the 12- 6 shift.

And one day I'm dealing with a toothache, and there's no painkillers of mine in the house, and my flatmate lends me aspirin, which I am unused to. I take them, fall back to sleep, and end up late, so I skip breakfast and haul arse. My bus hits the stop with 5 minutes to shift, and I run as hard as I can to get to the bar for 12. I make it, and I open up. It's cold enough that I light the gas fire. I'm sat by it, and all of a sudden the world goes weird. My head feels swollen and my body is coated with sweat and my heart is pounding and a strange synth tune is playing from the jukebox, a million miles away, and a high male voice is singing about conflict, and I stand up on legs that feel too high and too thin, and I fucking *wade* to the toilet through the song *Russians,* and as someone says 'we will bury you' I throw up and instantly feel better, just aspirin and a brisk run on an empty stomach, but Loz sees me and asks if I'm all right, or if I am on something, and I say no, and he says okay but it looked like I was, and if I was, I should stop, and I say that I'm fine, and I am, but for a second there, I really, really wasn't, and I've never forgotten it, and I never will.

"INSANITY IS HEALTHY"

COLUMBINE

One more story from pub land.

It's April 21st 1999. I've been working in the fucking pub for five months, and as you may recall, it sucks and I hate pretty much everything about it. Sure, it's better than Barnstaple. I am, at least, in London. Granted, I can't afford to do anything more than eat, sleep and work, but... it's better. London's alive, in a way Barnie wasn't. There's energy.

Still. It sucks, for all the reasons outlined in the previous chapter, and I am miserable. I've been banished to the Public Bar by this point – away from the hard work of the Sports Bar, true, but the trade-off is that I'm serving half a dozen (at most) hardcore alcoholics, and enduring seemingly endless conversations about what they'd like to do to Carol Vorderman, and whatever you're imagining, I can almost guarantee it's worse.

Boredom doesn't even begin to cover it. Things are so bad that... well, how's this? The brewery/chain that owns the pub made a deal sometime in the new year with *The Express* "newspaper", as a result of which, and no doubt in exchange for vastly inflating the purported circulation of said paper, part of my morning job involved placing a copy of that godforsaken rag on every single table in the bar before opening.

And I was so fucking bored that I read it. Cover to cover. Well, okay, no, not the sport, I have my standards.

Still.

And this particular day, I read it with far more care and attention than normal.

Because it was the day after the Columbine massacre.

I can't remember now how I first heard the news. I do remember the state of numbness, of shock. My flatmate and I. She was a few years older, working at a Uni. And, I mean, the bald, core facts are as simple and as dark as they come: two teenage boys murder a bunch of fellow teenagers before turning the guns on themselves. It's just one of those indigestible things, a happening you can neither unsee nor really reconcile yourself to. Or at least, I couldn't. Can't. It feels like a negation. A black pit where reason should be. An impossible horror.

But, of course, I *did* try to make some kind of sense out of it, alongside the millions of people who saw it on telly, and the thousands of families directly affected, and the circling news crews with hour after hour of airtime to fill, column inches to fill, literally everybody screaming the same useless question: Why?

Never mind *how*. Everybody knew *how*. In 1996, a gunman had walked into a classroom in the UK, shot thirty-one children, sixteen fatally, murdered the teacher, and then took his own life. I remember that day, too; the same sick numbness, sitting with my fellow invincible teenagers in the smoking cafeteria at college, totally unable to process. But we knew something would be done, and it was. Within a very small number of months, it was functionally close to impossible to own a handgun of any real deadly power in the UK. And though there have been murders, and the odd shooting, there's not been this kind of mass killing since.

And, I mean, fuck having the gun control debate again, who the hell am I going to win over, but I think even back then I knew US 'culture' was different and gun ownership far more normal, so when I say I knew how, well, that's what I mean. As soon as it happened, shocking to the core as it was, it also felt... inevitable. Something that should never happen, and yet was absolutely definitely going to happen at some point.

Because of the how.

But, *why?*

The answers were not long in coming. A picture was quickly emerging of a deeply toxic environment. Jocks that picked on goths and suspected queers. A bullied underclass of Marilyn Manson fans who sometimes wore black nail varnish, bullied beyond endurance; self-describing as The Trenchcoat Mafia, adopting a hateful, mocking nickname as their own.

The headline in *The Express* from that day was a pull quote from the Trenchcoat Mafia yearbook page (and really, that there *was* a yearbook page should surely have given some pause as to exactly how out there this group *really* was): "Insanity Is Healthy".

And, like, I'd seen *Heathers*, but more importantly, I'd somehow survived secondary school myself, and...

Well, as previously discussed in Chapter 13, school was a fairly hellish experience for me, for the usual banal reasons: short, over-enthusiastic, bright and not good at hiding it, lonely and socially awkward, you know how this tune goes. The music I loved the most – Manson came later, but not too late for me to connect – was full of spit and fury, and I honestly think it was a big part of how I stayed sane, in an environment that felt engineered to try and break me. And I realise how pathetically hyperbolic that may look, on the page, coming from the fingertips of a 40-something-year-old-man; but we've come way too far for bullshit, now, haven't we? And I tell you, it's the stone-cold truth of how I felt back then. Hell, I still think it's true. I still think it was. And I'm still pissed off about it.

Anyway.

The point is, sure, by the time Columbine happened I was out of school – hell, out of Devon, entirely, thank fuck; yes, sure, working a shitty job without the slightest clue what happened next, or how, but having faith, expectation, that there *was* a next, once I learned how to breathe and figured it out. On the other hand, I was still *not* out, in many important respects. I'd discovered the freedom to be not-a-lot in the place of my choosing, and of course that's not nothing... but nor is it to be anything approaching whole. The scars were there, and they ran deep, especially when a typical workday involved bullying co-workers who'd periodically threaten violence, indifferent bosses, and regulars who hated me for Existing While Male, Young, and Long Haired. I definitely felt stronger, and more confident... but not actually in any way strong or confident, if you can dig it. The hole had been very, very deep, and though progress was being made, I was a long way from daylight.

And then, this. This story of bullied kids and a bloody, pointless, destructive revenge. Like *Rage* or *Heathers,* but *real.*

I tried to imagine it. Tried to imagine being so overwhelmed by the despair and the fury and the shit that I just... gave up. Just decided fuck it, full nihilist, no nothing, write my suicide note in the blood of other people and ride out into the black.

And, well, if you've come this far, you'll know what I'm going to say next; I found to my crawling horror that I really, really could.

Dig it: I'd had this daydream since I was twelve. And the daydream was blowing up the school.

I knew just how I'd do it, too: break in at night, get to the science block, turn on every Bunsen burner gas tap in every lab, close the outside doors, wait for the building to fill with flammable fumes, light fuse, retire to a safe distance... boom! Or the other version: newly minted millionaire Kit Power (millionaire movie star? Oh, probably – back then, acting was still the thing) buys outright the entire school building complex, then has it wired with dynamite and razes it to the ground.

The more astute among you will have already spotted, I hope, the pretty important difference between these daydreams and what happened at Columbine (beyond the fact of them only ever being daydreams, of course, let's not lose sight of that); though my dreams ran destructive, they never ran *homicidal*. I wanted to destroy the site of my humiliation, and I wanted that destruction to be a spectacle, a statement... but I didn't want to hurt anyone, let alone everyone.

Not that I didn't also have violent fantasies, to be clear. Again, if you've read my fiction, you'll know I have a certain fascination, and maybe flare, for depictions of violence. Of this fact, I am neither proud nor ashamed, but I'm pretty sure I know where it comes from.

I'd rehearse fights. A lot. Almost certainly inspired by *Ender's Game* (see Chapter 9) and actively encouraged by The Ghost (see Chapter 33), I'd imagine myself delivering absolutely brutal beatings to particular bullies that had either threatened me or harmed me. The fantasy would always start with them throwing the first punch; me, moving instinctively, avoiding the blow; countering with a fist to the nose, throat, or gut, aiming the punch for several inches behind the target area to ensure my fist was still accelerating when it hit home (again, we can thank The Ghost for that little bit of dark wisdom); following up immediately with one of the other spots, causing the target to drop; after which a short speech about never, ever fucking with me again, liberally punctuated by kicks to the chest and gut, would complete the scene.

I'd run scenarios like this over and over and over and over. Picturing different settings, different opponents. I'm not going to say it made me feel good, because it didn't... not exactly. But it didn't *not,* either. The rationale was preparation, of course; to secure peace is to prepare for war, and all of that shit, and of course bullying wasn't an abstract threat, so, you know, I came by it honestly in that sense, but still... still...

Ah, hell. It is what it is, and it was what it was. And while none of the fights I got into ended up anywhere near that apocalyptic, I think the exercise did gift me a certain elevated sense of calm when the shit hit the fan; and perhaps more importantly, gave me a certain confidence that couldn't help but project, a bit. As we've discussed before, most bullies don't want a fight, they want to hand out a beating, and I think the little extra swagger these constant imaginings gave me, earned or not, sent just enough of a signal that this sheep might have some bite after all to see me passed over for a softer target.

So, as I read the coverage in the papers, this story of the bullied kids who snapped, and took their homemade bombs and firearms on a rampage, I felt those two vivid fantasies of my own collide in my head, and felt an awful, soul sickness. Jesus. It could have been me. Just a little less love at home, a little less support, a little less conscience, a little less self-belief... if I'd actually believed that school was forever, rather than a jail term it was my job to outlast...

Mat and/or Trey of *South Park*: "I remember just thinking, if only I could have told those kids... man, high school is a funhouse mirror, it's the opposite of real life. All those kids making your lives hell, they'll end up working in their daddy's garage, it's the weirdos and freaks who will become the kings of creation..."

And that empathy wrecked me, for weeks afterwards it felt like, especially as the regulars in the bar offered their considered verdict on what had happened ("they're just gone! In the 'ead!", okay, yeah, cheers for that insight, Otis). Again, to be crystal clear, not out of sorrow for the killers, but out of horror at what they'd done, the hideous abominations they'd felt, wrongly, they'd been pushed to. The idea that the pain could get big enough to obliterate all sense, all reason; that consciousness, life itself, might start to feel like a joke – worse, a trap... and that feeling could lead to the ultimate damnation, destruction and death as a last, desperate bid to scratch your name of the face of the world.

And it wasn't until decades later that I learned what perhaps you already know: almost everything I knew about Columbine, and the killers, was bullshit.

They weren't bullied. They weren't goths. They weren't Marilyn Manson fans. They didn't snap – they'd planned the massacre for months. Columbine itself was not some *Heathers* style dystopia – at least, no more than any high school is. Dylan was a kid with deep seated psychological problems: impressionable, unable to regulate his emotions, prone to depression, but not bullied, nor unloved or abused. And Eric was a one-in-a-million psychopath – a kid Dave Cullen, journalist, in his excellent book about the truth of what happened that day, describes as "like studying a virus" – someone impossible to relate to or empathise with, so alien was his interior.

Shock fucking horror, the press had lied to me – to us. Again (see Volume I).

To themselves, too? Oh, hell, probably, in some cases – though, given what their job is supposed to be, ask me if I give a shit. The point is, I – we – were sold a bill of goods that was completely false, and, speaking personally, I went through a wholly unnecessary bout of self-doubt and loathing as a result, agonising over what now seems, at the blessed distance of a couple of decades, as nothing more or less than the utterly banal, typical thought processes of a bullied teen.

And, yeah, sure, boo fucking hoo me, people actually fucking died. True. But, also true: we were all collectively gaslit in an absolutely gigantic way by people whose actual job it was to know and do better. And, check it: I am nothing approaching unique or special, especially as regard my experiences as a school child of the 90s. I strongly suspect many, many young people put themselves through the kind of mill I did; tried to process not only the trauma of the fact of what happened, but also a sickening sense of culpability, complicity, there but for the grace of... well, whoever.

Like most of us, I suspect, I've got enough guilt I earned honestly to work through. I didn't fucking need this, and if you're nodding along as you read this, neither did you.

In fiction, we don't have to tell the truth about monsters. We can, of course. Or, we can try to; try and reach across the empathy chasm, see inside the heart of the heartless, the mind of the mindless. Sure, we can. I think we'll almost always fail; I think we'll inevitably take too much of our own minds and hearts with us, and that what we come out with, whilst valuable, and 'entertaining' (for a given value of etc.) will bear as much relation to the reality as... well, as a portrait of a person does to a virus. But, try or not, it's fundamentally not our job, I don't think.

Journalists, on the other hand? Yeah. Yeah, I think it is their fucking job. And with a few honourable exceptions, it's a job they're failing at. Miserably. It hurt me then, in 1999, and here and now, in 2021, it's fucking killing us.

The Columbine massacre is a scar on the minds of everyone who lived through it, whether in person, or vicariously via the global coverage. It's trauma.

The lies we were told about that day, and the way those lies have perpetuated, normalised, become history in the minds of so, so many... that piles obscenity upon obscenity, degradation upon tragedy. It victimises the dead all over again, and by telling us a false story of what happened, stereotypes are perpetuated, misunderstandings are repeated as fact, and, as the wrong lessons are learned, further such killings gain a sick inevitability.

It's 2021. The planet is burning. 71% of global carbon emissions are made by just 100 companies.

And the papers are telling you that paper straws and electric cars are the only solution, and if you don't buy them, it's *you* that's killing the planet. Or, at least, us. Not *them*.

Us.

What do these stories have in common? The refusal of those with the platform, and the responsibility, the fucking *obligation,* to accurately name the problem. Whether through distaste, vested interest, or investment in the false narrative we've built for centuries around the power of individual action (but never collective action, god forbid The Baying Mob ever manifest) to somehow resist the awesome forces of human-shaped viruses with effectively limitless resources, we are fed a line of plausible sounding, emotionally resonant bullshit. And, because we care, because of our empathy, we absorb it, we internalise it, and we try to reckon with the distorted image these false stories give us of ourselves.

It's 2022. The planet is burning. We need better stories. Truer stories. And people with the courage to write those stories, in the face of all the social and financial incentives that push towards the status quo.

Good luck to us all.

This chapter is dedicated with respect and affection to the memory of Dawn Foster – A Real One who Got It. May she inspire us all to Do Better and Be Better.

WHADAYA GONNA DO?

CASINO

It's not like I don't *make* plans. That wouldn't be a fair observation at all.

It's more just that life keeps happening.

Example: I had a list. My Life In Horror was always conceived as a finite project, with a very definite end game, including a penultimate essay that, well, we'll get there, and when we do, please take the content note to heart. And at the time *this* essay was originally written we were, as its inclusion in Volume II implies, comfortably over the halfway mark.

So, there was a list. And, sure, it fluctuated. Things got added and, due to the finite nature of the project, that meant other things had to come off. It was a useful process, in a lot of ways – it forced me to focus a little, on a project that could otherwise become utterly and unforgivably indulgent – I had to keep asking myself, what are The Big Ones? Those moments – in childhood, as a teenager, in my twenties – that really got me where I lived, made me think, made me *feel?*

And this movie has been on and off the list from the very start.

There's a lot to not recommend it for the project. It's certainly not a horror movie, for starters (though obviously if you've come this far, you're likely chuckling at that – and no, you're right, that's never stopped me before). More seriously, the standard opening spiel just won't fit. I can't tell you how old I was, when and where, any of that. Truth to tell, though I've seen the movie a fair few times (being married to a woman who loves gangster movies has its perks), I really don't have a clear picture in my head of much of the piece as a whole, if I'm honest. Though I know it's not true, it feels quite a lot like a film

I've only ever seen from the middle, tuned into halfway through and then been unable to tune away.

That said, there's a reason I feel that way. There's a gravitational pull about the back half of this one – a black hole of awfulness that seems to eat light and crush mass. Which I suppose explains how it stuck around as long as it did, and why it flickered so often, on and off, on and off, as other ideas jockeyed for attention.

Still, it had recently come off the list. I thought for good.

And then Frank Vincent died.

I was surprised by how upset I was. And then, not long after, surprised by my surprise. After all, he'd peopled some of my favourite art of... well, shit, my life, really. *Raging Bull*, *Goodfellas*... And, of course, a show-stealing turn in the final couple of series of one of my Top 5 TV shows of all time, *The Sopranos*.

Sure, he was a character actor, and sure, the roles all had certain elements in common. That didn't change the fact that he was there, and not only did he not let the side down, he was an amazing asset to whatever story he was a part of. He had everything you'd want – charm, ruthlessness, intelligence, pride, even arrogance, and an aura of power and menace. He may never have had the lead role, but he was always a powerful addition to any crew, always someone you felt you had to watch.

So, yeah, I was sad. And as I thought more about why, I thought about him telling Pesci to go home and get his fuckin shine box, and I thought about how he explained to Tony Soprano about how he'd 'compromised', the chilling fury juuuuuust under the surface. The look on his face when he finally cornered Vito in the hotel room.

Most of all, though, I thought about this movie.

I thought about *Casino*.

Now, if you'd taken a look at the list of things I was going to write about for this column, and you'd seen *Casino*, I'm betting that you'd nod and say to yourself 'the vice scene'. Like *Reservoir Dogs* and the ear, it's the kind of totemic cinema moment that was whispered about on the playground – "Oh my God, did you see the bit where he...?"

And I'm not going to deny how fucking horrible that scene is. Nor am I going to deny how utterly gruesome the emotional car wreck of Rothstein's marriage to Ginger is, Sharon Stone and De Niro knocking it out of the park with their merciless, unflinching portrayal of a poisoned, poisonous relationship.

As you'll know, if you've seen the film, there's all of that and more – brutality upon brutality, and misery feeding misery.

It's all true, but none of that is why this movie sat on my list for so long, or why we're talking about it now.

No, we're talking about this fucking movie because of the climax in the wheatfield: the execution of Nicky Santoro and his brother.

Nicky – played by Pesci – has been pretty much vileness personified the entire movie. He's cheated and murdered and murdered and tortured his way all across Nevada and back. The head-in-a-vice scene? Nicky was the one cranking the handle.

Nicky is unrepentant. Nicky is irredeemable. Nicky is self-destruction in an expensive yet still tasteless suit. Which would be sort-of fine, if he wasn't also such a voracious, malevolent cancer for everyone who comes into contact with him.

By the closing of the movie, even he realises he's going to be persona non grata in Vegas for the rest of his life. Too many hits, too many missing people, just too fucking much. He understands this. In voiceover, he accepts it. And as the scene opens, he's driving up a dirt track in a corn field. The corn is tall – eight, ten feet maybe. The track leads to a clearing at the end. There's a few cars, maybe a dozen mobsters waiting. Nicky's crew.

With them, Nicky's right-hand man – the man who's been by his side throughout his decades of carnage. The man who lied to the big bosses about Nicky's transgressions – covered for him when he was fucking his best friend's wife.

The man's name is Frank Marino. Played by Frank Vincent.

As they drive up, Nicky explains the score to us, in voiceover, in that same arrogant, hectoring voice he's used throughout the movie. Sure, Vegas is too hot for *him,* so he's here with his brother, to hand over the reins. He's going to introduce him around, make sure the gang – his gang, Nicky's people – know what's what. As he and his brother get out of the car, and the group starts to huddle around them, he says, to us, "what's right is right..."

And then, mid-sentence, there's a dull clunk, and he says "Oww!".

He drops to his knees, clutching his head, a look of stunned confusion on his face.

My stomach drops right with him. An express elevator, going all the way down.

Two of them grab Nicky's arms, hold him down on his knees. They grab his brother, drag him away. His brother is yelling, furious, scared, "You rat bastards!".

They force Nicky's head up. Nicky looks.

He looks at his brother. Maybe the only other human being on the planet Nicky has any genuine feelings for. Helpless. Trapped. Yelling.

He looks up, eyes following the baseball bat, up to the impassive face of Frank.

His friend. His right hand man.

Frank looks back at him. And his face...his face is a mask.

Nicky – this sociopath, this monster, this vile brutal killer, hardened by a lifetime of unchecked fury and sadism... Nicky starts to beg.

Frank nods, once. Then he swings the bat.

The bat falls again and again. Others join in. The sound is relentless – metal colliding with meat. Nicky sobs. He tries to look away. They won't let him.

By the time they stop, his brother is unrecognisable – his face a mask of blood, his body shattered. Nicky, sobbing, keeps begging. "Please, he's strong, he's still breathing, leave him..." Begging Frank. Frank looks at him. "Yeah?!?" He brings down the bat once more on Nicky's brother's skull.

He walks over to Nicky, now just begging, the same word "please", over and over, a broken machine. Frank shows him his brother's ragged, still breathing form once more. Then he swings the bat at Nicky's head.

The cuts start to fracture now, as the attacks rain down on Nicky. Freeze framing, then cutting forward – as though we're sharing the concussive effects of the blows with our former narrator. Finally, De Niro comes on, in voice over, telling us what we already know – that Nicky had taken it too far, and that an example was made.

As the bodies are stripped, torsos blue and purple from their battering, as the two no-longer-men are thrown into a hole in the ground, there's a final, gut twisting moment. As a shovel of dirt falls over the blood-caked faces, a puff of breath from one of the broken jaws disturbs the soil, sending it out in a plume.

"They buried them alive", De Niro intones, just in case your mind is somehow refusing the information your eyes are sending it.

And sure, it's horrific on a number of levels. The sadism of it reaches levels even Nicky couldn't – yes, he trapped a man's head in a vice to get information from him, and he murdered lots of people… but battering a loved one beyond repair in front of someone, forcing them to watch, in the knowledge that they are next – and, crucially, that there is nothing they can do to stop it, escape it, even hasten the outcome? Even for a sick fuck like Nicky, that is some next level brutality.

And let's not forget the extra/meta-textual fuckery that Scorsese pulls here. Every time I think about that voiceover being interrupted by the *thunk* of a bat, and the surprised *ow* that follows, the hairs on my arm stand up – and not in a good way. It's a rule of cinema so ironclad, so ingrained, we think of it not at all, never examine or question it. And then he oh-so casually violates it, in a moment absolutely calculated to deliver maximum shock. It's a bold, punk, brutal, unfair moment of unbridled cinema genius, and I cannot immediately think of a better example of understanding just when, and how, and how hard you can break the rules, providing that you are doing so with a purpose. It's also a trick that can probably only be done once – but fuck me, what a moment.

So there's that. And there's also the fact that it plays on the mind, long after it's done. Because, dig it: it's a lesson for who, exactly? Nicky? His brother? They are going in the ground and they ain't coming back. If the lesson is for them, a bullet would do the job.

No, this horror show is to send a message. But to who? The men who did this would have to be very fucking careful who they talked to about it. Orders came from on high, sure, but still, loose lips sink ships. They will talk, of course – worse than a sewing circle, as a famous moll will memorably put it, in a movie that we discussed back in chapter 20 – still, it's not something you'd exactly feel good bragging about, I don't think.

No, the real horror is this: the message is for each other. For Nicky's whole crew.

And the message is: fuck up like your friend did, and this is what your friends will do to *you*.

Which brings us back to Frank. Nicky's right-hand man, who has protected and enabled and shielded and covered, again and again.

Frank Marino. Played by Frank Vincent. His face a mask, as he meets Nicky's eyes. Telling him everything he needs to know about what the rest of his short life will consist of. There's little emotion – either regret or rage, sorrow or anger.

But there is something. Something glittering, deep down in those eyes. Something dark and strong and real.

It's a look I will never, ever forget. It's a look that will haunt me, as long as I draw breath.

Here's to you, Frank Vincent.

Here's to you.

THIS PLANET BELONGS TO ME AND THIS HIPPY WITH LONG HAIR

DEVIL WITHOUT A CAUSE

Well, well, well. The year 2000 AD, get down with your bad self.

Things have gotten better. I quit working at the fucking pub. I didn't have a job to go to, but I simply wasn't prepared to work millennium eve in that place for the princely sum of double the national minimum wage. It's interesting; obviously through the strict lens of transactional logic, it was a bad move, in that I ended up earning nothing and being unemployed. But, you know, I knew I was worth more.

Yeah. That's what mattered.

Anyhow, three months of being unemployed wasn't fun, but then I landed an admin job at London Guildhall University, initially processing forms in their registration department. It was a nine-month fixed-term contract job. For the first time in my life, I was being paid monthly.

And I was earning – after tax, mark you – £1000 a month.

My rent, on the shared house I was living in with The Ghost, was £270.

I felt like a fucking millionaire.

I started there because I'd assumed this was the point I acquired this album. Like, I remember my first Saturday after payday (fuck, weekends were *mine* now, rather than being the busiest and most soul-crushing days of my week), riding the tube to the west end, going into HMV on Oxford Street and grabbing a fucking basket; like, I am here to buy some damn music.

I denied myself nothing, and I walked out £120 lighter, and with a canvas bag bulging with jewel cases.

And I got some beauties that day, some all-time hall-of-famers: Queens of the Stone Age's *Rated R*, NiN's *The Fragile*, and Slipknot's debut (later that year, I'd queue for hours in that same store to get it signed by the band, when they were doing their first UK tour. I still have it). Sure, some misses too: the cover art for Limp Bizkit's *Significant Other* got me over the line, and it spent frankly too long in rotation; it wasn't until I saw the band playing at Leeds in 2000 that the scales fell and I realised I'd been mugged off. But, you know, hey, they can't all pay off. Overall, it was a roaring success, and one of the most straightforwardly happy days of my life.

And I really thought I must have picked this one up then, but I checked the dates, and that cannot be the case.

See, I bought *Devil Without a Cause* as a present for The Ghost – likely as a birthday present. And it must have been soon after it came out, because I'd picked it up as a result of XFM playing the absolute shit out of 'Cowboy' for weeks, which must have been in 1998.

Except… I wasn't working in the pub until December 98, because I phoned in sick for Christmas. I remember, because when I put in my notice in December 99, the boss said "Wow, that's two Christmasses you've fucked me over". So…

Jesus, you know what? I think 'Cowboy' must have lodged in my head so badly that I went and hunted the album out once I had money. Like, I think that almost has to be it. I know I had the album by the time I was at Guildhall because I remember talking with people about it, so…

Okay, so either that shopping trip, or one of the subsequent ones.

Back in the room. Jesus, I know the past is a foreign country, but why does it have to be such a fucking maze?

Anyway. The Ghost had access to a CD burner and a colour photocopier, so I knew anything I was buying for him, I was also basically buying for myself, and sure enough I still have the burned copy, somewhere on a shelf or in a drawer.

And I fell pretty hard.

Now, in my defence, my entire experience of rap music to this point was *Rage Against the Machine* and Insane Clown Posse's *The Great Milenko* (see Chapter 24), and the aforementioned LB record. And I was – hell, am – primarily a metalhead. Sure, my respect for hip hop as a form has grown over the years, and I've lately been listening to a lot of it, so one might fairly point out that this album was almost cynically tailormade to appeal to me. Hip hop, but with slamming rock/metal guitars and a lead singer rapping about being a white trash trailer kid? How could I resist?

And I'm listening to it now, and you know, it's about as well produced as any rap/rock album from 1998 could possibly be. The guitars on 'Fist of Rage', 'Bawitdaba', and 'I Am the Bullgod' chug and crunch like you want them to, and 'Fist of Rage' actually has a pretty good riff going on.

At the same time...

So, you'll recall back when we were talking about *The Lost Boys* (see Volume I), I posited the entirely uncontroversial fact that it's just a bad movie, regardless of what your nostalgia may be telling you? Well, I stuck *Devil Without a Cause* on a few months back, looking for some aggressive music to help me pretend I wasn't hating every second on the crosstrainer, and despite knowing every word, I found myself itching to hit the skip button about halfway through 'Cowboy'... then again as 'Devil Without a Cause' entered its 17th minute... Until I skipped 'Rollin' into 'Wasting Time', and just noped out entirely.

I have a shocking and terrible news flash from 1998: this album may have sold 11 million copies in the US, to widespread critical acclaim, but it's actually not very good.

I know. Try and contain your shock.

The why of the badness is trivial. To start with, there aren't enough good songs; that's a pretty fundamental issue. 'Bawitdaba' is a strong opening; it builds well to the chorus intro, and the first verse sets out the stall well; it comes off like a classic chest-beater, but there's a bit more going on under the hood. *This is for the questions that don't have any answers* is a fucking good opening line, and the parade of misfits the song (album?) is dedicated to (*the Gs with the 40s and the chicks with beepers, wild mustangs / The porno flicks / and all my homies in the county in cell block 6*) feels like if Fun Loving Criminals were going dirty on this one, and the riff is solid. 'Cowboy' is what it is; it was a good choice for a single, but it's certainly run through its replay value for me, at this point. Good comedy makes you laugh; truly great comedy makes you laugh the thousandth time you hear it. 'Cowboy' no longer makes me crack a smile, though I remember why it once did.

But then we get to the title track, and the problems start to surface.

Like, it's not terrible or anything, but it *is* just a bit too long. The Joe C verse is cute, and contains probably the best single line on the album (*I'm a freak, don't call me sick / three foot nine, with a ten foot dick!*), but there's one too many tours through the chorus. I understand this is something about which reasonable people can differ, but, for me, a rap metal song that has you checking how much longer it has to run has failed some pretty elemental test.

'I Am the Bullgod' makes some strange production choices with the guitar sound, an issue that's exacerbated on subsequent tracks; by the end of the record, I feel like I've heard seven or eight different producers who have aggressively different approaches to the job, which in turn generates a track-to-track dissonance that I find tiring. That said, 'Bullgod' makes a good case for Kid Rock's drug consumption; it's also the last straightforwardly good song on the album.

The issue from here is pretty simple: I've heard everything Kid Rock has to offer. The entire gamut of his emotions, the limits of his rhyme schemes, the subject matter (having sex, taking drugs, being White Trash, going platinum, okay). But the album still has 15 tracks to go. And a combination of lyrical diminishing returns and the aforementioned tonal production and beat/tune choices mean that I'm both bored and oddly exhausted by the time the risible 'Welcome to the Party' and faux-cool 'I Got One For Ya' kick in. Marking the halfway point.

The back half isn't devoid of charm; 'Fist of Rage' has a sub-sub-RATM quality that still has enough blood in its veins to bring on a nod, and 'Fuck Off' sees KR audibly upping his game, in a vain attempt to not be demolished by his special guest MC. It's the definition of a doomed effort, but it does at least give you a glimpse of what could have been, if KR had put more effort into *being* The Hottest Shit Ever, instead of merely declaring it, like every success-visualising huckster in the embarrassing history of capitalism.

Oh, also, in the final track, 'Black Girl, White Guy', Kid Rock casually drops the n-bomb.

So, you know. There's that.

And, no, of course I'm not sat here in 2022 trying to get Kid Rock cancelled; frankly, if, here in 2022, you're still enjoying Kid Rock, you're welcome to each other's company, and it's none of my damn business.

What I am curious about is why I liked this so much, at the time and place when I did, given how transparently mediocre it always was. Like, I had RATM's debut when I was twelve or thirteen. *Fear of a Black Planet* existed, *Straight Outta Compton* existed, and in two years and one chapter's time, A Certain LP is going to demonstrate just what a white boy from Detroit can do in the realm of hip hop, and without being some middle-class twat cosplaying as a drug dealer.

So, let's start here; it's not good, but it's not aggressively and unremittingly awful; if I also enjoyed Limp Bizkit and, heh, Methods of Mayhem, maybe I should just cut myself some slack. Like, there's some legit good guitar playing here, and the band behind him is rock solid. All hip hop is essentially new to me at this point, so I had no way of knowing just how reliant Kid Rock was on what had gone before. I was still green, about the past and the present-as-was; the point of the big shopping trip was to take some risks, see what was out there. I was terminally easily impressed, and the rap/metal thing was still new enough (and rap in general still essentially unknown enough) for the thrill of discovery to whitewash a multitude of sins.

Also, I guess let's kick this about for a second: it's the same record I heard in 1998. Not a note has changed. What's changed is me; my positionality to the work, and therefore my relationship to it. The stuff I loved is all still there; if I love it no longer, is that just because I've since heard so much done so much better that what seemed impressive now sounds mediocre?

Sure, that's part of it. Shit, this one goes all the way back to our early conversation about the music of WASP back in Volume I, doesn't it? I loved that too, and, well, yeah.

And intellectually, that's a perfectly reasonable, defensible position to hold. I was young. I'm no longer as young. Considering how long it's been with some of the work I've covered here, it's honestly astonishing this hasn't happened more often.

Sure. But also...

Well, look, I think, even by the subterranean standards of hip hop and metal, this album is kind of frighteningly misogynistic. Not that other titles in this series so far covered and still to come don't have their share of, erm, issues, but fuck me, this guy just has nothing else to talk about. This is a man who, like Fred Durst, appears to hate women because his sex drive means he has to be in their company but *they just won't stop talking.* Seriously. And, like, sure, welcome to patriarchy, welcome to toxic masculinity, and it's not like it isn't a crowded field. But with Rock it stands out so starkly, for me, because of the paucity of the rest of the material; when your entire persona is pimp/street hustler, and you don't have the creative chops or imagination or confidence to ever move outside of that, it becomes a kind of relentless dirge of self-loathing, the party anthems feeling like dead eyed embracing of nihilistic abuse just to feel *something*.

Only, you know, a bit shit.

Like, I bought this for The Ghost, a horrifically misogynistic man, and I remember he loved it but was surprised that I'd know he'd like it because rap wasn't his thing (oh, yeah, he was a *massive* WASP fan). And for those of you staring at me in Guns N' Roses (see Volume I, twice), sure, but in my defence, I called it out there, too. And I think what bugs me – and I admit this is subjective, but – is just how deeply felt the assumptions appear to be, just how much it feels like KR thinks these are simply Facts Of Life, obvious truths.

I dunno. I came here to work out why there was this gap between early 20s me and mid 40s me and I feel like I'm trying to grasp smoke.

That fucking n-bomb does bother me too, though. And it bothers me a lot that it didn't bother me at the time. Like, I didn't even remember it, so little impression did it make. And, again, not trying to relitigate 1998, but at the same time, that's not a fucking hundred years ago, is it? Did it not bother anyone because Kid Rock was clearly just an awful person, or because he has a black son and therefore can't be racist, or... what, exactly? Like, of course he *could* say it, but, I mean...

Like, Axl Rose has spent decades, now, rightly apologising for 'One in a Million', and here we are ten years on from that song's release, and a white middle class kid cosplaying as a street hustler drops it in a song talking about his relationship with the black mother of his son, and... crickets all round? I dunno, man, it feels fucking odd to me, and definitely kind of shameful that I wasn't more uncomfortable about it at the time.

Because what it comes down to is a faint bad taste the whole thing leaves in the mouth, for me, at this point. I don't like Kid Rock, as a human; and that's okay, there's plenty of artists whose work I love who I don't like either... but the work is pretty mediocre too, and that's what I think pisses me off. It's one thing to get taken in by a blinding talent that happens to be owned by a garbage human, but when it's a garbage human who also doesn't have a huge amount going on creatively; when it's an album that, in retrospect, feels like a cynical rebranding of a struggling hip-hop artist who saw the nu-metal wave starting to crest just in time to grab it, creating an album that feels oddly half-baked and inchoate... yeah, then it's just a little bit upsetting to have gotten caught up it that, taken along by it.

I'm sure it won't be the last time, but even so.

Still, there is one big fat, silver lining. On track 14, with the pleasingly direct title of 'Fuck Off', Rock delivers his best bars on the album, over a truly snarling guitar line. The subject matter's the same as ever – getting fucked up, getting laid, determined to be The Biggest – but it's delivered with more conviction and skill than anywhere else on the record; you kind of get the sense of why the suits thought they could make use of this guy.

And then, at the end of the song, he calls in his guest MC.

And for the first time in my life, I hear the high, nasal voice of someone KR introduces on the track as Slim Shady.

And in a few short bars, I get a sense of what this form can *really* deliver.

Everything he's doing is next level. He does Kid Rock's same subject matter but there's an edge to it; the flow is more assured, more intelligent, the rhyme scheme far more complex, and yet the overall flow sounds effortless, as though he's making it up on the spot. And it's *funny* in a way that Rock's 2D machismo simply isn't capable of. Slim sounds like a whiny brat, the anti-cool, the nerd kid, only with more skill than everyone put together, a swagger that knocks Kid Rock off the stage with one hip swing, borne not from a need to rooster strut to cover for insecurity, but from a place of total, furious confidence – *I got this shit, I own this joint, just you sit back and let me go* (if my sources are to be believed, at least some of that swagger came from young Mr Mathers enjoying a rare encounter with cocaine, supplied at Rock's studio prior to recording). The track bleeds away behind him as he closes the song out (*so when you see me on your block, you'd better lock your cars/ 'cause you know I'm losin' it when I'm rappin' to rock guitars!*) and he closes with an electrifying dedication/call to arms that sets me off in a way nothing has since *Rage Against the Machine*.

So, sure, I think *Devil Without a Cause* sucks, and Kid Rock sucks, and I'm embarrassed that I loved this deeply mediocre artist and album, as a young man.

But, on the other hand, it did introduce me to Eminem.

To be continued…

AM I TOO LOUD FOR YOU?

THE MARSHALL MATHERS LP

Content note: discussions of violence, including sexual violence, misogyny, homophobia and the use of homophobic slurs.

The first time I heard the name was the year 1999. I was still working in the pub.

It was White Natalie who told me about him. We were talking about music, and I was trying to explain to this in-her-early-20s London girl about metal, and she was trying to tell me about chart dance and hip hop, and I don't think we were really communicating at all, to be honest, but we had much time to pass, so we talked.

Or, more accurately, she talked, and I mocked.
"Like the chocolate?"
"No…"
"He's named after a fucking sweet?"
"No! It's…"
"What's his first name, peanut?"
"Fuck off! His name's Marshall…"
"Like the amplifier?"
"I don't know what that is. No, Marshall Mathers, that's where the name comes from – m in m, see?"
"That's the stupidest fucking thing I ever heard."
"But he also calls himself Slim Shady…"
"I stand corrected."
"Piss off!"

And so on. The conversation turned to acts whose names may have seemed less silly to me at the time, but were clearly less memorable at 20 years' distance, and, secure in my metal meathead snobbery that she didn't have the first clue what she was talking about when it came to quality music, I gave it not a single moment's further thought.

Sorry, White Natalie. You were right, and I was wrong. At least about this chap.

Fast forward a year. I'm now working at Guildhall University, earning a grand a month and feeling like a millionaire. Monday night D&D is the highlight of the week; The Ghost has assembled a great bunch of lads, all late twenties/early thirties, and I take over DMing, running an epic classic D&D greatest hits campaign, hitting the party with a Quantum Leap curse so I can take them through Castle Greyhawk, The Temple Of Elemental Evil, and any other campaign I can get my mitts on, continuity be damned. The Ghost has an extensive collection. I have ambitions to take them into Ravenloft eventually. And, as previously mentioned, after the wage poverty drought of The Pub Year, I'm making up for it now by dumping a non-trivial percentage of my disposable income in HMV Oxford Street every month.

And one of the gang – let's call him Drew – mentions the name again. Drew has music taste a lot wider and a fair bit more indie focused than me, but he knows his onions, and he says Eminem is Actually Good, and this time, I listen, but mentally add an asterisk that reads 'for a rapper', because yeah, sure, Kid Rock's cool (and, yes, Eminem's verse on that album is superb), and Bodycount are awesome, but rapping *without* guitars? I dunno, man, life *is* pretty short, you know?

And then, Marilyn Manson happens.

I mean, he's been happening for some time, for me. And, yes, to address the elephant in the room, I am aware of the many credible accusations that allege him to be a gigantically vile asshole, I believe victims and no longer consider myself a fan... but it's the year 2000, and I know about none of this, but I do know *Holy Wood*, his third-in-a-trilogy album that started with *Antichrist Superstar* and whose second entry, *Mechanical Animals*, was at least partly responsible for lifting me out of a pretty deep teenage depression, is coming out that summer, and hoo, boy, the Marilyn Manson BBS service is buzzing with the dripdripdrip of promo images and sound clips and whatnot. And somewhere in that pre-hype moment, Manson makes reference to having completed some collaboration with Eminem 'that nobody knows about yet' and sad to say, that did the trick for me.

And look, in my defence, like Anton LeVay before him, Manson had an absolute genius for attaching himself to bigger cultural figures, who, likewise, were titillated by being photographed with the Antichrist Superstar. And the 'collaboration' turned out to be no more than a blink-and-you'll-miss-it appearance in Eminem's 'The Way I Am' video, as Em, in a bar talking about Columbine, says *They blame it on Marilyn, And the heroin, But where were the parents at? And look where it's at*. Chuck in a hilariously pixelated video clip from Manson's site where he joined Eminem on stage for the final chorus of the song, followed by an embrace between the two stars, and suddenly I'm very interested in this rapper named after a chocolate.

Drew lends The *Slim Shady* and *Marshall Mathers LP*s to The Ghost, he burns me copies with colour photocopies of the cover art, and all of a sudden, Eminem takes up residence in my stereo and my internal cultural landscape.

I quickly gravitated to *MMLP*. It's not that *SSLP* is bad (and these days, settling into mellow middle age, I actually prefer it, in all its wild Tex Avery On Angel Dust Technicolour energy) but the darker edge of Marshall Mathers is obviously going to exert the stronger pull to a twenty-year-old Marilyn Manson fan. And so it goes.

Not that it's *not* funny; there's a thick seam of dark comedy that runs through the whole album. I have a vivid memory of sitting with The Ghost's daughter, one of my early listens, and I think her first, and the pair of us collapsing into delighted giggles all the way through 'Kill You'. It's an instructive moment; up until then, the song had always hit me queasy. I couldn't fully parse it, was the thing. I mean, it was clearly, obviously a joke. Trivially so. It's also a manifesto for the album, in a lot of ways – 'oh, you thought *The Slim Shady LP* went too far? Strap in, kids!'…

And yet.

The anger in the performance is visceral, as are the descriptions of violence. By the end of the first verse, he's described strangling a prostitute and 'raping his own mother', before flinging it back in the face of the audiences and critics who have turned him into a megastar

"Oh, now he's raping his own mother, abusing a whore, snorting coke, and we gave him the Rolling Stone cover?" You're goddamn right bitch, and now it's too late! I'm triple platinum and tragedies happen in two states! and on, and sure, in his sober career he'll achieve linguistic gymnastics and pacing that put this in the shade, but...

There's still something uncomfortably breath-taking about it, for me. There's a relentlessness to the delivery, and the start-stop, sparse, almost nursery rhyme beat creates so much space that you can't help but hear each machine gun syllable as it's delivered. And I remember just... not knowing what the fuck to make of it. The anger called to me, as it had with Guns N' Roses and all the rock and metal bands since. And along with that, the cartoon misogyny did trigger a laugh impulse. Given how I was raised, woman hatred was both alien and a powerful taboo, and so art that was, to me, transgressive in this way (and I do of course now realise that it's anything but transgressive in the wider world, and that's a significant part of the problem, but) had an incredible impact.

But it was scary, too. Because on *The Slim Shady LP*, the comic leaning is more clearly signposted, from the nasal, childlike vocal delivery down to the cartoonish imagery. Gross things happen on *SSLP*, for sure, but it's done with a playful glee, the sound of a kid delighting in saying shit (and, indeed 'shit') for the sake of it. And on one level, 'Kill You' (and the *MMLP* taken as a whole) is just that turned up to eleven... but the act of turning it up to eleven changes the delivery, and created, for me, an uneasy sinister undertone that made/ makes me queasy.

What's really amazing is, right now, I'm listening to the album, and I can still feel that reaction. Normally, I can't revisit the initial emotional impact of a work once I've seen it in a new mode. Like we discussed back in the *Pulp Fiction* chapter, that overdose scene fucked me up the first time... but only the first time. Once I was in on the joke, I've only ever been able to enjoy it as one of the greatest comedy scenes in modern cinema. Not a complaint, to be clear, just an observation.

What's incredible to me about *The Marshall Mathers LP* is that, even following that listening with The Ghost's daughter, as her laughter allowed me to see that the shock was the joke, that the po-faced angry delivery was that of a comedy rant and the laughter came tearing out of me, an explosion of relief and joy as, suddenly, I Got It, I can still flip back to that stomach sunk discomfort of those initial solo listens.

One of the interesting things about Eminem, I think, is how he's simultaneously massively commercially successful and, in many circles, considered a kind of embarrassing artist to admit to liking. I've joked a couple of times with the couple of friends I have that I know are fellow fans that it's music you love to listen to on your own, but would be mortified to listen to in company. And that's true in one sense; I've reconnected with Eminem's more recent output over the last year, and I think a lot of it is absolutely phenomenal, but I honestly cannot imagine sitting and listening to it with my wife or kid. The same shit that makes me grin ear to ear as it blasts through my headphones while I walk the dog or endure an exercise session on the hated cross trainer would make me curl up with embarrassment in the company of many of my nearest and dearest. Hell, that may even be part of the pull, right? Slim as a persona is pure id, pure self-destructive impulse, pure 'say-the-thing-you-think-but-would-never-say' smart arsery; dude's the fucking court jester of pop culture, poking ribald fun at everyone and everything, including himself.

At the same time, it took that communal experience, listening with another, to unlock the comedy reaction, and let me make the mental flip from uneased awe to grinning enjoyment. The permission to laugh at the most awful, heinous shit, because that was the point.

I wasn't laughing because it *wasn't* horrible, but because it *was.*

And we're in this strange cultural moment, right now, in 2022. A billion bullshit column inches have been spilled about 'woke' and 'cancel culture', and almost all of it is fucking awful scaremongering non-issues... but artists, especially artists of A Certain Age (like, to be precise, my age and older) remember perhaps a little too well the moment in the 90s when the PMRC were trying to shut down metal and hip hop, or at least make it inaccessible to kids, while in the UK, the 'video nasties' scare was outlawing movies out of some preposterous suggestion of moral corruption. And, to be clear, these actually *were* dark moments for freedom of speech and artistic expression; we were right to be worried and fight back against government encroachments on those freedoms.

The trouble is, the muscle memory of those days runs deep. And so, in 2022, when members of marginalised communities start talking about problematic portrayals, especially in art created by artists not part of the community that they are writing in/commenting on, or YA publishers start employing specialist editors to try and ensure that such issues get identified and fixed prior to publication, a lot of artists my age and older have an almost knee-jerk negative reaction.

It's not a good or healthy reaction, of course, and a second's thought would tell you why. Because the difference between a community exercising its freedom of speech to interrogate and criticise art and *congressional hearings and confiscation of videotapes by the state* is… ah, I can't even be bothered to complete the sentence, you've got the point.

Still, I bring it up because one of the things people my age and older seem to say an awful lot about the art of our youth is "oh yeah, but/and you wouldn't be able to get away with that these days". And Eminem's often held up as an example; the number of otherwise intelligent reaction video makers who say endless variations on "if Eminem was coming up today, he'd be so cancelled".

And, like, newsflash, motherfuckers: four years ago the US managed to elect a racist to the highest office in the land, and despite then having one of the most hilariously corrupt and inept terms of office in the history of the presidency, as of the time of writing, that motherfucker still isn't wearing an orange jumpsuit, and may indeed run again next time, and win again. So get the fuck out of here with your bullshit 'both sides are just as bad, you couldn't do that These Days' cause it's fucking *happening*, you can literally do that shit *in the white house,* and appoint supreme court justices who will do that shit from the bench, and one side wants to introduce fascism to the US, and the other side wants you to know that Lovecraft was a racist, and **those are not equivalent fucking problems.**

And in the specific case of Eminem, it's worth noting that Bill Clinton was slagging him off in speeches in the late 90s, the Feds almost certainly opened a file on him when he started going after Bush on his *The Eminem Show* and *Encore* albums, and Trump got so upset by his later work that Em got a visit at his studio from the Secret Service; all *actual* threats of 'cancel culture' that are fucking dangerous coming from government overreach, and mostly from, surprise surprise, the authoritarian right. The other problem with this argument relating to Eminem is that he's still going strong, and still putting out cartoonishly offensive songs, with a level of technical ability so high as to have become peerless. Cancelled by "the wokeratti" my *entire* arse.

And, look, yes, absolutely, *The Marshall Mathers LP* contains a lot of misogyny, and lyrics that describe misogynistic violence. There's also a lot of homophobia, including numerous uses of 'f*g' and variants as an insult, and do I have to say that's clearly Not Okay? Because it's clearly Not Okay, and I'm fine saying it, and I have no interest at all in getting into some spurious justification/apologia about whether or not he 'really means it' or is 'just' saying it for shock value (or even, at the far end, 'playing a homophobic character' which I'm sure someone's tried on as a justification), for the simple reason that, in context, it doesn't make any difference, because it's clear we're meant to laugh along with the homophobe, and not at him, and once more, that's Not Okay, earlier point about taboos notwithstanding.

In fact, let's put a finger right on the squirming hypocrisy of this moment; in the song 'Criminal', Eminem spends the entire first verse on a homophobic (and, in an ahead-of-his-time-in-a-bad-way moment, transphobic) tirade, claiming gay people don't like him not because he's homophobic but because they're 'heterophobic' (and also want to fuck him, obviously). And I want to be clear, here: I do think, like with 'Kill You', he's playing it 'for laughs' (the introduction to 'Criminal' has Em stating 'A lot of people think that because I say something in a record, I believe in it, or I'm really gonna do it'), and I will admit that, like with 'Kill You', I can 'hear' it in both modes, the intended comedic and the grossly offensive and disturbing versions.

But here's the thing: if we're going to defend this song on the basis that it's 'okay' for him to perform this verse because 'freedom of speech, he's playing a character saying slurs' (which in and of itself, yeah, I buy that's what's happening) what are we to make of the moment in the second verse where he edges right up to saying the N word, leaving the tape blank at the crucial moment?

I drink more liquor to fuck you up quicker / Than you'd wanna fuck me up for sayin' the word ...

I feel like with a real commitment to the bit, you say the word. But *of course,* he doesn't. Because, of course, he knows there *are* some things he 'can't' say.

Except that's not quite right. He *could* say it. But he knows that it would be bad. It would have material social consequences. And, presumably, the black artists he had around him made it clear to him that saying that word on a track was a really terrible idea. Or he was bright enough to work it out for himself.

But an entire verse of queer-bashing, using homophobic slurs? Go for your life, mate. And an entire album where women are punchline punchbags? Genius.

And yet. I call myself an Eminem fan. I listen to his music a lot, especially lately.

And I can point to why. He's an insanely talented songwriter and performer, and some of what he does lyrically, here and especially later in his career, leaves me breathless with the skill and audacity deployed. If the word genius has any meaning when applied to art, Eminem is a genius hip-hop artist.

That's not a justification, nor is it an excuse. It's just a thing that's also true.

And I can appreciate and enjoy the man's work without defending the bullshit.

Which brings us neatly to the dark heart of *The Marshall Mathers LP*, and the reason I can justify talking about one of the biggest hip hop albums in the world as part of a book ostensibly about horror. Because *MMLP* contains, for my money, one of the most straight-up brilliant dark non-supernatural short horror stories in all of genre fiction.

It's time to talk about 'Kim'.

Let's first observe, with a dark humour worthy of the subject, that this isn't the first song on which Eminem spins a narrative in which he murders his then-wife, Kim. On *The Slim Shady LP*, there's a track called "'97 Bonnie and Clyde', in which Em baby talks to his infant daughter Hayley, and it gradually becomes apparent that:

- He and Kim have separated
- Kim has hooked up with a new man, who has a son
- Eminem has 'fixed' this by murdering Kim, her new boyfriend/husband, and her new boyfriend/husband's son, and the bodies of all three are in the trunk of the car he's driving
- He's taken Hayley to the pier, where he's going to dump the bodies before driving off with his daughter into the sunset

And it's hilarious.

Okay, okay, sure, humour is subjective, my giggle is your yuck, probably should have gotten into that earlier. If you find ''97 Bonnie and Clyde' horrific and/or disturbing, I'm not going to tell you you're wrong to do so. But I've got to say that it absolutely cracks my shit up.

It's mainly about the deployment of voice, I think. His tone is so soft, loving, cooing at his infant child as she gurgles and giggles, at one point interrupting his flow to ask her if she needs her diaper changing. And that same tone describes momma having 'spilt ketchup down her shirt' and how there's 'a lovely bed for momma at the bottom of the lake' and when I type it out this sounds skin-crawlingly creepy, so maybe I am just a hilariously sick and broken person, but eh, we've come this far; I find it both funny and brilliant. YMMV.

'Kim' starts the same way. A piano plays a melancholic but childish melody, evoking nursery rhymes, and Em's talking-to-baby voice cuts in, describing how his daughter has grown so much, telling his sleeping two-year-old how proud he is of her... And then suddenly he's yelling, angrier than we've ever heard: "Sit down bitch! You move again I'll beat the shit out of you!"

In an album not short of shocking moments, this is next level. All the smirking glee is gone, and what's left is pure fury, hatred. It's the moment in the crime thriller when the mask of the charming stranger slips and we see the killer beneath. As he continues to rant and rave his voice begins to crack, running through a litany of grievances; she's left him, moved her new man into their house. A woman sobs as his fury builds, as he screams at her to "look at your new husband now!" It's not stated explicitly, but the picture is painted; I see him grabbing her head, forcing her to look at the body on the floor, face red and flushed, tears in his eyes, spit flying as he yells. The sound of shattering furniture adds to the scene, as the woman begs him to stop, telling him he's drunk, and that he'll never get away with it. The fear in her voice is absolute, abject; as much a prisoner of miserable emotion as he is; two snarling, sobbing animals.

I realise this is probably a redundant statement, but it's absolutely fucking horrifying.

After a chorus sung in a dead flat monotone that is, if anything, scarier than the yelled verses

("So long, bitch you did me so wrong, I don't wanna go on, living in this world without you") the couple are in a car, driving. He's still yelling, she's still begging for her life; the row is intercut with moments of road rage, Em unravelling, mind racing, distracted, yelling at other drivers, at the song on the radio, at her; there's an absolutely gut sinking moment when he shrieks her name, voice crackling and distorting, before asking, in a quiet, childlike, teary voice "Why don't you like me?" She tries to reply, but he cuts her off, fury building again: "You think I'm ugly, don't you? You think I'm ugly! Get the fuck away from me!"

By this point in my life, as we discussed previously (see Chapter 27), I've already had my one sustained brush with a human being I genuinely believe was both sociopathic and wished me harm, and while the circumstances were very different (and the outcome, of course, considerably less dramatic) I can tell you that the psychological realism of this moment has me fucking reeling every time. It is viscerally, elementally shocking; and, if we're going to be honest (and we should, because the wordcount grows long and the hour late), it's also shocking because while I've never physically attacked anyone in my life outside of self-defence (my preferred outlet for this kind of pain and despair being self-destruction, a path not without its issues but one I find, on the whole, preferable morally), I've sure *felt* angry enough to do so on a few occasions, and this is a pretty accurate description of what the inside of my brain sounded and felt like in those moments of rage.

And, like, here we are, horror fans; is this not (part of) what we're here for? Beyond the sick thrill of getting to witness monstrosity unleashed in a 'safe' environment, aren't we also here to be challenged by these moments of even more sickening recognition, as something of the darkness we are encountering in the text finds a resonating frequency with a darkness within ourselves?

I think so. It's certainly part of what I'm here for, part of why I write horror and dark crime, and it is my sincere wish that at least some of you, sometimes, will wince when you read a tale of mine, not just in sympathetic shock, but also uncomfortable recognition. And, to go even deeper, writing can be an act of radical empathy, an attempt to make sense of that which we don't immediately understand or find relatable; some of my best work, fiction or nonfiction, comes from my reading or seeing something and thinking 'I can't imagine how/why someone would...' and then just digging in and saying 'well, let's find out'.

Kim is absolutely one of the most viscerally disturbing pieces of art I've ever encountered. The fact that Eminem is playing both voices in the song, his own murderously jealous self-destruction and his crying, screaming victim, heightens that skin crawl, as does the fact that Kim is the name of his real-world then-wife. And again, for the avoidance of any doubt, that's a very fucked up thing indeed, and morally reprehensible. Do I think he had the right to write and produce the song? I think so, on balance. Morally, should he have done it? Absolutely fuck no, he shouldn't.

Would I rather he hadn't, then?

Ah, fuck.

Kim is horrific entirely on its own terms, as a depiction of something that happens with depressing regularity: an angry man murdering his wife. It's as raw and unvarnished a depiction of this particular mundane, pervasive toxic masculine horror as I can immediately recall, and when you consider it's happening within the structure of a hip hop song, complete with a need for coherent rhyme scheme, internal rhythm, and all the other structural constraints that implies, I feel like that makes the case for describing this piece as an authentic masterpiece. It's also a song written by a man about his real-life wife, at a point when their marriage was in turmoil, in part because of infidelity and incidences of domestic violence and abuse on both sides.

Here's where it gets super, super messy. Because the invocation of Eminem's rage, both in the lyrics and performance, comes from what sounds and feels like an authentic place. It's the guts of the power of the piece. At the same time, when it was recorded and released, a real-life actual woman had to deal with her megastar husband putting out a song which depicts him dragging her out into a forest and cutting her throat. And at the risk of repeating the endlessly obvious, that is incredibly fucked up and wrong and hurtful and he shouldn't have done it.

And *Kim* is a masterpiece – of hip hop, of storytelling, of horror, of performance art.

And it may sound like a copout, but what I really want is a world where people aren't so fucked up that this horror is a part of everyday life. I want a world where jealous husbands murdering their wives is exclusively an occurrence of fiction, as opposed to an annual statistic that makes me want to see the entire species wiped out and go back in time to single-cell organisms and just figure out a whole different way to get to guitar solos and chips that doesn't also contain All This. And I do not accept that it's some irreducible part of our nature to be like this, either. The fuck away from me with that defeatist, hand washing, fash adjacent essentialist bullshit.

Ramsey Campbell says of horror that it is the one genre where it is sometimes permissible to go Too Far. I don't think there is a reasonable yardstick by which anyone could claim *Kim*, and by extension, *The Marshall Mathers LP* as a whole, doesn't go Too Far.

Was there a way a version of this song could exist that hadn't targeted and traumatised a real-life woman? I feel like the answer has to be yes, but I can't actually say that for sure, because Eminem's creative process is utterly inaccessible to me. So much of what he does is excoriating self-exploration, he's such a prominent character in his own work, that it's impossible to say he could have accessed the same emotional depth if he hadn't put her in the song. And if his creative process is such that abstraction wouldn't have worked, should he simply have not written it, not recorded it, not put it out?

I think, morally, on balance, yes, he shouldn't have.

Would I be without it?

Reader, judge me if you will, but I would not.

I would not.

PS: My friend, Holly, is about to produce the best piece of sustained critical writing on the work of Eminem the planet has ever seen. Follow her now on Twitter – @fireh9lly – so you're set for when the awesome starts flowing. You won't regret it.

I NEVER HAD A SON

GANGS OF NEW YORK

A love story this time, as we start to round the final bend.

It's the winter of 2003, and my living arrangements have gotten... interesting. Having relocated from London to Milton Keynes, in the successful pursuit of indoor work with no heavy lifting, the guitarist from my first band, his girlfriend and I are living in a huge two-storey terraced house in an area of town the landlady optimistically calls 'up and coming'. It's walking distance from work, which is nice, and the rent split three ways is cheap, and it's big.

But not, it's transpiring, big enough for the three of us.

The Girlfriend and I, predictably enough, do not get on. She's a neat freak, I'm kind of a slob. She's a big fan of passive aggression, and while I can ignore it when aimed against her chap, I can't tolerate it coming my way, and she increasingly can't control herself.

And then, there's Bill.

Bill is a refugee from The Girlfriend's place of work. He's seventeen or eighteen, and literally the red headed stepson. And he does not get on with his stepdad. The Girlfriend asks if he can stay in the spare room on the ground floor for a while, and of course we say yes, and of course once he's in, well, he's in.

He's not a bad kid, to be clear. In fact, I grow to really like him. He has a tendency to get into scraps of a weekend, he smokes copious amounts of weed, but he also shares generously, and never brings the aggro home, and what the hell, he's young and adrift and a bit angry, and I'm never going to seriously condemn someone for any of that.

Anyhow.

As relations deteriorate in the house, between myself and The Girlfriend, and from there with The Guitarist, I see less of Bill – Bill and The Guitarist by this time being weed brothers, and me only ever a very occasional smoker, it was inevitable, really. Still, we remain friendly. And my recollection is I recommended the movie to him, even though I'd yet to see it.

Nope, I couldn't tell you why. But that's what happened.

And he went to see it.

And he loved it.

I mean, as in, it was all he could go on about the next time we met. Being, well, who he was, he couldn't go a great job of articulating why it was so good – bless him, he knew it too, and his frustration was palpable – but, well, passion has its own language, and it was clear this movie had done a pretty serious number on him. So, having talked him into seeing it, he went on to talk me into it.

So I went. And I saw.

And I, too, fell in love.

Goddamn, this movie. I mean, it has its critics, and it's hardly considered a classic of the director's work, but holy shit, what an energy, a ferocity, this thing has. The opening sells it completely, this huge, rotting structure of timber peopled with dirty, desperate people. The camera just pulls back and back and back, revealing bedlam. It's kinetic chaos, way too much going on, swarming, noisy. And yeah, it feels like you can almost smell the worked-in grime.

I remember Liam Neeson, in leather armour cut to represent a priest's robes, entrusting his medallion to his son ("Who is this, boy?" "St. Michael!" "And what did he do?" "He cast Satan out of paradise!" "Good boy!").

(Brief digression – there's a fun synchronicity regarding Neeson, here the slain father figure and cause of Leo's long quest for vengeance, given how much he will later become the face and voice of THE revenge flick of the last ten years, *Taken*.)

The priest leads a parade through this murky torch-lit underworld, more and more figures joining his ranks, all tooled up for hand-to-hand combat. The drums are drumming, the pipes are blowing, and the air crackles with violence. They take communion, and then a final mercenary waits by the door. After a brief exchange, the priest and he agree a price per head, and then the door is kicked open...

It's a huge city square, under a blanket of snow. It's breath-taking. The army marches out, lines up. Plumes of mist as they breathe, waiting.

They wait. And then, the Natives arrive.

They are led by a tall man, made even taller by the stovepipe hat. He has a classic silent movie villain moustache, and his face is hard. He also has a glass eye with an American eagle at the centre.

He and the priest regard each other across the tundra.

At first, his gang seems pitifully outnumbered by the Catholic army. His men resemble him, similar stove pipes, blue striped trousers, military style tunics. Then, more appear. Many more. They emerge from the buildings, like termites pouring from a mound, all armed with brutal looking, crude melee weapons, and by the time they are lined up, they fill the widescreen.

I remember my mouth dry, hairs on my arms standing up, scalp fucking tingling. Utterly transfixed.

The two leaders exchange dialogue, making it clear this is a turf war to decide ("for good and all") who control the area of the city known as The Five Points. The man with the stovepipe hat invokes God, asking him to guide his hand as he strikes down his enemies. Liam Neeson pulls a long dagger from his staff and yells "prepare to receive the true Lord!"

And then, all hell breaks loose.

The two armies collide and it's just fucking carnage. Blood flies. Skulls are fractured. Ears are bitten off. Men are stabbed, beaten, bludgeoned. The snow turns brown with mud, crimson with spilt blood. A man is fish-hooked, his cheek pulled from inside until it splits. Through it all, the man with the glass eye and the priest move towards each other, dispatching members of the opposing army en route, before clashing. The combat is brief, and at the end, Liam Neeson is impaled through the chest on the end of the other man's knife. His son watches on, tears in his eyes, as the other man stops the fight, before executing the priest.

And ten minutes into *Gangs Of New York*, I've fallen in love.

I really can't do justice to the epic scale of this movie in words. And frankly, nor can the DVD release. This is a cinema film and it demands the cinema experience. It really is the only context under which it makes sense. It's massive, overwhelming, and that only works if you're in an environment where it *can* overwhelm you. Daniel Day Lewis got some stick for the hamminess of his performance, but it's only hammy on the small screen. When his leering face fills the entire wall, sneering out at you with such clarity that you can see small blobs of wax in his moustache hair, it manages to go through big and out the other side; it utterly transcends camp and becomes terrifying. Bill the Butcher is one of THE great movie villains, for me – not least because he doesn't remotely see himself as a villain.

And really, I spent the rest of the movie in a state of shock as it battered me, with the soundtrack, the setting – my God, the setting! – the performances. I am not a big DiCaprio fan, and I think he's the weak link in the film, especially the second half, but he's good enough, and everyone else is so far off the chart good that it simply doesn't matter. Also, it becomes clearer and clearer as the story goes on that he's not necessarily the hero anyway – more just another rat caught in the trap of history, of violence, of fury and vengeance.

Because the real monster, the real horror of the story, isn't Bill the Butcher, or the gangs in general.

History is the real monster that sits at the centre of this tale, the bloody beast with chomping jaws and an insatiable appetite for human flesh. It is merciless, and by the end of the running time almost every character we meet that isn't killed by it will be permanently disfigured.

That which doesn't kill us, makes us older, and sadder, and weaker.

There's a microcosm within the movie itself, told in a single tracking shot that for my money is Scorsese's finest – better even than the moment when Henry Hill and Karen walk through the back door of the Copacabana in *Goodfellas*. Yeah, really.

The shot starts with the immigrants from Ireland, coming off the boats at the docks. It follows them as they shuffle in a line off the ships into the waiting arms of the army recruiters, who are signing them up to go and fight The South. The camera pans over from that queue to the next, showing more men, now lined up in their uniforms, boarding another boat to take them to the fighting. As the camera pans over them and up to the boat, an Irish voice says "Do you think they'll feed us now?" As the words, plaintive and resigned, reach our ears, the camera pans up for the grizzly punchline – the coffins being unloaded from that same boat, returning the fallen to New York.

And of course, worse is to come, as Leo first befriends Bill the Butcher, and then is betrayed to him, before finally raising his own army to take on the man who killed his father, while in the background the rumblings and anxieties of the population explode into the draft riots. It's another mesmerising, breath-taking sequence, Scorsese pulling out all the stops as only he can, the cutting, music, action creating a symphony of discordant, nightmarish violence before the union conscripts arrive back in their hometown and simply gun down the rioters in the street.

Like I always say, you can't make up a horror story that can hold a candle to human history – a point underlined with brutal poignancy in the closing shot of the movie. The graves of Bill the Butcher and The Priest are slowly overgrown by weeds, as a series of fades shows the bridge, river, and landscape transform from the mouldering slums to the Manhattan skyline. And there's a final blow, as the very last crossfade shows the twin towers reaching into the sky and out of shot, before the final fade to black. And I have no idea if that was always the final shot and they just left it in, or if it was a last-minute addition, but I have to tell you, in January 2002 it packed one hell of a punch.

Ah, who am I kidding? It still does.

It's a long movie – but I have to say, it didn't feel long. Epic, but not long. I was utterly transfixed, and I knew when I left the cinema that I had to go and see it again.

And I did. Three more times. It's the only movie I've seen that many times at the cinema, and I bitterly regret not going more. Because it's utterly a cinema movie, and the small screen – even the big small screens of today, with the surround sound and sub – do not, cannot, convey the power of this film.

Some things, only cinema can do. *Gangs Of New York* is one of Scorsese's best movies, and one of the finest horror movies ever made. But if you've only seen it on the small screen, you'll never understand why.

You really had to be there, I guess.

NO TURNING BACK

THE GHOST

Content note: frank discussion and description of child sexual exploitation and abuse.

And I'll never forget the way I feel right now... with you... no way...

I'm somewhere between 16 and 19.

I'm lying in his bed. It's early afternoon and I haven't been awake long. I have, blessedly, nothing to do, and nowhere to be. No college to go to, no parents to bug me, no flatmates to wind up or disappoint.

I'm free.

I stick on Meatloaf's *Bat Out of Hell II* album and slide back under the thick, warm duvet, light up a Marlboro Red, and let the music wash over me.

Later, I'll say to The Ghost's roommate (a kind and blameless man, to be clear – he didn't know what was going on, and how could he? I didn't either) how great it is to smoke a cigarette whilst listening to Meatloaf after a long sleep, and he'll tip me a wink and grin and say something like 'it's even better if you've had a reason to wake up!' and I'll grin and nod back and work out his actual meaning about a day and a half later.

But that's later. For now, I'm in that room, in that warm bed, drawing the smoke deep into my lungs, snuggled in the warmth of the sheets.

The Ghost is an early riser. I am, at this point in my life, not so much a night owl as a creature of chaos living a series of 28-30 hour days. There's a mattress on the floor, my 'official' bed, but I'll often share his, or else take his spot when his early start inevitably wakes me, preferring the firmness of his mattress, and the thickness of his duvet.

I remember the smell. In the room itself, it should be air freshener vs. cigarette ash, a titanic, whoever-wins-we-lose battle for the ages, but it isn't somehow... or at least, not to me and my smoker's nose. I like it. And then there's the smell of him on the sheets; soap and store own-brand deodorant with just the mildest undercurrent of his own odour.

This smell, too, I like. It's a smell of comfort. Of safety.

Of love.

At this point, we've been together for somewhere between five and seven years. In this room, so much of my ultimately futile magical training will take place.

Hanging from the wardrobe door is an oil painting his brother made. It depicts the flying creature from the Donington '94 Monsters Of Rock poster, complete with the circled, winged A symbol of that year's headliner, Aerosmith. We'd attended that show together, camping out the night before. It was one of the best live shows of my life.

On my left, in the space where the fireplace used to be in this Victorian London house, is his altar. There is a chalice, a tarot card (The Magician, of course), other things I can't recall, probably an owl ornament of some kind, and a bronze spearhead.

I grew up around altars. My mum had one. I, at this point, have one. It's normal.

One evening, before or after this cigarette, this morning, we will be having one of our rambling conversations, and he will ask me about my night owl ways, and I, full of teenage bullshit romanticism and faux darkness, will describe Night as containing "a wondrous savagery".

The Ghost straightens up, becomes commanding. "Come here". I'm in bed, in just my boxer shorts, or possibly nude ('anyone who sleeps in clothes when they don't have to is an idiot', he's always insisted) but I immediately go to him.

"Turn around."

I do. He takes my shoulders, pulling me back and down, so I'm sat on the edge of his bed, facing the wall, back to him. He moves away, rummages. I sit, looking forward, waiting. This is instruction, he's in Telling Mode

(earlier, he'll tell me about The Voice, the power to command – his gran had it, he explains, and it's something he can do too; he'll claim he used it on me when he caught me attempting to steal his cigarettes in my mum's house, and I'll believe him)

and so I wait.

His arm comes into view over my shoulder. He's holding the arrowhead in his fist.

(it has Celtic designs on it. He claims it's ancient, that he found it hiking on Dartmoor. I believe him)

He presses the tip to the centre of my chest, not hard. The cold, blunt, rounded point of metal rests at the top of my collarbone. Then, slowly but deliberately, the point moves down. It traces the central divide of my ribcage, then down to my stomach. He brings it to rest just above my belly button. He holds it there. Then he says okay.

His arm goes away. I turn around. As he replaces the arrowhead on the altar, he explains: that my statement had made him worry that I might be moving toward The Dark, that what just happened was a test, "nobody of The Dark would allow that, you'd have stopped me when it was clear where it was going, you wouldn't have been able to help yourself".

He asks me how I'd felt during the test. I tell him the truth; that I felt calm, but at a heightened, elevated level; intense. He nods, smiles, happy.

I think we smoke. I ask him what would have happened if I had reacted, pulled away. He tells me our training would have trailed off gradually, and he'd have found a way to drift away from me. I accept this without further question.

In this room, he'll lead me on many guided meditations, attempting to get me to astral project; the breakthrough proof he knows I'm craving, that will move the magic from something I desire and infer to something tangible. In this room, he'll explain to me how lowering my inhibitions is crucial to my obtaining the openness I need to let go. In this room, under his verbal guidance, and the power of my own imagination, I'll experience something agonisingly close to the things he's described to me in vivid detail, only to find myself surrounded by a roaring, booming sound that starts me out of my trance. He'll explain it was my heart; that I'd Travelled Within, as the meditation led me to, but I'd ended up inside a chamber of my heart, and the experience had overwhelmed me. He'll tell me I'm really close to a breakthrough, though in reality, this is as near as I ever get.

In this room, he'll tell me to masturbate in the bed on the floor, while he lies in his own bed.

He'll tell me it's part of the training. That sexual energy is a kind of magic, and masturbation is a way to channel it. He'll advise me that there might be magical spells or rites I'll be able to complete as part of sexual congress with my then-girlfriend, if I want – "you might be sitting face to face, fully inside her, but not moving" I remember him saying, a stray fragment from conversations in The Room.

He'll tell me, too, that my own sexual energy is potent, can affect the mood of others. One evening, after I've masturbated, lying on the mattress on the floor next to his bed, he'll tell me about how he'd heard the man in the flat upstairs reinitiate sex with his girlfriend, triggered by my jerking it in the room below. I believe him. Later, I'll try and deploy this power to get his flatmate to go to bed with his girlfriend so I can play on his PC, jerking off in the bathroom next to the living room where his flatmate and the computer are situated. I will be disappointed when it doesn't work, and when I tell The Ghost, so is he.

In this room, he'll give me instructions on how to masturbate better. He's backed me into a rhetorical corner, by this point: there's no logical reason for me to resist the lesson. It won't be sexual for either one of us, and he's concerned I might be hurting myself, wants to help.

As I present my erect penis to him, he explains that the skin is unusually tight and that I should be gentle to avoid chafing. I can't remember much of what he told me; I can mainly recall how my concentration was on breathing normally, treating the situation with casual indifference, no big deal. I do remember at one point his finger touches me, as he points out an area of particular sensitivity.

Two decades later, I'll see the two women police officers exchange a glance at the moment I describe this, an unspoken communication passing between them.

In this room, we'll have countless conversations. I'll pour out my heart, my desires, my hopes, my fears. We'll talk about things fantastic and mundane.

Among many other things – computer games and role-playing games, and music, and books – we'll talk about maturity and the age of consent.

He'll patiently explain to me that it's arbitrary; that different people mature, physically and emotionally, at different ages, so the law just draws a line because it has to be drawn somewhere, and that's okay, because children do have to be protected against predators.

He really doesn't like paedophiles.

In one of our conversations, he claims he, with some friends (the implication is magical friends, fellow shamen, but I can't remember now if he ever made that explicit) castrated a paedophile once, in Ireland. I don't remember if I asked if the man survived, or what his reply was. I suspect I didn't ask. I suspect I just nodded at this obviously just turn of events.

Anyhow. Consent is important. Consent is *key*. Physical and emotional maturity might make a sexual relationship possible, but never without consent. Rapists must die.

How old, he asks me, must someone be before a sexual relationship can be considered?

I know it sounds like a copout, but I swear it's the truth – I cannot remember what reply 16, or 17, or at the outside 18-year-old me gave.

But I do remember his answer.

Twelve years old. Not, in point of fact, because of physical or emotional considerations, it turns out (some girls start puberty as young as nine, he tells me, and I nod, believing him), but because 'nobody under the age of twelve can be trusted to keep it secret'.

Yeah.

What about your childhood? It's defective!

I was ten years old, I think, when I first met The Ghost.

I met him at a Live Roleplaying event put on by my local youth theatre group (see Chapter 18). He was attached by some means to a local troop, even though he was living in London at the time. I can't remember, now, what his role was; he had a wizard character who was quite powerful and involved in that system, but was he any part of that first event? As I think more, I suspect not. Kez was, for sure – a bear of a man who had the job of guide for our party. And that event was the primary vs teenager theatre kids, and they massacred us in the final encounter.

Yeah, I think maybe The Ghost wasn't at that event, but a later one.

Anyway, the LARP bug had well and truly bitten, and for the next ten years, attending LARP weekend events would be a significant part of my social calendar.

And The Ghost would take me.

It's the summer of 1992. I am 14 years old.

Summerfest has loomed large in my imagination since I first heard the name; a vast event taking in thousands of attendants for a weekend of drinking, bonfires, and latex swords and silly costumes. It sounded like heaven, and The Ghost, possibly already dating my mother at this point, scores permission to take me. Due to a political and/or rules-based schism, a new group is formed, and so, for my first large event, I am attending not Summerfest, but The Gathering – the first event to hold this name.

In the long car journey from North Devon to the Derbyshire scout camp that hosts the event, I smoke my first cigarette (see Chapter 13).

I just ask him if I can have one, and he says yes. I smoke it like I know what I'm doing, but of course, I don't, and when I confess at the end it was my first, he tells me he knew. I remember the feeling so clearly; a warmth in my cheeks, the flush of the forbidden, the comforting smell of tobacco smoke, now reborn as a taste, my mouth full of saliva.

"If you start to feel like you actually need them, cut back, and if you feel your breathing being affected, just stop," is his sage advice. I nod. When I get home and tell Bev and Freddie, they'll both be delighted, and we'll immediately form the village underage smokers club, sneaking cigarettes from the vending machine in the village pub – Marlboro Reds, same as Slash smoked.

...I want to show you how to use it...

Either that trip, or the next one, we'll become blood brothers.

We've been talking about it for months. He's told me all about it; how we're both old souls, who have shared many past lives together. "In many of those lives, we've been lovers. You can call me a dirty old man, I don't care" he says at one point, defiant.

I don't say it. I don't even think it.

I don't want a physical relationship, but I do love him. It's all the clichés you'd expect; he combines the best elements of my mates with all the advantages of being a Grown Up. Sure, access – to cigarettes, whiskey, LARP events, concerts, plus a pretty mean music collection on cassette. But it's not just that. It's access to wisdom. The Ghost *knows* stuff. He's *from* the adult world, but not really *of* it; he tells me what my secret heart already knows; that all that grown-up bullshit is bullshit; magic is real, hidden just beneath the surface, and those of us that can do it, ah... the rules don't have to apply to us. And of course, I'm not just a magician, but one of unusual power; there are just seven this generation that have the kind of power I do, and I haven't been this powerful since I was Taliesin.

And he and I have known each other before. Life and life again, we find each other. Sometimes men, sometimes women, sometimes one of each. Always friends, always together, often lovers.

And I feel it.

So we do the ceremony. Naked, at his insistence, we sit in the tent, facing each other, lit by candle flame. We use needles in our fingertips to draw the blood we mingle. "Normally, at the end, we'd have an open-mouthed kiss. To prove our trust in each other," he'd told me earlier, and I'd snorted before replying "yeah, that's not going to happen". We do, however, embrace, naked in the tent, blood brothers now, the ceremony completed again, ensuring the cycle will perpetuate, and we'll be reconnected in the next life.

We sleep together, naked, in two sleeping bags zipped together. We smoke in the pitch dark, and he teaches me to read symbols in the glow of the ember.

...it'll kill you right back...

It's the summer after, 1993. I am fifteen years old. Two amazing live shows in the space of a week – my beloved Guns N' Roses, on the third leg of their mammoth *Use Your Illusion* tour, with The Cult as the main support band, and Metallica touring the black album (with Megadeth in tow) the following Saturday. I'm fifteen years old. I go to these shows with friends. The Ghost is not in attendance. I stay with my father, and I have an amazing time at both gigs.

In the week in between, The Ghost takes me to another show. Ugly Kid Joe, at The Island in Islington. Screaming Jets in support.

At the show, there is a group of girls, a similar age to me. I think they are beautiful. The conversation starts teasing, but they actually warm up to me after a while. I tell them The Ghost is my father, and that he lets me smoke. They're venue regulars, and they flat-out do not believe Ugly Kid Joe are actually playing there. "They won't show up, I mean, why would they?", she insists.

But they do, and It Is Good.

After, we're walking back. I remember – God, it's wild, what comes back – passing a Burger King, the lights on, but the door locked. A leather-jacketed man rattles the door angrily, drawing wary glances from the staff inside. He turns to his companion, and with a tone of whining exasperation and an angry smile says "If they'd just had a little imagination…!"

On the way back, I talk about the girls a lot, excited. They really seemed to like me. I wonder if we could go back sometime. He demurs, saying the acts there are usually dance bands. I cool on the idea quickly, but not without regret. He laughs and says "anyway, you're getting a bit ambitious for someone that hasn't even painted the ceiling yet!"

I'm taken back to The Ghost's house. He lives with his parents in a block of flats. He explains that they're not here, and they don't know I'm staying. He explains that he won't tell them, because his dad's brother had a thing for boys, and so his parents were hypervigilant about that kind of thing.

I smile, laugh, nod.

We share a bed that night. Naked. We laugh and joke around. At one point, he pulls me onto his chest, so we're lying face to face, me on top of him. "Come here!" he says. "Why?" I ask. "Because I want to control you!" he says, still smiling.

Something in my stomach flips over.

I say something, and flee the bed. He immediately apologises, says it was a joke. He says my reaction is good, he says it was a test, and I've passed. He says that if I'd responded positively, he'd have known he was on for a love affair, rather than a magical trainee. "It's a shame, though, I could have done with a love affair," he says, mock wistfully, and I laugh at his silliness.

And looking back on moments like this, knowing what I know now, for just a second, I can feel a glimpse of what it must have been like, for him. What he must have imagined, desperately hoped, was about to happen there. I don't know if he really loved me – to be honest, I'm not sure he's capable of love, in a way you or I would recognise – but I do believe that he *believed* that he loved me, and that his desire came from that love. It's the only way I can make sense of his fetishisation of consent; though as I type that, of course, it's possible it was nothing more than survival instinct, right? Consent makes the waters muddy, if it ever comes to that; gives shame as leverage, makes talking at all less likely.

Let's face it, I was never supposed to write this down. You were never supposed to read it.

The next morning, the conversation ends up coming around to self-defence, a perennial obsession of mine at that age, in the final year of an unhappy school career. He says he can help with that. He holds a large cushion against the wall and instructs me to punch it.

Naked, of course. So he can properly see what my body is doing, how it moves. Boxers often train naked, he assures me.

I believe him.

... they'll never let a night like tonight go to waste...

It's the only way it'll work, he tells me. We're back in The Room.

The meditations are going nowhere; following the Big Heart moment, I can't get close to that state again. I'm frustrated. So is he.

He insists the issue is sexual. By this stage, I have a girlfriend. In point of fact, he's in my home, the night I lose my virginity, and the following morning, he sits on the end of the single bed we're curled up in, beaming with pride. That she took this in her stride seemed inconsequential at the time, and seems nothing short of miraculous today.

Anyway.

I need to 'really let go'. I can't do that with her, but I can with him, because he'll let me. He lays it out. "You can do whatever you want. If you want to touch me, you can. If you want me to touch you, I will. If you want to penetrate me, you can. If you want me to penetrate you, absolutely not." It will be safe, he insists. I need it, he is clear, and it's the only way it'll work.

And there's simply no way.

The proposition is the opposite of appealing. I don't want to 'let go', be out of control sexually. Why would I? Why would anyone? I've only been having sex for five minutes, but it's already clear to me that the more attentive and responsive you are, the better for both of you. And anyway, it's *him,* and as much as I love him there's not a single remote spark of physical attraction.

Do I want the astral projection, that power, that proof? Sure... but, you know, not *that* much.

I've been unsparing in terms of showing you my credulity to this point, but I have to give myself a bit of credit, here; I was firmly in touch with my own desires and, despite years of careful path laying and preparation and manipulation and lies, despite that enormous investment of time, and energy, and imagination, it all crashed against the solid wall of implacable Do Not Want, leaving not so much as a mark.

I don't know for sure where that selfish, unmovable core came from, but, obviously, I'm grateful.

There's much more I could tell, but this book is already running long, and honestly, I don't think he's worth it. But I do need to share one further moment because it's very, very instructive; and a big part of me finally writing this out is, as always, an attempt to answer a question. Unusually for this series, however, the question this time isn't 'why', but 'how'.

So.

...baby, we could talk all night...

It's sometime between 2009 and 2010. I'm married, and settled, baby on the way or possibly recently arrived. And I get a phone call out of the blue from one of the old LARP crew that's stayed in touch.

And he's got questions for me about The Ghost.

Turns out, The Ghost has gotten cosied up with another family. This time, it's a girl child he's getting close to. The parents are concerned; the kid won't talk.

And it's at *that* moment, over twenty years after we first met, ten years after I stopped living with him in London, in the flat we shared and split the rent and ran D&D games and bickered like an old married couple as we drifted apart; as I became more and more aware of how regularly and pointlessly he lied, about everything; as any talk of magic and magical training faded before drying up entirely; ten fucking years after we parted, still on friendly terms, still Facebook friends, still the guy I thought of as my brother...

It's that exact fucking moment, and not one second before, that the scales fall.

And, you know, I've gotten better at this writing gig, thanks in no small part to eight years at this particular coal face (thanks again, Jim), but, sorry, gang, I cannot fully put it into words what that moment did to me. Hell, real talk, what it's *still* doing to me.

Because, all at once, it was so gobsmackingly obvious – what he'd really been, what he'd done, what I'd almost done – that the overriding initial tide of emotion that hit me – before the shame, before the baffled anger, before the sorrow – was *embarrassment.*

'You were a kid. You couldn't have known. You're not supposed to need to. That's how it works.' Well-meaning loved ones and counsellors. And of course, they're not wrong... but it didn't happen to them. It happened to me.

And I fucking should have known.

I should have. It was screamingly obvious. I mean, you've come this far, you know. And, not a clue; not as a kid (understandable), but also not as a grown ass, in-his-thirties-with-a-wife-and-career-and-kids adult; and that's the part that's still a little hard to swallow, some nights.

And then there's the guilt.

As you'll have gathered, I went to the police, the phone call from my friend ringing in my ears. The two officers were incredibly sympathetic and sensitive. I told as much of the story as I could remember – less than I've told tonight, as I've had more time, since, to think about it, and the events that surrounded it, to piece together at least some of the chronology – but enough.

A couple of weeks later, I get a phone call from another officer. They tell me they're not pressing charges. They interviewed him, and he denied everything, and it's word against word, and that's it. They were tempted to go for it anyway, they said, because I was a compelling witness, but in the end they felt without a single piece of corroborating evidence there was no way forward.

I think about that a lot. About the fake secret I knew I was carrying, and the real secret I didn't. How he hid in plain sight so well, I couldn't see it until I found out I was neither the first, nor the last.

Yeah, I think about that a lot, when I can't help it.

The police said they'd keep my testimony on file; they'd made it clear to him that they had an eye on him, and he was no longer welcome at live role-playing events. "You came forward because you thought it might corroborate what was going on with someone else, but sadly it looks like it's the other way around" said the officer on the phone; or something very like that, anyway.

And at some point came the twist of the knife I should have expected. The officer told me that The Ghost had denied it all, of course, and then; "he did say that he'd always thought of you as like a younger brother".

Yeah. Yeah, me too, you fucker.

Me too.

Anyway.

Oh, he had at least one prior conviction for child sex offences, I learned that, too. That's where the 'not the first' revelation came from. And if the stories his daughter told me are true – and I have no reason to disbelieve her – his father was also an abuser. I remember replaying the conversation in his parents' flat, about the dodgy uncle.

Right there, in plain sight. Fucking hell.

I don't know what happened with the family he was cosying up to, the child he'd clearly started working on. They were not people I knew or had direct contact with. I don't have their names. I do know he vanished from social media days after I went to the cops, and my understanding is that he can no longer take part in UK LARP events, though I don't know how they'd enforce that.

I suppose, technically, I don't know if he's alive or dead. Though my money's on alive. Sure, he was starting to develop a middle-age spread by the time we parted company, but he was in pretty good shape. Maybe the smokes got him in the end, or will do soon; but I think, if he were gone, word would have gotten back to me by now. Hell, there's even a part of me, a holdover from that believer kid, that thinks I'll know, when it does finally happen.

Still, I hope he is dead, or dying. Not because the thought gives me any satisfaction – I'd say if it did, without shame, it just doesn't – but for a simpler reason; once he's dead, he can't do it anymore.

Because that's the weight of this thing that I can't ever quite shift. I remember a friend actually saying to me "I don't feel safe having him around my niece" and thinking, hard, and replying "I don't think he'd do anything intentionally to harm her", and God help me, I meant it, and what the fuck does that say about me? I knew about everything you've read above, and I fucking said that. And, you know, not for nothing, but I went through an aggressive, ugly New Atheist phase, around 9/11, and somehow I was also carrying this entire doublethink about my 'brother' in my head that exact same time, and I dunno, you guys, I think maybe, in certain fundamental and important respects, I'm just not that bright.

...endless winters, and the dreams would freeze...

I don't like knowing he's still out there, and still a danger, that's the beginning and end of it.

And I guess this is where we draw the lesson, right? And I think – *I think* – the lesson might be this: no secrets.

Or. no, that's too proscriptive; too radical, even for the guy who wrote *A Song For The End*.

Okay, how about this? Interrogate your secrets; especially the secrets others want you to keep.

Because it felt so plausible. That's the thing. Because I was bright, and imaginative, and angry, and rebellious, and a kid. And because he knew just what to say. "You know if you'd been into football, it'd have been football", a wise friend told me, and she was right, of course, but I couldn't see how it was tailored for me, because it *was* tailored for me; such a perfect fit, I'd wear it long and far past the point I should have known better.

There's one last thing I've got to share, too, because it's too perfectly macabre, and I'm a horror writer, but also, it's a true thing, and it's this: increasingly, I look like him.

I've got long hair (though mine is already thinner than his was, damn his eyes). I've got the glasses. Since lockdown and working from home, I've even started working on the belly, now I'm not cycling 40 miles a week in commute. And when the beard's short, it's okay, but I gotta tell you, lately, when it fills out, and I catch myself in the mirror… well.

Because I'm about the age he was when he met me.

And that's when the sadness comes in.

What I think is, he was empty, in some fundamental way. Empty in a way that can't be fixed, can't be filled. I don't think he was capable of love, as you or I would understand it.

But I was. I am.

And I loved him.

And that's why nobody knew what was going on. Because *I* didn't know what was going on. Because I trusted him, and I loved him, and so I knew the secrets he needed me to keep were good, were right.

I dunno. I'd hoped when I got to this point, I'd have something useful to say. I'd imagined there'd be something I could say to the parents and kids who don't know they've invited a predator into their lives; some wisdom from what I lived through that might stop some kid from making bad choices, or help twitch the antenna of some well-meaning parent.

I really thought I'd get there.

Well, okay, how about this? My sister – who knew nothing of any of this until decades later – told my mum, at the time The Ghost was courting her, that if he moved in, she'd run away. And Mum broke off the relationship, though whether or not it was in response to that, I don't know, and frankly don't want to ask, at this distance.

But.

She didn't know. Obviously.

But she knew *something*.

And who knows how this story plays out, if he'd moved in?

I'll say this too, for whatever it's worth, and if you've come this far, you may see this as a weakness or defect rather than a strength, and fine, whatever, but; I refuse to reject my capacity to love. Because love may have trapped me into lying for someone who didn't have my best interests at heart... but it also saved me, over and over. And it's still saving me, as I spend the rest of my life wrestling with the fact that the most important relationship to me, in my most formative years, was with a man who was a pathological liar with a sexual interest in children.

...does it get any better, can it get any worse?

I am acutely aware that, as I type this, there are people – children and adults alike – who are suffering at a level that renders what I've described as trivial. I say that neither to aggrandise or diminish my own story, merely to acknowledge reality. I wouldn't wish what was done to me upon anyone, and I was profoundly lucky, and both these things are true.

Just… look out for each other, okay?

And okay, maybe, maybe…

Maybe we need to be even more fearless about expressing what we know to be true.

Because this is a dark time; maybe the darkest our species, and our planet, has endured since a big space rock did for the dinosaurs. Our kids, if they live at all, are going to live through cataclysms not merely outside of living memory, but actually unprecedented. And, as a father, I can relate on a cellular level to the desire to protect, to shield.

But.

I think, maybe, that's not always the best way to go.

Because I think, maybe, that if we resist that urge, and instead speak painful truths, we'll give those kids a fighting chance to be the beacons of hope we're all desperately going to need, in the decades we're cursed to face.

And, as an added bonus, we will, hopefully, leave them less vulnerable to those skilled, brilliant operators who will mix lies with truth, in service of appetites incomprehensible to those of us with souls. Because, while such people are blessedly rare, they do exist, and left unchecked, they can do an awful lot of damage.

And I feel like that's probably worth doing. Given where we are.

…objects in the rearview mirror may appear closer than they are…

Thanks for coming this far. Good luck out there.

PS: There are a few – a vanishingly few, I suspect – who knew me back then and might come across this. Know that I'm okay, and also, respectfully, I don't want to talk about it. If you know, you know. If not… let's leave it here, okay? Thank you.

STILL, IT WOULD BE SUCH A LOVELY RIDE

'THAT HELLBOUND TRAIN'

Let's end with something short and sweet. The first short horror story I can remember reading.

Most of the recreational time at my father's house was spent in front of screens, both big and small. In my day-to-day life in Devon, trips to the cinema were financially impossible; hell, as we discussed back in Volume I, TV didn't actually enter my life until well into my seventh year. But at Dad's house there were cinema trips (and theatre trips, though truthfully they made less of an impression), a big old colour TV with a VHS player, *and* my beloved ZX Spectrum. This last was, in the fullness of time, replaced by an Amiga 500, and I think if you'd asked me, I'd have told you I'd have been happy to sit and play that thing until the end of time, with just the odd breaks for eating, sleeping, and so forth.

Only, you know, not really. Turns out, somewhere around the fourth or fifth day, my mind would crave something different.

When the urge hit, I'd leave the ground floor bedroom that housed the Amiga, and walk into the room next door. Which contained the piano, and, more importantly, two walls of bookcases.

I think I've mentioned earlier in this series that my father's current house actually contains a room called 'the small library', and yes, that is to differentiate it from the main library one floor up. The set up in this house of my childhood was marginally less grand; still, though, there were a *lot* of books. I have fond memories of two paperback runs in particular; the minimalist black and white Iain Banks collection (yes, this is where I scored that fateful copy of *The Wasp Factory*, see Volume I for more), and the glorious Josh Kirby Discworld covers. In due course, I'd tear through both collections, and Jim Thompson, James Ellroy and Elmore Leonard besides, and I learned a lot from all of them.

But this particular day – I suspect I'm shy of ten years old – none of them jump out at me. Instead, I'm drawn to a pile of annual-sized books piled on their side. Asterix? Tintin? Something in that wheelhouse, I think.

And then, next to them, I see…

What is that? The cover says *Venture,* and it's just about book-thick, but the size is all wrong. Plus the cover – a colour image of an old, white man's face surrounded by stars, under a title in yellow letters (*Space is a lonely place*, apparently, which, you know, probably that's true) – is paper thin, like on those Commando comics I sometimes saw in newsagents.

It is a comic, then? A space comic? I pick it up, carefully. The top left corner of the cover next to the spine has been torn, and the pages are yellowed with age. As I open it up and take a quick flick through, I register disappointment at the pages of small type text. "No comics, Harry," I think, in Tom Baker's voice from 'Genesis of the Daleks'. I turn back to the table of contents. Just what exactly is a Novelette, anyway? And how can a 128-page book possibly have room for three of them, plus short stories?

And then I read the story titles.

And on one of them, I feel The Pull.

It's gotta be a horror story, surely, with a title like that? And I'm sure my mind is also cross-referencing Bruce Springsteen's 'Downbound Train', a heartbreaking short story for the ages.

And so it is, at nine years old, that I read my first short horror. The author is Robert Bloch, and the title is 'That Hellbound Train'.

And I'm captivated from the off.

It's the voice, of course; colloquial, welcoming. I wouldn't have recognised how quintessentially American it is, but the simplicity would have appealed; there's a Just So quality to it that really pulls me in. And the efficiency of the storytelling is astonishing; by the time we've turned the first page, we know protagonist Martin is, effectively, an orphan (father dead from a combination of drink and railroad tracks, momma run off, and Martin an escapee from the state home he was put in), in his early twenties, has recently done time, it's heavily implied as a result of committing petty theft in an effort to keep body and soul together. The telling is neither cold nor cloying; Martin is not unsympathetic, but his simple stoicism seems to transmit itself to the reader, or, at least, this reader. I'm caught up, that's all, same way Terrence Dicks and Stephen King and John Christopher and all the greats will catch me up; my father's house and library and TV and Amiga 500 are fading away, and I'm instead walking with Martin down a cold railroad track, wondering what's next. And Martin is just considering signing up with the Salvation Army – anything for a warm set of clothes, at this point – when he hears a train coming; and from the wrong direction, given the hour.

We've already heard, in the opening paragraph of the story, that Martin's father would sometimes sing a song about That Hellbound Train when in his cups, and how Martin would sometimes envisage the passengers, imagining what a fine bunch of fellows they must be; how nice it would be to hang with them, if not for the destination... and when the train pulls up, the brakes screaming with suspicious levels of menace, I knew exactly the same time as Martin what was going on.

The conversation that follows is glorious; the Devil is never named, referred to by Martin as 'The Conductor', and the verbal jousting delighted my child's mind – especially the moment where Martin refers to the devil as a 'used car salesmen' before immediately apologising, seeing the hurt look on the conductor's face. It's brilliant, as is the Devil's reason for turning up, namely Martin's consideration of approaching the Salvation Army – "I'd hate to lose you after thinking of you as my own, all these years", he says, wistfully. Initially, The Conductor initially merely offers Martin a lift, but eventually allows himself to be drawn into a bargain.

The layers, here. Martin frankly admits that he's given this moment a lot of thought. The Devil jousts and feints and feigns, and I remember feeling this incredible push/pull, because Martin *can't* be smart enough to have worked out an angle... can he? The Devil must surely have his measure... right?

And then Martin lays out his proposition.

Martin wants the ability to stop time. For him only, obviously. The world will continue to turn, time's arrow will continue to fly forward...

but not for Martin. Martin will remain, frozen forever, at the moment of his choosing.

And the Devil agrees. He hands Martin a pocket watch. Twist the stopper, says the Devil, and when the clock runs down, your moment will freeze.

My memory – treacherous thing, this far out, not something we can rely on, but – is that, delightedly, I'd seen it before Martin articulates the point – once he uses the watch, time, for him, freezes forever, and he'll never have to ride The Train.

He's made a deal with the Devil, and he's already won.

Goddamn.

And does the Devil know it? As he turns his back, his voice is choked, and his shoulders shake with what could be sobbing.

I remember the thrill of this moment so, so clearly. I knew he had the devil beat, you see. It was simplicity itself, and my child mind delighted.

And, at the same time, I think I was just old enough to pick up on the ambiguity in the moment, in the Devil's reaction.

Crying?

Or laughing?

We're almost exactly halfway through the word count.

What follows is one of the most elegantly told stories-of-a-life-lived I've ever encountered. With a new purpose in his heart – in point of fact, that most American of purposes, as I reflect upon it, The Pursuit Of Happiness – Martin sets off to Chicago, where he becomes, as the narrator wryly notes, first a better class of panhandler, then, eventually, scores a job.

Employment secures a place of his own, a promotion secures a car, and a car allows for the possibility of taking ladies out on dates. And with child's eyes, the contours of the story felt instinctive, a needle following a well-worn, familiar groove. It's only now, with adult eyes, I see the shape of a way of life that must have seemed eternal to the post-war generation, and yet turned out to be a chimera – for many of that generation too, of course, but most assuredly for those of us that came after. It's a simple fate, destiny, utterly unremarkable; get a job, get a place, get a better job, get a girl, eventually meet the *right* girl, fall in love, get married, get a yet better place. It's the circle of life; or, actually, the death spiral of capitalism, but here in good old 1953, who could have predicted?

I think it's the moment that he has a child that I start to work out maybe he's screwed up. I'm young enough that sex is effectively an abstract concept, but also steeped enough in the pop culture of the 80s that I understand it's basically The Best Thing Ever. So the moment he doesn't pull the pin while consummating the love of his life, I suspect the first trickle of unease started to creep in for me. But when the kid turns up...

I saw it in my own parents, is the thing. My mum, and most especially my dad, who, in retrospect, clearly could barely wait for me to get to the point where I was capable of more-or-less rational conversation. I saw how both of them, in their own ways, centred my sister and I, and I understood that (again, pop culture playing its part) to be the natural order of things. Once you have a kid, I thought, you're always going to want to see what happens next.

Interestingly, it turns out for our Martin that impulse only lasts until the boy is of age, at which point his concerns become once more about the material. The facets of the character that I'm sure the author intended to be, and saw as, weaknesses, rear their heads, and the moment with his mistress is cut short by the private detective and then the divorce lawyers, and once his wife has cleaned him out, it turns out the mistress is less enamoured than she might have led him to believe.

And that's his last opportune moment; the slide from there is slow but sure. He makes back his money eventually, but he's too old to really enjoy it, and also too old to make the lifelong friends that might have provided the companionship he realises now is the real key to happiness. And anyway, it's too late; he overdoes it trying to make friends at some holiday destination, and his body gives out.

There's an amazing moment, right near the end of the story, where Martin finds himself outside, near the trainline, almost exactly back where he started, reaching for the watch... and then the stroke or heart attack that is to end him hits, and he has the chance to complete the action, and he realises the notion of forever in this state does not compare favourably with hell... and so he doesn't.

And the train pulls up. And the Devil pops out.

And Martin has lost.

I felt crushed for him, but also like I'd encountered something approaching wisdom; how his pursuit of The Moment meant he actually completely lost track of Now, of being. That happiness, contentment, whatever such weasel words even mean, are both states that coexist with other feelings, impossible to isolate; but also that these terms actually describe a process, not a state, steady or otherwise.

So sure, I was sad for Martin, as he boarded the train and the Devil asked repeatedly for his watch back, but I also felt the tale had been just; and, at the end of the day, when you deal with the devil, you kinda do always lose, and probably you should, at that.

But Bloch, that bloody genius, had one final card to play.

As Martin finds himself in the pullman carriage, he looks around. At his fellow travellers. The gamblers. The womanisers. The drunks and dreamers. The sinners, all bound for the same dark destination, all determined to wring every last drop out of their journey.

And at that moment, Martin realises, at last, he's found his moment. And he turns the key.

Amazingly, in the copy of *Venture* in which I first read the story, the text ends at that precise moment, with a rather bland notification to turn to page 183 for the rest. And it's doubly odd because there's just one paragraph to go, a couple of sentences, the Devil incensed – 'we'll never reach our destination now!' – and Martin taking on the role of brakeman on That Hellbound Train, on its never-ending journey to the underworld.

And really, what finer a place could there be to end My Life In Horror? My first short horror story. A meditation on life, and the living of it, and what we pursue, and what we win and lose in the pursuit. How we all face the same destiny, at some unknown but all-too-soon future moment.

And how a story, well told, can crystalise a moment in time.

These essays, and the two volumes of books that came out of them, are my Hellbound Train. My modest hope is that they live beyond me; a signal across generations. A faithful attempt to describe the contours of a fundamentally unremarkable life in a manner that commanded your attention for as long as I demanded it – and, sure, an attempt to scratch my name, however faintly, in the hard rock of human history.

I was here. We were here. We lived, and this is what it was like, to try and live, in this time and place.

This was My Life In Horror.

Thank you for choosing to share it with me.

I REFUSE TO SHUT UP AND DIE

EXQUISITE CORPSE

Always a bit of a risky proposition, this. The encore you're not sure anyone's really asking for. Then again, if the chap who's written more than 60 essays about the idiosyncratic works that messed him up as a kid for the sheer unhinged joy of it is starting to worry about coming over self-indulgent, probably best to acknowledge that particular horse has not just bolted, but fled to another country where it lives under an assumed identity, and has raised a family of foals with little if any idea of what Daddy Did In The War.

Anyhow. This whole project has been about jumping off a cliff, honestly; learning to write nonfiction, learning to write criticism and autobiography; sitting down at the keyboard and figuring out why I felt strongly enough about, say, *One Flew Over the Cuckoo's Nest* or the *Escape From Colditz* board game to commit an evening and a few thousand words to talking about it. And then there was the crowdfunder, and then the second crowdfunder, and at the time of writing I don't know if it's been successful, because, for reasons that will become clear, I'm putting this essay down a bit ahead of publication (and, indeed, before the last two you just read; wibbly wobbly timey wimey). Did it land? Will Volume II get a mass-market release and a limited edition pressing? Who knows? So far, so good, said the falling man; the view is so beautiful, all the way down.

Still. Thanks for coming this far, all of you who have.

Postscript – and thanks for making sure my landing was safe. Again. You're the best.

And let me beg your indulgence as we take one last trip down memory lane.

It's 1997, so I must be 19 years old, and my memory is that I'm in a WHSmiths, possibly Christmas shopping on a painful budget. But it's me and a bookshop, so the odds of my not picking up something for myself are always pretty damn low.

They plummet to zero when I see the cover.

I have no familiarity with the author. But that is one hell of a title. And is there a Barker or King cover quote? Maybe. *Something* sure draws me in, enough to part with some incredibly limited discretionary spending budget from my Job Seekers Allowance. Interestingly, I remember no especial fear or trepidation; the author and narrative were both unknown to me, unlike some past entries where reputations proceeded. Anyway, I was a veteran of *IT*, and *The Wasp Factory*, and *Hellraiser*: how bad could it get, really?

And so I dived straight in, with nary a thought to how deep, dark and cold things were about to get.

And it starts off so slow, oddly almost low-key. Sure, our narrator is a serial killer, but he's in jail, at the end of his career, and I remember wondering if this was going to be one of those 'told in reverse' type deals, where we learn about the crimes via flashback, safe in the knowledge that it all ends in a cell... and then, almost immediately, it gets really fucking weird.

Turns out our man has taught himself how to put himself into a coma, indistinguishable from death, and he can do it so successfully that he wakes up in the prison morgue. It's an incredible piece of writing, describing the process from the inside, backing right up to the very edge of the supernatural, before taking a hard right into *Silence of the Lambs* territory, as our narrator effects a bloody, daring escape.

And then, suddenly, we're in New Orleans, and it's like going from monochrome to technicolour as the palette and cast expand like the opening minutes of the big bang, and I have absolutely no idea what is going on but the author has my attention and I am *here for it*.

And then, while our man is cruising the quarter, looking for likely victims, he encounters a fellow predator.

I REFUSE TO SHUT UP AND DIE

There's a moment when they meet – I've never forgotten it – where our narrator shakes hands and, in a gesture he tells us he's used countless times as a way of gauging someone's potential as a submissive victim, moves his hand down to briefly encircle the other man's wrist... only this time, the shakee does the same thing.

I am doing the moment painfully insufficient justice, here, because Poppy Z. Brite is a world-class horror author, brilliant at pretty much every aspect of novel writing, from characterisation to voice to description to plot to emotion. So, please, just trust me; it's a hairs-on-the-back-of-your-neck moment for the ages, and nothing's even happened yet.

But I remember feeling, with a moral certainty, that shit was about to go down.

I was very much not wrong.

Before it does, though, the novel cuts away, and we meet recently split up Lucas and Tran. Lucas becomes an instantly totemic character, for 19-year-old me; when we meet him, he's ranting and raving on a pirate radio station, angrily condemning straight people as 'breeders', with a persona called Lush Rimbaud. It quickly becomes apparent that he's furious because he's HIV positive (and this is why he's split from Tran), and he's determined to articulate that fury in a world where a plague that only seems to kill gay men is treated as something between a minor inconvenience and a blessing.

Lucas is not a good person. His anger often spills into outright violence, and during his darkest, most self-pitying moment, he comes perilously close to infecting Tran with his own blood; a fantastic example of toxic romanticism that has some eerie echoes with the flowering relationship between the two killers, I have literally just realised as I type this. Nonetheless, this guy really spoke to me; responding to the brutal injustices life had dealt him with a defiant spit and fury that felt honestly come by, if a little indiscriminate in expression. Not the first time I've felt the pull of such a figure, of course, as you'll be well aware, if you've come this far.

You know, I'm really not feeling so good.

Anyway.

And then there's Tran, whose situation is less immediately mortal, but no less gut-wrenching; as we meet him, he's in the process of becoming homeless, thrown out by his parents after they discover that he's gay. A major part of the brutality comes from the matter-of-fact way Tran absorbs this; he's always known that if they found out, he'd be kicked to the kerb, and his stoicism in the face of the loss and ostracism is honestly kind of heartbreaking.

And then I learn, with a dreadful sinking feeling, that Tran not only knows the NO-based killer but intends to throw himself at his mercy, imagining he might be able to stay with him, at least for a while.

It's a brutal twist of the narrative knife, creating huge tension for the reader, an awful sense of impending doom, and inexorable pulling together of darkness and innocence that...

Oh.

Oh, yes, I see.

Sorry. I knew this was getting a bit risky. I've stayed too long. Pushed it too hard. Thanks for coming this far, but I'm going to have to leave it there. Sorry. I know it's a bit abrupt, but I suspect it'll be for the best.

It's the end. But the moment has been prepared for...

Now then, where were we? Oh yes: *Innocence and darkness.*

It's a strange thing to say of any character in this book – indeed, of any in Billy Martin/Poppy Z. Brite's work – but insofar as *innocence* exists in this world, it exists in Tran.

And that doesn't mean, by the by, that the child is sinless, certainly not from the perspective of the aggressively heteronormative culture in which he operates. He, like so many of us, is a child – and victim – of his forebear's misunderstanding; one of the many lonely, disconnected queer children of the early 1990s, seeking out acceptance, affection and fraternity wherever he can find it.

Like all of *Exquisite Corpse's* cast, he is a hedonist; a sensual creature of sex and aesthetic beauty, of casual narcotic consumption and stray relationships. To the average straight, cisgender reader of the era, Tran's motif of innocence might well have proven baffling.

But to those of us that bleed and weep rainbows, it's heart-breaking in its earnestness.

Tran is the very icon of children many of us older queers know and that we once were; the hedonistic congregation of orphans, the outcast and exiled from our family hearths by dints of our natures, forced to seek and *carve* community from our fellow strays; the lovers, exes and siblings we find for ourselves in neon limbo. His innocence isn't founded in some Christianic virginity or prescribed ignorance; for a young man of his age, he's already a cynic by many standards, having known and lost love many times, having experienced losses and traumas – not to mention pleasures and revelations – that many of his straight brothers and sisters will likely never know.

His innocence, just like the darkness that ultimately consumes it, is explicitly, achingly queer. His appetites, his free and easy sensuality, aren't antithetical to it, but *essential.*

And exquisite.

In the wake of the long, collective trauma left on the LGBTQ psyche by the AIDS epidemic (and our abandonment to it by societies and systems that were only too happy to have rid of us by any means), queer communities adopted angelic motifs in much of our panoply and symbolism (much to the chagrin of our traditional enemies).

Tran manifests that symbolism in so many ways: a child of the late 1980s, only just blossomed into adulthood in the 1990s, he's old enough to feel the lingering, morbid resonance of the disease, to be *afraid* of it, yet to have just avoided the plague-like pestilence that beset his forebears in the late 1970s and throughout the 1980s.

In that, Tran is *us*; the queer readers who share a similar birthday, who were also children of the 1980s and 1990s, for whom the disease and its effects are both hideous reality and morbid myth. He is our blitheness and disconnection, our troubled positioning within our family units, our demonisation by the popular media and cynical, scapegoating political forces.

And what happens to him is thus so, so much more than just another murder in a horror novel. It is the witless, unthinking consumption and desecration of something beautiful, something emblematic of tomorrow's beauty; the innocence and state of grace that might be possible in the years to come.

That Tran is so atrociously undone – ostensibly – by members of his own tribe is perhaps the most trenchant misanthropy: here are men old enough to have suffered everything Tran was spared, to have been outcast, demonised, diseased, beaten, abused, who, in the case of Dennis Nilsen-inspired Andrew Compton, is a victim of the AIDS epidemic himself.

But that, as a result of their natures, are blind to Tran's innocence. Or, to put it more accurately, perceive that innocence as a wolf might be the weakness of the lamb.

In their own cruel, peculiar, twisted ways, the atrocities they wreak upon Tran – from their betrayal of him to the cuts, bites and incisions that ultimately unravel him – are acts of reverence; acknowledgments of that essential innocence that straight culture cannot perceive. They would not have selected him to be so intimately their victim were that not the case. But, rather than love and adore him, as any half-way sane queer soul would, their affections are expressed in the manner of cats having cornered some rare and exotic bird.

They are such twisted, diseased, execrable examples of the human animal, the only way they can express their appreciation is through sadism and cannibal consumption. To them, the moment is one of supreme love and religious observance; transcendent in its sensual intensity, infernal in consequence.

That Martin/Brite invites us to share not only Tran's despair and pain, the black murder of his innocence, but also the demonic ecstasies of his killers is the contradictory soul of this book made explicit. Throughout, but nowhere moreso than in this heart-breaking crescendo, Martin/Brite revels in the sensual intensity of both, drawing no distinction between the excesses to be found in sex or murder.

It's a Luciferian relationship this book draws with its readers, queer or otherwise, inviting us to share the souls of the most tainted human beings imaginable; to revel in their strange appetites, the undoing of innocence and the cannibal consumption of beauty. To understand them as we understand ourselves, in our darkest and most nihilistic moments.

In that, the book is an excoriating condemnation of the politics and cultural circumstances that provide both the breeding and hunting grounds for this strange, sadistic species: Tran, along with every victim of Andrew Compton and Jay Byrne, are as much victims of the societies to which they were born as they are the killers themselves.

And nowhere is that made more explicit than in the book's closing chapters, in which Martin/Brite actively recreates an actual scenario that occurred during the height of Jeffrey Dahmer's killing spree amongst the gay community of Milwaukee throughout the late 1970s and early 1980s:

Having barely escaped Jay's sadistic clutches, Tran stumbles naked, drugged and bleeding down the street, only to be met by two police officers, who actively hand Tran back into his tormentor's custody with little in the way of convincing, and proceed to beat senseless the only man who might've saved him.

This is not only a thinly veiled reference to a very similar situation that occurred with Dahmer's – underage – victim, Konerak Sinthasomphone, but also a metaphor for our status as queer children in cultures either indifferent to our brutalisation or actively engaged in cultivating it.

For all of Martin/Brite's gleeful descent into the abyss of Byrne and Compton's sadism, there is a righteous fury kindling in every sentence and syllable of this book, that readers definitely don't have to be queer to understand, but that speaks to us directly, drawing echoes with our lived experience so acutely, it is often as traumatic and painful an experience as it is arousing and sensual.

Yet, the better part of that fury isn't for the serial killers themselves: monstrous as they are, Brite/Martin finds the humanity, even the vulnerability, in these most inhumane of individuals. They are merely symptoms of wider societal sickness; as much products of circumstances beyond their control as any of us (indeed, Andrew Compton in particular evinces deep descents into internal abysses, where he loses himself in existential considerations as to his nature and alien appetites).

The author's fury finds expression in Tran's former lover, the writer and AIDS victim, Lucas Ransom. If there is an author insert in the book, a character who manifests the raw anger and abandonment of older generations of queer men in the early 1990s, it's Lucas. Whilst technically Tran's ex, Lucas hails from a prior generation of gay men, one whose hedonistic legacy is well-drawn and detailed in the book, and for which he has paid far too high a price. Considering himself amongst the walking dead, a creature as in despair of his existence as, perversely, Byrne and Compton are as in love with theirs, Lucas is a creature of violent passions; the outcast child in all of us railing at the injustice of society and creation as a whole. He has little but contempt for the culture that has reduced him to his current circumstances and, indeed, condemns him for what he is, loves and suffers. Unlike Tran, who is our innocence, Lucas is the Romantic opposite; a walking avatar of bleaker queer experience, that cannot help but destroy what it loves more than anything in the world. The desolation of Lucas Ransom, his impotent, violent fury at the world, is something any queer reader will relate to. Unlike Tran, he's also a manifestation of that – to heteronormative culture – most troubling of queer characters; the one who conforms to no particular prescription or stereotype. Unlike angel-boy Tran, who is identifiable from a glance, Lucas is rugged, masculine and physically imposing; the kind of gay man that straight women have a marked tendency to fall for and, in extreme cases, be offended by his manifest disinterest.

He is the self-defined splinter in the flank of prescriptive culture; he refuses the places and slots society grudgingly allows for us, seeking to – often traumatically – carve out his own from its necrotic flesh. In this, he is inevitably punished; if there is a character in the book whose desolation has no rock bottom, who exemplifies the depths of disgrace culture will submit us to if we allow it, it's Lucas. By the end of the narrative, he is one of the last men standing, but only – as Andrew Compton almost supernaturally sniffs out – because he doesn't want to be; because he has nothing left but suffering, despair and a loveless death waiting for him.

Lucas is our suicidal ideation and self-destructive rage, our broken, jagged spirits and the danger that is born from our near-constant cultural abuse. It's little wonder that he seeks balm in the arms of Tran, whose innocence is his contrasting opposite; the sober Yin to his furious Yang.

That their story together – the lost love that still flickers, despite circumstances conspiring to smother it – ends in the bleakest tragedy is Martin/Brite's commentary on, and condemnation of, the disgrace that tradition and conservative culture would submit us all to, if it had license, and a stark reminder that the fight is far from over.

That such a book even exists, that a writer such as Billy Martin/Poppy Z. Brite has license, as a gay trans man, to write about our collective experience in such an intimate, flagrant and sincere manner, was a revelation to me, and continues to be so. Like Barker before him, Martin/Brite blew apart my preconceptions of what is possible in fiction, and inspired me to write with a sincerity that cannot help but make the reader share our passions, no matter what form they take.

George Daniel Lea

AFTERWORD

A life in horror. Readers who don't know better might come to a work that promises elucidation on such assuming it to be a discourse on dread, trauma and wholly negative experience. A cursory reading of the myriad articles, essays and pieces m'colleague Kit Power has created over the last half a decade – compiled here over two volumes – betrays that misapprehension.

Whilst there are indeed examinations of trauma here – experience and media input that shudders and disturbs – even those are expressed in terms of their *potential*; what they meant for Kit's state of mind and identity, both in the original consumption and later, in retrospect. In that, these volumes provide a species of psychic communication; a self-autopsy of a psyche informed by material ostensibly considered horrific in nature. That underlying imperative – to communicate what we are; what gives birth to us, alters us, shapes and sculpts us – is the baseline of writing (fictional or otherwise), of art itself.

We want to be known. We want to be, in Clive Barker-ian terms, flayed alive, slit at the seams and exposed to one another, in manners more intimate than sex or surgery can ever contrive. Mind to mind, soul to soul. We ache to be split out of the insane-asylum cells of our skulls and meet one another in purer conditions, where we can not merely *empathise* but understand what it is to experience the world from entirely other states of mind.

That is what *My Life in Horror* represents for me, as a reader and sometime participant in the project. The self-exposure, the auto-*dissection* that these collections manifest might be, at times, shocking in its earnestness; distressing as only sincere intimacy can be. Without that element, were the project merely superficial or performative, it would fail. The willingness to expose the raw nerve, to touch joy and trauma and perceive the sublime poetry in both, is what lends this project its wings, and has allowed it to sustain over multiple years of near-unbroken production.

Having interacted with Kit and been included in multiple projects over the last several years, we've come to understand one another in ways that might seem peculiar, given that, at the time of writing, we've yet to physically meet. Through the articles that comprise *My Life in Horror*, audio-visual projects such as *What The Hell is Wrong With Us?*, *Seasons of the Crow*, *Clive Barker's Books of Blood* and more, we've come to know one another via the medium of our passions; what brings us joy, what inspires and elevates, what disgusts and excoriates. Again, the meeting of minds that such a relationship represents is here, in these volumes, manifested in a communal form: Kit seeks not merely to express his own engagement with these materials – that range from literature to popular music albums – but actively invites the reader to consider and share their own responses. There is a subtextual hunger underpinning the entire project, that pulses beneath the text of every article: a desire not merely to be known, but to *know* in turn.

The reader is not a passive participant here: they are seduced, indeed *obliged*, to consider their own media experiences and how they inform their assumptions of identity; how they are shaped, sculpted by what they consume, and, in turn, the consequent malleability of their own states of mind.

Throughout the project, Kit exclaims upon experiences that changed who he was; that, in effect, murdered the human beings of before, made ghosts of them, from whose ruins a new entity walked away, occasionally bemused by the lingering echoes of previous incarnations. This isn't merely a journalistic examination of one man's experiences with media, it's a manifesto on our changeling natures; the fact that we trail ghosts of dead selves with every breath and step of our lives, that art, stories and music are the instruments of that -sometimes ecstatic, always traumatic- renaissance.

In that, there is an urgency here; a sincere desire to inspire and facilitate that transformation in others, for those reading to transgress into heretofore unknown contexts via the engagement. By looking back at his own experience – or rather, the stories that memory tells – Kit enjoins us to do likewise, not necessarily for the same media or materials, but generally, in terms of our own mental topographies –

AFTERWORD

what shapes and states our internal landscapes take (not to mention what ructions and cataclysms they are prone to).

This is an act of writing as self-analysis; a look inward, into states and recesses that, arguably, are rarely perceived, much less acknowledged, in our day-to-day experiences (certainly not as part of the prescribed systems in which we operate). As a result, it runs the gamut of human emotion and experience (often within the space of a single article). Ambiguity and inconstancy are givens here; what were once beloved and highly significant works transform as our perceptions alter, as our contexts swell. That process too is examined here, in all of its pain and ubiquity. Whilst certain works and creators remain as significant and powerful as they ever were – their import only swelling with time – others come packaged in a patina of affectionate melancholy, their significance to younger incarnations diminished or abandoned wholesale as new and less celebratory facets of work and creators both become apparent. In that, there is a "coming of age" quality to the collections that almost all readers will chime with, the experience of which is nigh-universal, not to mention essential if we are to develop beyond our abstract and ideological adolescence.

To have been invited to adopt the project now that Kit has determined the conclusion of his own examinations is both an incredible honour and a matter of some anxiety. My abiding hope is that, going forward, I can invest it with the same earnestness, sincerity and power that Kit consistently has, and demonstrate that a life lived in horror can be one worthy of celebration.

George Daniel Lea
19/10/2022

ACKNOWLEDGEMENTS

First and foremost, of course, you'd have read none of the proceeding without Jim "Gingernuts" Mcleod. I don't think either of us had a clue that this project would grow in the way it has; I couldn't be happier about what My Life In Horror has become, and I'll be eternally grateful for the chance Jim took on me, and for giving me access to such a brilliant platform to host my work. Far more importantly, it was the forging of what I feel sure will be a lifelong friendship with one of the most driven, passionate, and generous souls I've ever known.

In a similar vein, I couldn't be more thrilled that My Life In Horror will be continuing under the wise and passionate pen of my dear friend and long term podcast collaborator George Daniel Lea. I've had the enormous privilege of reading the first essay in the new series, and I gotta tell y'all, you're in for a *ride*. It's going to be a thrill to be in the audience. Thanks for agreeing to take the torch forward, George; it couldn't be in better hands.

Similarly, I was honored beyond words that no less a talent than Alasdair Stewart agreed to write the foreword for this volume. His multi-award-nominated newsletter The Full Lid (alasdairstuart.com/the-full-lid) contains some of the best pop culture genre criticism I've ever read: enthusiastic, frighteningly knowledgeable, and with a generosity of spirit tied to an incredible talent for really digging under the skin of a piece of work… you know, as I type, I'm realizing you can go off some people. Only not really, or at least not Alasdair, because he's simply made of awesome, and so is his work.

You may have noticed this book has a brilliant cover that is absolutely gorgeous to look at, and that the content is both brilliantly formatted and basically error free. You have Steve J Shaw of Black Shuck Books and WhiteSpace (white-space.uk) to thank for that. And so do I. So, thanks, Steve. Amazing work.

I want to thank my podcasting crews, who have been so vital to my emotional and mental wellbeing, especially since lockdown. Thanks and love to Jack Graham, Daniel Harper, Holly, James Slater Murphy, George Daniel Lea (again), and my fellow benevolent overlord of Writeopolis, RJ Barker, the much-fired Scott K Andrews, and especially all the beloved and generous citizens of that teeming metropolis.

Similarly, my thanks to the wider horror and SFF community, both in the UK and globally. There are far too many of you to name, but know that I've appreciated every single like, share, retweet and supportive comment throughout this project. It really does feel like a family, and I'm so grateful for how welcoming you've all been to me and my work.

And finally, as ever, thanks to my wonderful wife and brilliant, brilliant children. It's all for you, fam. Thank you. You are my world.

And actually finally, you. Yes, you. Thanks for taking the time to read My Life In Horror Volume II. I hope I held your attention for as long as I demanded it. And if you did have a good time, spread the word - every single star rating/one sentence review on Amazon or Goodreads makes a difference and helps other people find this book, as will any recommendations on social media, or for that matter by what I'm given to understand is still called conversation. And if you had a good time, do check out my other work. Merry meet, merry part, and merry meet again.

So may it be.

ABOUT THE AUTHOR

Kit Power lives in Milton Keynes and writes horror and dark crime fiction, with occasional forays into dystopian science fiction. His fiction work includes a novel, *Godbomb!*, and a novella collection *Breaking Point*, two short story collections (*A Warning About Your Future Enslavement That You WIll Dismiss As A Collection Of Short Fiction And Essays By Kit Power* and *Voices*) and novellas *The Finite* and *A Song For The End*. His non-fiction work includes a limited edition hardback on the Ken Russell/The Who movie *Tommy* (from PS Publishing) and regular posts at Gingernuts of Horror (the series you've just read, and also a first-read response series to the work of Brian Keene).

In his increasingly inaccurately-labeled spare time, he podcasts – as one third of the apparently indescribable fortnightly Discord show Writeopolis (@Writeopolis), one half of What The Hell Is Wrong With Us? with George Daniel Lea, and on a Patreon-exclusive show on the Sherlock Holmes canon with the legendary Jack Graham and Daniel Harper.

For monthly updates on what he's getting up to, sign up to his newsletter at: https://powertothepoeple.substack.com/

For weekly early access to his fiction, non-fiction, and podcasting work, visit www.patreon.com/kitpower

www.ingramcontent.com/pod-product-compliance
Lightning Source LLC
Chambersburg PA
CBHW030106240426
43661CB00001B/29